Students Aspire to Inspire

Co-Authored by 35 Inspiring Leaders at Lassiter High School

Copyright © 2014 by Gary Martin Hays and Adam Weart.
All Rights Reserved.

Published by We Published That, L.L.C., Duluth, Georgia

No part of this book may be copied, reproduced or used in any way without obtaining prior written consent by the Authors or Publisher.

Limit of Liability/Disclaimer of Warranty: While the publisher and authors have used their best efforts in preparing this book, they make no representations or warranties with respect to the accuracy or completeness of the contents of this book and specifically disclaim any implied warranties of merchantability or fitness for a particular purpose. No warranty may be created or extended by sales representatives or written sales materials. The advice and strategies contained herein may not be suitable for your situation. You should consult with a professional where appropriate. Neither the publisher nor authors shall be liable for any loss of profit or any other commercial damages, including but not limited to special, incidental consequential, or other damages.

ISBN: 978-0-9885523-9-5

For more information, please write:

We Published That, L.L.C.

c/o Adam Weart

PO Box 956669

Duluth, GA 30095

Foreword

It all began at the Academic Letter Ceremony with the guest speaker – Gary Martin Hays. Lassiter High School students who received all "A's" for the Fall Semester and the Spring Semester are honored at the Academic Letter Ceremony with an academic letter. It's a pretty big deal since Lassiter has been named one of the best schools in the state of Georgia and to earn all "A's" is a huge accomplishment. The ceremony takes months of planning and coordinating to show respect for these students. Janet Bentley and Art Walsh (parents) have worked tirelessly for years to sustain the program. As a school counselor, I supply the lists, requisitions and communication for the school.

Weeks of preparation went into the 2013 ceremony. Once the ceremony began, Janet, Art & I sat on the stage to listen to the guest speaker – Gary Martin Hays. Because the microphone speakers projected outward to the audience, we did not hear the offer that Gary made to the students – write a chapter about what you will do to give back to society and the chapter will be published in a book. Stunning! The opportunity to be published author before high school graduation – this was so tempting to high achieving students. Students congregated around Gary after his speech and we began to see the crowds and hear about his generous offer.

After the ceremony, Gary sheepishly asked Dr. Richie (principal) for permission and I was asked to coordinate communication, meetings and photo sessions with the interested students. High achieving students always accept a challenge, however, finding the extra time to plan and work on a 2,500 word chapter was difficult. Many students were interested but could not manage the time. (Those students who could not complete the chapter stopped by my office to explain and apologize.) Dr. Wylie Brown, English teacher, offered incentives which accounts for the majority of sophomores who participated. These young authors were challenged to commit to making a difference and by giving up their time and efforts to write the commitment, I think they have made a difference. These students are the next generation of adults and I feel secure in our future.

ANN RIVES, ED. D.
Professional School Counselor
Lassiter High School

Table Of Contents

1 - Introduction - Gary Martin Hays — 1
    Gary's Bio — 10
    35 Student Authors — 13

2 - I Will Make a Difference - Rebekah Lippens — 14
    Rebekah's Bio — 23

3 - Helping Others - Olivia Camillo — 24
    Olivia's Bio — 32

4 - For the Children of China - Abby Overstreet — 34
    Abby's Bio — 42

5 - I Will Make a Difference - Lauren O'Malley — 43
    Lauren's Bio — 51

6 - A Change in Perspective - Nick Willett — 52
    Nick's Bio — 62

7 - The Butterfly Effect - Rachel I. Cohn — 64
    Rachel's Bio — 74

8 - Dropping the Ball - Ryker Martin — 75
    Ryker's Bio — 84

9 - I Will Make a Difference - Hannah Sbaity — 85
    Hannah's Bio — 94

10 - Promoting Healthy Habits Throughout Schools - Adam Ward — 96
    Adam's Bio — 107

11 - The Gift of Soccer - Bailey Peacock — 108
    Bailey's Bio — 114

12 – Change the World – Shannon DeSantis	115
Shannon's Bio	123
13 – I Will Make a Difference – Katelyn Balevic	125
Katelyn's Bio	137
14 – Global Cultural and Religious Education – Robert Longyear	138
Robert's Bio	148
15 – Called to Serve – Julia Miller	149
Julia's Bio	162
16 – What's Your Dream – Catherine Olivia Sicard	163
Catherine's Bio	172
17 – Second Chance to Life – Lucy Singer	174
Lucy's Bio	183
18 – Finding My Niche – Samantha Sanderford	184
Samantha's Bio	192
19 – The Music in Everyone – Anna Wang	193
Anna's Bio	203
20 – The Story of a Victim – Erica Copenhaver	204
Erica's Bio	217
21 – The Precious Gift of Life – Paige Walsh	218
Paige's Bio	227
22 – To Change the World – Galilah Woubshet	228
Galilah's Bio	237
23 – Make a Difference – Kelsey Freshour	238
Kelsey's Bio	250
24 – Aiding Our Elders – Nisha Lee	251
Nisha's Bio	260

25 - I Will Make a Difference - Annalise Dressel	261
Annalise's Bio	268
26 - The Invisible People - Emmalyn Dressel	269
Emmalyn's Bio	276
27 - Start a Chain Reaction - Danielle Okonta	277
Danielle's Bio	287
28 - Be Kind - Paige Gorski	289
Paige's Bio	295
29 - Helping to Inspire Future Generations - Sarah Lezaj	296
Sarah's Bio	304
30 - The Power of a Simple Choice - Caroline Knight	305
Caroline's Bio	314
31 - Giving to the Less Fortunate - Varsha Padmanabhan	315
Varsha's Bio	322
32 - Improving Your Quality of Life - Erica Jackson	323
Erica's Bio	333
33 - The Power of Reading - Luke Bentley	334
Luke's Bio	343
34 - Enviro-Girl - MacKenna Butler	345
MacKenna's Bio	355
35 - Random Acts of Kindness - Stephanie Lilly	356
Stephanie's Bio	364
36 - An Ever Changing World - Madeleine Sewall	366
Madeleine's Bio	373
37 - Final Thoughts - Adam Weart	374
Adam's Bio	380

Introduction
Gary Martin Hays

CHAPTER 1 - Introduction

I WILL MAKE A DIFFERENCE

"One person can make a difference,

and every person must try."

*   John F. Kennedy, in a speech to a group of students
at the University of Michigan on September 22, 1960
as he was campaigning as a candidate
for President of the United States.

This statement from John F. Kennedy is one of my favorite motivational quotes. To me, it is a call to action. It is a rallying cry for each of us to get our butts off the couch and to get out and make a difference in our community. But it is not enough to "talk" about making a difference. We need to make it happen.

On October 10, 2013, I had the honor and privilege of speaking to 337 students and their parents at Lassiter High School in Marietta, Georgia. These exceptional young men and women were receiving "Academic Letters" because of their outstanding grades. These students were being recognized for having a 4.0 or better grade point average for the entire previous academic year. Lassiter is one of only a few schools in the state to give students an opportunity to earn a "letter" in academics. I wish more schools would follow Lassiter's lead as I think this is an amazing way to publicly recognize these students for their hard work.

While driving to their school on the morning of the event, I was thinking about the speech I had prepared. I certainly planned on acknowledging their amazing academic accomplishments. It was also my desire, however, to let them know it was not time to rest on their laurels as there was so much ahead of them to do. There were three main points I wanted to stress to the students:

(1) What can I do to make a positive difference today?
(2) Never be afraid to take chances!
(3) Just do it!

Something felt like it was missing, though. And then it hit me as I pulled into the school parking lot.

I parked my car and then dialed Adam Weart, my business partner in a publishing company that we started in 2012 named "We Published That." I shared with Adam the talking points of my speech, but I told him I felt like more was needed. I wanted us to lead by example. In that phone call, I shared with Adam my desire for our company to give these students a tangible example of how we could make a difference - for them. Without hesitation, he agreed and approved of what I wanted to add to my speech. Now the only question left would be how would I present the opportunity to the students - and to the school administration.

When I walked inside the beautiful new Concert Hall at Lassiter High School, I was amazed. The hall was packed with parents, grandparents, teachers and students - all there to celebrate the academic success of 337 young men and women. I was introduced to several members of the faculty, including the Principal, Dr. Chris Richie, and Dr. Ann Rives, who serves on the school counseling staff. We were then ushered on stage and I was introduced.

I began my speech telling the crowd that I had three important points I wanted to talk about - things that I have learned over my 24 year career as an attorney. But I also told them I wanted to add one more point that really hit home for me that morning.

> "I love my wife. She has such a helpful spirit about her. In fact, without me asking, she grabbed every one of my suits and took them to the cleaners for me. Sheri is a remarkable woman."

I told them that this was such a wonderful gesture on her part. The downside of this was the lack of communication between us regarding this trip to the dry cleaners. She was not aware that I would need it for the awards ceremony that day at Lassiter. I was left without a suit and appeared in front of that large audience in the concert hall in jeans and a sport coat.

****

The following is a paraphrase of the 3 themes I addressed:

(1) <u>What can I do to make a positive difference today</u>?

I shared with them President Kennedy's quote and challenged them to ask that question each day. It does not have to be some huge production of spending a day working in a soup kitchen or mowing the older woman's yard in your neighborhood. It can be something so simple as taking the time to say an encouraging word.

Whenever you wake up in the morning, ask yourself:

What can I do today to make a positive impact in this world - however small it may be?

Is it taking the time to say hello to someone you ordinarily wouldn't speak to as you are passing them in the hall?

You have no idea how much one kind word can make in someone else's day.

Think about it. I'm sure everyone of you had someone encourage you - someone that believed in you - to help you get where you are today.

Why can't you be that person that encourages someone today?

There are reasons you should be nice and encourage others.

- It is the right thing to do! First and foremost.
- You never know just how much of an impact your positive encouragement could be to someone.
- Who knows who that person will become - they could be your boss one day!

One person can make a difference. I think you can be that person. So do it!

(2) <u>Never be afraid to take chances</u>!

You have no idea the things that you will miss if you don't!

In my first year of law school, I heard about a band that was forming in Macon.

I used my student loan checks to purchase a keyboard and an amplifier.

> I auditioned for the band and made it. And for the next three years, I had an amazing time playing different music venues. Performing in the band really helped me feel comfortable speaking to groups and trying cases. Because of that experience, I was able to perform in April 2013 with the award winning band Chicago at the St. Augustine Amphitheatre.

This never would have happened if I didn't take that chance to spend the money I was supposed to use to pay for law school on that music equipment.

(3) <u>Just do it</u>!

I love the simplicity of Nike's slogan. Just do it. Don't talk about it - DO IT!

It is easy for people to share their plans and dreams with you. So many in this world are "getting ready to get ready." The overwhelming majority will "talk the talk", but very few will "walk the walk." The way to separate yourself from the masses is to actually make something happen. Put one foot in front of the other and take action.

I have always wanted to write a book, but I could never find the time. In 2010, I decided the talk was over and I needed to do it. So I put a plan in place where I found the time. And I did it. In the past 3 years, I've authored or co-authored 10 best selling books. I even started a publishing company so I could do this myself instead of working with a publisher.

****

When I finished the three points, I told the students I had a special opportunity I wanted to make available to them. This was not something I previously discussed with Dr. Richie or with anyone at Lassiter High School. I thought it would be better to ask for forgiveness later than to seek prior approval.

In the spirit of "Making A Difference", I told them I wanted to lead by example. Adam Weart and I offered to each of the students an opportunity to co-author a book with us. We would hold their hands every step of the way and give them a "behind the scenes" look at the entire process. We would give them tools to help them with the writing process, and we would meet with them to discuss their progress. I even paid to have a professional photographer come to the school to capture their headshots for their chapter biographies. All of this was being offered to them FREE OF CHARGE.

It was my hope that this would be a tangible example to them of my company helping to make a difference. We were willing to donate our time, resources and expertise to help them become authors of a book. All that would be required of them was for them to take chance, write a chapter, and tell us HOW they planned on making a difference.

This book is a culmination of their dedicated, hard work. I am so very proud of these amazing students. After you read their stories, I am sure you will feel the same way. These young men and women will inspire you with their chapters - their dreams and their aspirations. It makes me rest a little easier knowing the quality of character that our future leaders possess today.

I want to thank Dr. Richie, Dr. Rives, and the faculty and staff of Lassiter High School for making this opportunity possible - not just for the students, but for myself. This has been a truly humbling experience working with such amazing young men and women. I have received far more in return than I have given in this endeavor. For that, I am truly thankful and forever grateful.

****

I shall conclude with something I wrote in the first book I co-authored entitled "Trendsetters":

We should all take to heart and practice the old Chinese proverb:

> "If you want happiness for an hour, take a nap. If you want happiness for a day, go fishing. If you want happiness for a lifetime, help somebody."

So now I ask this final important question:

I *will* make a difference. Will *you*?

Gary Martin Hays - Bio

Gary Martin Hays is not only a successful lawyer, but is a nationally recognized safety advocate who works tirelessly to educate our families and children on issues ranging from bullying to internet safety to abduction prevention. He currently serves on the Board of Directors of the Elizabeth Smart Foundation. Gary has been seen on countless television stations, including CNN Headline News, ABC, CBS, NBC and FOX affiliates. He has appeared on over 110 radio stations, including the Georgia News Network, discussing legal topics and providing safety tips to families. In the past he hosted *Georgia Behind The Scenes* on the CW Atlanta TV Network and has been quoted in USA Today, The Wall Street Journal, and featured on over 250 online sites including Morningstar.com, CBS News's MoneyWatch.com, the Boston Globe, The Miami Herald, The New York Daily News, and The Miami Herald. Gary is currently the host of Atlanta's only weekly lawyer TV show, *Do I Need a Lawyer* on the CW Atlanta, airing weekday mornings.

He is also co-author of the best-selling books "TRENDSETTERS - The World's Leading Experts Reveal Top Trends To Help You Achieve Health, Wealth and Success", "CHAMPIONS - Knockout Strategies For Health, Wealth and Success", "SOLD - The World's Leading Real Estate Experts Reveal The Secrets To Selling Your Home For Top Dollar In Record Time", and "Protect And Defend: Proven Strategies From America's Leading Attorneys to Help You Protect and Defend you Business, Family And Wealth;" and "The Success Secret: The World's Leading Experts Reveal Their Secrets for Success In Business And In Life"; "The Authority On Tout";

"The Authority On Child Safety", "Consumer Advocate: Today's Leading Attorneys Share Their Secrets On Finding Justice For Those Who've Been Wronged & Protecting Those In The Right," and most recently the sole author of the best-selling book "The Authority on Personal Injury Claims in Georgia."

Gary graduated from Emory University in 1986 with a B.A. degree in Political Science and a minor in Afro-American and African Studies. In 1989, he received his law degree from the Walter F. George School of Law of Mercer University, Macon, Georgia. His outstanding academic achievements landed him a position on Mercer's Law Review. He also served the school as Vice President of the Student Bar Association.

His legal accomplishments include being a member of the prestigious Multi Million Dollar Advocate's Forum, a society limited to those attorneys who have received a settlement or verdict of at least $2 Million Dollars. He has been recognized in Atlanta Magazine as one of Georgia's top workers' compensation lawyers. Gary frequently lectures to other attorneys in Georgia on continuing education topics. He has been recognized as one of the Top 100 Trial Lawyers in Georgia since 2007 by the American Trial Lawyers Association, and recognized by Lawdragon as one of the leading Plaintiffs' Lawyers in America. His firm specializes in personal injury, wrongful death, workers' compensation, and pharmaceutical claims. Since 1993, his firm has helped over 32,000 victims and their families recover over $250 Million dollars.

In 2008, Gary started the non-profit organization Keep Georgia Safe with the mission to provide safety education and crime prevention training in Georgia. Keep Georgia Safe has trained over 80 state and local law enforcement officers in CART (Child Abduction Response Teams) so our first responders will know what to do in the event a child is abducted in Georgia. Gary has completed Child Abduction Response Team training with the

National AMBER Alert program through the U.S. Department of Justice and Fox Valley Technical College. He is a certified instructor in the radKIDS curriculum. His law firm has given away 1,000 bicycle helmets and 14 college scholarships.

His website addresses are http://www.GaryMartinHays.com

and http://www.KeepGeorgiaSafe.org.

35 Students Present How They Will Make a Difference

The following chapters combine to

create a literary collection of the

hopes and dreams of young adults today.

"The surest way to corrupt a youth is to instruct him to hold in higher esteem those who think alike than those who think differently."
Friedrich Nietzsche

I Will Make a Difference
Rebekah Lippens

CHAPTER 2 – I Will Make a Difference

Mark Twain said it best: "The devil's aversion to holy water is a light matter compared with a despot's dread of a newspaper that laughs." The power of the press was something Twain, a veteran reporter himself, knew like the back of his hand -- and, as he remarked, countless oppressive governments and other not-so-upright personalities have learned as well. Especially today, when media has exploded and exists on a more massive scale than ever before, there is much power to be wielded in the proverbial pen.

It is through that power to make a dent in the injustice and general conflict stemming from basic and not-so-basic misunderstandings in the world that I seek to make a difference. I have found a passion in this method of communicating ideas and knowledge about the world around us through words, a method as vital as it is potent. Journalism is my favorite outlet for creating change, and it certainly has a track record that speaks for itself.

Muckrakers

It is impossible to talk about making a difference through journalism without touching upon the muckraking journalists of the Progressive Era, a time of massive reform at the beginning of the last century. One of my favorites is Ida Tarbell, who took on one of the most powerful and wealthy men in the history of the world and won. As a child, she watched as her father learned firsthand of John D. Rockefeller's highly unethical business practices in expanding his leviathan Standard Oil Company; later on in life, she returned to the subject in a three-part magazine series entitled "The History of Standard Oil." The instant and incredible popularity of the series led to its extension, and it ultimately became a nineteen-part expose that set the monolithic corporation on the path to a landmark court battle that shattered the trust.

Ida Tarbell was able to level the playing field at least a little in terms of economic opportunity for millions of Americans through the change she served as a catalyst to bring about. She managed to do all this at a time when her personal political rights as a woman did not even allow her to vote for the judge who would ultimately preside over the Standard Oil Co. v. United States case. When most women were limited to making dinner, she was making a difference in her country and in history.

Tarbell's fellow "muckrakers," a term coined by President Theodore Roosevelt, dug up the filthy tactics of corrupt industries and exposed the dreadful state of millions of Americans. Their efforts are part of what earned their period the moniker the "Progressive Era" and ushered in an entirely new way of thinking about economic life in America and the role of the government. They changed the course of journalism and serve as a constant reminder of the power of communication, a power that is every bit as relevant today.

Modern Examples

In the decades since the Progressive Era, a burgeoning media presence has shaped world events time and time again. During the '60s, a relatively new journalistic medium, the television, brought current events right into the living rooms of thousands upon thousands of people who may otherwise have felt themselves unaffected. During the Civil Rights Movement, news footage of the atrocities committed against peaceful protesters in towns like Birmingham, Alabama spurred national sentiment towards equality. People who otherwise would not have thought twice about the plight of African Americans living under Jim Crow segregation were suddenly forced to craft an opinion on the subject as it was brought to their attention in such an intensely up-close-and-personal way. As journalism has grown and evolved, its influence has grown and evolved with it.

These past few years have once again reminded us of the power of the news media to spur change as the events of the Arab Spring have sent shockwaves through the Middle East and left the rest of the world fascinated as events have continued to unfold. Beginning in December 2010, protest movements against well-entrenched regimes caught on like wildfire over the course of a year that brought widespread change to an entire region. Cell phone videos posted to the internet of protesters and police brutality as well as other first-person accounts practically unprecedented for protests of this type were picked up and circulated by major international news outlets until it seemed everyone the world over knew what was going on in the streets of Cairo and Tunis, Tripoli and Damascus. In a part of the world where freedom of the press was regularly ignored and repressed, regimes were facing a gush of media coverage they could do nothing to stem, one that undoubtedly played a major role in shaping the political change that swept these countries (and is, in many cases, still in the process of sweeping over them).

The potency of journalism in bringing about change has not been diluted over the years but grown stronger, as the events of the last fifty years have illustrated time and again. Even as people turn away from traditional sources like newspapers in favor of the internet, the news media is a serious force to be reckoned with for foreign and domestic sources of turmoil alike.

Personal Experience

If participating in student journalism has taught me one thing, it is how much I love this medium of communication. As a senior, I am honored to serve as the co-editor-in-chief of both the newspaper and the yearbook. The newspaper staff especially carries a sense of responsibility to our readership to produce relevant, quality content that will spark interest and thought wherever it may be distributed. Of course, as with many adults in the real world, high school students tend to be largely apathetic to long columns of print, so our staff is constantly challenging ourselves to bring fresh and intriguing ideas to the paper we so love.

This year in particular, we decided as a staff to depart from the safe, familiar realm of general high school material -- lack of sleep among teens, front page articles about

Homecoming -- and take our monthly periodical a little deeper. Despite the strong legacy of our paper in terms of quality and the pride we all felt in every issue we had streaked our fingers in ink handing out of a Friday morning, we made the decision as a staff to begin reporting on the issues we face as a school and a generation. Enter: the cheating article.

In October, we decided to report as evenly and honestly as we could on the realities of academic honesty in a 21st-century high school. Our coverage included an anonymous editorial on one student's personal track record with cheating, a list of Onion-style "cheating tips" in the comedy section, a two-page spread of facts and figures related to the phenomenon, and, of course, a front page article which clocked in at about 850 words and included polls and comments about academic honesty. Of course, much of it was rather academic *dis*honesty -- one poll found that an overwhelming majority of students had cheated on homework or another assignment at some point during their high school career. The results may not have been surprising to the students, at least, but they did provoke some thought into how students viewed cheating.

I am very grateful to attend a high school where the administration believes in its student journalism programs enough to allow us to explore topics many schools would consider thoroughly taboo. That article, if nothing else, gave me a taste for what passes at this level as investigative journalism -- gathering interviews and quotes from students, teachers, and administrators alike, taking comprehensive student polls, and researching cheating scandals at leading universities. Writing the article was also an exercise in maintaining as unbiased and professional a voice as possible and working as a team to ensure my article was properly edited and fact-checked. What was most exciting about the process, though, was the sense of purpose and drive I got out of reporting on a subject that is so highly relevant and important to our readers.

Thanks to the response from the school community after the release of the October issue, our paper has pressed onward to issues that are somewhat more sensitive than traditional high school fare. Through reporting on school Red Ribbon Week activities, we addressed student drug use. Future projects include a story on eating disorders. There is a definite feeling among staff members that we can leverage our position in the school to spark discussion among both students and adults. And, of course, there can be no change without discussion.

In the Future

Because of my Christian faith and upbringing, I firmly believe that God bestows upon each of us a particular set of talents and skills that He plans for us to use to better the lives of others during our time on earth. We are all given the potential to make a difference from the onset; it then becomes a question of whether or not we make use of the opportunities that come our way to fulfill that potential.

I believe that written communication is one of the God-given skills I possess to create an impact in the world around me, however small that impact may be. The more I explore and expand upon that skill, the more I fall in love with it. No matter where my life may go from here, I cannot imagine it going anywhere journalistic writing does not play an integral role.

For years, adults like to ask young children what they want to be when they grow up. When those children reach their senior year of high school, those adults start asking again. My dream job is to work as a reporter for a top national newspaper, reporting on issues of major significance, bringing light to things people might not otherwise know or fully understand. Whether those issues are political turmoil, corruption in the business sphere, or even something far more local and lighter than that, I know it is something I would find rewarding.

Journalism is the opportunity to voice the stories of others as they happen; to bring in another Mark Twain quote, "News is history in its first and best form, its vivid and fascinating form, and… history is the pale and tranquil reflection of it." To have the opportunity to record histories, be they international or individual, is an immense opportunity to bring people together. In an age where we share everything via photo collages and 140-character blips, written news media is still one of the foremost avenues we have to construct a coherent account of our experiences and opinions, and as such, remains one of the most powerful forms of communication.

Even if I do not write for a major news outlet, the internet has introduced myriad new ways to practice journalism and make a difference through words. The advent of blogging opens up the field of journalism to anyone with a computer and a message. Keeping up with a personal blog is an opportunity to reflect upon events and share your perspective with the world around you. Just like a traditional printed periodical, a blog allows both its author and its readership to connect to current events and the world they occur in.

    Journalism does not make a difference simply because it gives voice to stories. If that was where it ended, reporters would be no different than someone shouting his or her opinions into thin air. Where journalists, whether they write for the New York Times or for Blogspot, are given the chance to make a difference is when people take what they read and use it to spur discussion. A story might break the silence, but it is up to that story's audience to fill the void with meaningful debate on how we can use that new information to propel society forward. That is the true role of journalism -- to foster discussions that lead to new ideas and opinions. By using my voice to add to this ongoing and constant debate, I will make a difference.

Rebekah Lippens - Bio

Rebekah Lippens is a high school senior and knitting enthusiast whose favorite authors include Mark Twain, Charles Dickens, Gabriel Garcia-Marquez, and Toni Morrison. She lives with her parents, who have always encouraged her to pursue her writing, two younger siblings, and a much-beloved cat of questionable breed named Minnie. She will be attending the University of Chicago in the fall.

Helping Others
Olivia Camillo

CHAPTER 3 - Helping Others

When kids are young they are asked who they want to be and what they want to do when they are older. Perhaps they will say the President of the United States, a teacher, a firefighter or even maybe a pop star, but in reality, they are not sure. Truth is, I am a sophomore in high school and still do not yet know completely what I want to study in college or how I can make a difference in our world today. Although I do not know exactly how I can make a difference, I do know that I want to help those who are not as privileged as others. Whether it is helping to build hospitals and water-wells, donating money, clothes, and glasses so people are able to see, teaching children how to read and write, or even teaching them the simple sport of lacrosse; I do know this: I want to make an impact on their lives.

Ever since I was little I have known that I wanted to travel the world to see China, Africa, the Middle East, and even smaller islands like the Philippines and Hawaii. If I were to study abroad in college, I would be able to visit multiple countries around the world. In these countries I could learn perhaps a language or two, enabling me to communicate with foreigners in the future. Being born in the U.S, my first language is English. I am currently learning the Spanish language and plan on taking at least one semester of Latin before I graduate high school. Taking AP world history and world literature may be difficult classes, but I enjoy learning about the cultures of each continent and their history. I would love to be able to visit the ancient, yet still thriving, cities of Athens, Baghdad or possibly Rome.

How I would make a difference in these areas I have still not figured out, but I am keeping as many options open as possible. After traveling abroad in college, I would like to travel to a country of my choosing and help them in whatever way I could (based off of what I get a degree for). For example, if Japan had another earthquake, I would like to provide them with relief efforts and help to rebuild their community. As for any other country suffering due to disease or famine, I would hope to hire a doctor to give them shots or in the case of famine, a farmer to buy them food.

I could make a difference now starting with donating. There is a 'Toys for Tots' bin in my school that I could spend a few dollars on buying toys for the less fortunate children. There are also clothes, winter coats, and shoes being donated to needy children around the world. Next to my gym, school, and grocery store, there is a bin to donate these clothes, winter coats, and shoes, so I can make a difference now by donating my old shoes to those rather than simply throwing them away. Another way to help would be to donate money to humanitarian organizations that will use donated money wisely. Such organizations include UNICEF and Red Cross, who aid the sick and alleviate their pain with shots, cures, or just support. Even glasses are donated to help children who are unable to see but cannot afford glasses or contacts themselves. I could donate to the Lions Club (a club that donates eyeglasses) because I have glasses myself and own at least two old pairs that other children need much more than me.

In my school, there are multiple clubs that volunteer to help ease the pain in other peoples' lives. In these clubs, members go to help families buy pets at animal shelters, sell candy for money to send to third world countries, set up fundraising events like runs, carnivals, and concerts, and participate in many food and toy drives. They even host bake sales, art shows, raffles, and participate in car washes. Although I have missed the deadline to join any of these clubs this year, I plan to make a difference next year by becoming a part of at least two of these clubs-Interact Club and Beta Club.

When I am older, I can also donate any books I know I will not read again to the Rotary Club. The Rotary Club is an organization that sends any donated books to third world countries. Having four kids in our family we have plenty of books in the house that we will eventually be able to donate to the club so they can give them to those who cannot afford books. After high school or maybe college, I could donate these books to the Club and ask any of my friends or neighbors if they have any books they do not want any more.

Donating clothes, toys, glasses and books are not the only way to help the less fortunate around the world. One way I could possibly help to make a difference today is by volunteering at a soup kitchen or donating cans of food to a canned food drive. I remember in elementary school our class donated the most amounts of cans to a drive in the whole school. Just knowing that we saved some peoples' lives and provided them with a meal was uplifting and made me feel so much joy, even as a kid. I was so eager to help other children at the time I must have brought in at least two or three cans of food in every day for two weeks.

Aside from teaching the less fortunate around the world how to build, make pottery, or play lacrosse, I could also donate money to health organizations, in order to ensure that they have clean and sanitary water or buy toys to give to needy children. The 'Toys For Tots' donation sends toys to the less fortunate children. Another thing I could possibly do is donate money to health organizations so they can raise enough money to research these diseases and allow them to buy plenty of equipment, enabling them to find cures to diseases throughout the world. As far as unsafe water is concerned, I could teach them how to cleanse the water and give them enough materials to be able to make sure their water from rivers or oceans is clean and safe. So many people die every year due to unsanitary water that cleansing their water could help them immensely. Next to that, approximately 40,000 kids die a day due to lack of food and the diseases that are caused by it.

Volunteering to become part of the Peace Corps when I am older would be another great way to make a difference. The Peace Corps is an American association where Americans volunteer to travel around the world to help those in need. The people involved in the Peace Corps not only teach other children about America, but also help in whatever way they can. Whether they teach education to these children, help to build classrooms, hospitals, or water-wells, or provide them with technical training, they always do the best they can to help. I would like to become part of this organization when I am older because this sounds exactly like what I want to do and whom I want to be when I grow up.

One way I could make a difference is by helping backward places become modern by building more advanced buildings and teaching them skillsets such as how to make pottery or fish, creating a market that will contribute to the beginning of trade. If hospitals were built in these areas, diseases such as malaria and could be cured and environmental sanitation could become cleaner. I am in ceramics now, so if I minor in ceramics in college, I could teach them how to dig up their clay from the ground, make products, and glaze them. Then, after I teach a few, they can teach others who will think off of these ideas, and soon will start to even paint or draw. This could possibly create a new type of art incorporated with their culture and influence them further. If I could help them learn a few skills, such as reading, writing, and maybe pottery, then they could take it from there and begin to thrive. I could also become part of the United Nation's World Health Organization (WHO) and help treat diseases such as malaria, dengue, HIV, smallpox, and/or even infectious skin disease. The famous 'tree-man' has suffered from the infectious skin disease since he cut himself as a kid and due to his poor immune system (because of his poor community) doctors are unable to help the man.

Another way I plan to make a difference is by teaching those in other countries how to read and write, raising their literacy rate and allowing smarter people to arise, creating motivation for competition, allowing a stronger economy to develop. I plan on getting a degree in college for teaching as well. If I get a teaching degree, I could help build schools, teach children how to read and write, and help create the foundation of a new, smarter community. Introducing books and paintings and poetry by famous artisans could inspire the children to do something like these works, creating an interest in education. This interest in education would promote jobs and further their economy. With a stronger economy, trading could emerge as an outcome and create relationships with other richer countries.

My lacrosse coach from this past summer is currently in England teaching kids there how to play lacrosse. This really inspired me and I hope to be able to do that myself one day. Lacrosse was not a very popular sport when I was born but it has been spreading, but only to the places of the United States, Japan, Australia, and Canada Teaching other countries how to play would be very fun and would help spread the game of lacrosse. Just like soccer at first, lacrosse is not as popular as football or even basketball. Now, soccer has risen and I plan on doing the same with lacrosse. There are many areas in the world where lacrosse has still not spread to yet, and I think I could make a difference, after graduating college, by teaching another new sport to other countries.

While I know I cannot do every one of these things, I would like to try. Teaching and coaching lacrosse, becoming part of the Peace Corps, donating items or money, building class rooms and hospitals, and teaching children how to read in other countries all sound like amazing opportunities to make a difference. If I get degrees in college for ceramics and teaching, study abroad in college, and graduate, then I think I could accomplish these tasks, however long they may take. When I read about the Peace Corps, I looked the organization up. I found their website and watched a video of a woman who went to

Uganda and helped to build a classroom and provided technical training. This video opened my eyes and made me realize this really is something I want to do when I grow up. While I do not have it all exactly planned out now, I do know that I would like to join the Peace Corps and teach lacrosse on the side. I love playing lacrosse now and would never want to give it up, so joining the Peace Corps organization when I am older would be the perfect opportunity for me to do both; helping others in need and playing the sport I love at the same time. So, while I thought there was no way I could make a difference at the beginning of this year, I now think that helping the less fortunate around the world by teaching them in lacrosse, education, and skills such as pottery and fishing is exactly the way I can and will make a difference in our world.

Olivia Camillo – Bio

Olivia Camillo is a sophomore at Lassiter High School. She has three siblings, two dogs, a lizard, and fish. Olivia also had Sam, a dog, and Lulu, a guinea pig, but they both died. She shares a room with her sister, Abby, who is 18 years old. Her two brothers are Peter (16) and Henry (13). On August 28, 1998, Olivia was born at Northside Hospital. Her family moved to Tennessee for a while, but moved back to Georgia shortly after.

When she was 3 years old, she began playing soccer at the YMCA. After pre-school, she went to Shallowford Falls Elementary. In elementary school she ran cross-country with her siblings, participated in drama club, safety patrol, and fox trotters (a dance club), and played soccer until middle school.

After elementary school, Olivia went to Simpson Middle School. During sixth grade, her best friend, Katelyn, moved to Switzerland. Katelyn and her still email each other whenever they have time. In seventh grade, Olivia joined Hotlanta, a summer lacrosse team and has played on the team ever since. Through Hotlanta, she has traveled to tournaments in Florida, Tennessee, North Carolina, Chicago, and Maryland. In eighth grade, her cousin, Kati, asked Olivia to be her bridesmaid. It was a very fun experience for her because she had a J-Crew dress and had her nails and hair done.

Olivia caught bronchitis before freshman year, which has turned into exercise-induced asthma. Freshman year she received her varsity letter in cross-country with her friend, Mary-Alice, and in lacrosse with her friend, Sabrina. Last summer, her friend, Kaitlyn, took her to the X-Games in Los Angeles. Because Kaitlyn's aunt worked at ESPN, they even got VIP passes. She is currently taking AP world history, honors world literature, and ceramics.

For the Children of China
Abby Overstreet

CHAPTER 4 – For the Children of China

I am a dreamer. I am full of ambitions.

My mind is constantly running, and my imagination is always in play. Like the late Martin Luther King Jr. once said, "I have a dream." Dr. King and I are similar, as I, too, have a dream... a dream that will hopefully one day be fulfilled. My dream is to bring about change. It is to take the world and give it a little shake of inspiration and hope. I'll explain more about my dream a little later.

The Origins of an Orphaned Child and What Fuels the Inspiration for Change

When I was little, up until I was 18 months old, I was an orphaned child. I was born in rural China, a country that prefers male children over female, so for that reason, I was orphaned. While I don't remember the tremendous poverty in China, my parents spoke of it and of course I have learned about this for many years in school. I am always greatly saddened and affected by what I see and have learned. I understand that in any of the pictures I have seen over these years, it easily could have been a picture of me.

Growing up, I was a very jealous child. I saw children as bundles of annoyance instead of bundles of joy. I wanted nothing to do with them. I especially didn't like how much attention they got from my parents. In fact, I was so jealous that I thought children would brainwash my parents to like them more than they liked me. The child imagination is crazy sometimes.

Now that I am older, I understand where my feelings of jealousy came from. At a young age, I was left by my biological parents near my home city's orphanage in the Hunan Province of China. I am one of the lucky ones because I was adopted by two amazing parents who lived in America and could provide me with a full belly, roof over my head, and clothes on my back. Perhaps, my jealousy came from the inside feeling of abandonment. I thought my adoptive parents would see me second to the other kids because physically they had more in common. Although my parents and I are different in looks, I couldn't be happier to call them my real parents. I am very blessed for them. Somewhere along the way to adolescence, I realized that children were not as evil as I put them out to be. Maybe this realization happened when I was around them more such as when I hung out with my baby cousins over the holidays. Personally, I love children. I love to see them smile and laugh and play, but fact that I love kids comes as a big shock to me.

That is where my inspiration and dream of change comes from. My goal is to better the situation for the boys and girls out there who are living the life in poverty, in foster care, on the streets, or any child that is screaming for help but remain voiceless. I want to be their voice for them.

Actions Speak Louder than Words: What Needs to Be Done

Since my roots are from rural China, my main focus is to better the lives of the children living in the small Chinese villages like the one I was born in. When my mother came to China in 1999, the year I was adopted, she recalls that there was flooding issues coming from the Yangzi River and many homes were destroyed. The destroyed homes left poor living conditions for the children growing up in the villages; they could lead to diseases, further child abandonment, homelessness, and death. China, on estimate, has around 3 million orphans, and about two out of five that come into an orphanage will end up dying. There are more female orphans because of China's One Child Policy, and because of that, sons are in higher demand because they will end up caring for their parents while a daughter will go off to live with her husband and his family. Males are usually orphans only if they are unable to care for their parents in the future because of a disability or sickness.

Along with the struggle to rebuild their homes, the Chinese are faced with providing for their families. About 50%-55% of the Chinese population is living in rural areas, which continue to be destroyed annually from the floods. Also, their income, usually from agriculture or mining, is significantly less than that of the Chinese living in urbanized areas. I want to help out the boys and girls of the poorer provinces in China by helping rebuild homes that have been destroyed by the annual floods. I want to provide them with a home that is acceptable to live in, one that can withstand a flood. I want to give them a home that they can create good memories in throughout their entire childhood. Not only do I want to set up individual sturdy homes for the families that can afford one, but I want to also build better and bigger orphanages and utilize more foster homes. This should help the children that are currently living the lifestyle without their parental guidance. As my mother once told me, "You can give a house to someone, but that won't give them a life."

My next step is to build schools for the children. A school will provide them with the education needed for their futures. More than half the inspiration a child gets is from their teachers and from a learning environment. A few years back I read a memoir about a young girl growing up in a small Chinese village, and she said that her school was a couple miles away from her home. I want to build schools closer to children's homes and communities, so they have an easier time going to and from school. Along with the schools built, I want to bring in educators and volunteers to fill the minds of the children with knowledge that they will use to hopefully find internal inspiration. Education is the key to success and a future.

I also want to set up separate education programs where professionals volunteer their time to teach the children that cannot afford to go to regular school. The educational programs will teach specific subjects such as the core subjects of math, sciences, social studies, and literature, but I also feel that children should be provided with "life-skill" classes, such as cooking, art, music or sewing. Another way children need to grow is to have good social interactions with their peers around them. A way to bring together the children would be to create playgrounds and sports fields. Set up local coed sports teams or games so the children can get out all their juvenile energy. This will help them make important life connections with the people around them. With the education systems in play, I hope to better the child's life because with education they are given the opportunities to branch out wherever they chose and they will be able to choose what their future will be like at an early stage.

Follow the Leader! A Call to Anyone Willing to Help

As an individual, it is difficult to change the lives of children living in poverty. My goal is to inspire others in my generation and future generations to follow me and help, but not only in China, but in other countries such as India, many of the African countries, and even The Americas. When a child is born, we do not know if the child will do great things to the world. They are the start of the process of life, and they are the key to change, but since they are so young and innocent, current generations need to educate them with the right mindset to change the world.

Regardless of what change a person makes, many of them had an inspiration growing up; someone they wanted to be like. Some create organizations that end up impacting the entire world in a very positive manner, but some act alone to trigger inspiration in others. I hope to teach children that they can act alone if they want change or they can even act in small steps to bring change to the world.

When I was in middle school, a teacher gave me a poem called "Drop a Pebble in the Water." It's the ripple effect. When a pebble is being dropped in the water, ripples form shortly after it comes into contact with the surface of the water. The same is with life. It starts with one. That one will go out and change a person's life to inspire them to go out and do the same. I want many individuals to go out and start their own ripple of inspiration so then a big wave of change can splash onto the beaches of a new world.

Kids are the light of life and the future to our world. It is up to my generation to protect the next generation and so on, even though we are still children ourselves. We all can grow up and inspire to be or do something great, or do nothing at all.

Now to my dream; I have a dream that I want to inspire the kids of my generation to grow up and do something great, and for them to help others of our generation and younger to provide better living conditions for the world. I want the children who are placed in the orphanages and foster care to not fear the dark that life might bring onto them. I want them to know that life will eventually get better if we all work together.

My dream is to help inspire the children of the world to do great things, for other people. That is where true "success" comes from. I've seen many documentaries and have heard stories of kids who are living sad lives that they shouldn't be living, but somehow they make it through. Some of these kids find internal aspiration in them that drives them in this positive direction. Most find it in education, but others find it in music or a special talent of theirs. These children, still so young and innocent, can still laugh or smile or play, even with the living conditions they have, so hopefully the smiles on the children faces can fuel the will in others to go out and help them.

My entry is my "check-list" for my adult self. I am writing down what I want to do and what I want to accomplish. When I'm old I can look back on this book and instead of reading it as, "I want to…," I can check it off as, "I did."

Abby Overstreet – Bio

Abby Overstreet was born in a small village in rural China. She was adopted by her two parents at 18 months old and was brought to the United States. She grew up in Colorado for her early years, but she has lived mostly in Georgia, which is where she lives currently with her parents, brother, and two dogs. Abby is an honor student at her high school, getting mostly As and few Bs on her transcript. Abby loves to play with kids and spends lots of her time with them. Her goal is to help the children in rural China that are living in similar situations as she did when she was born. She also hopes to spark inspiration in others by doing this. Her plans for the future are to attend a four year college at University of Georgia and then get her masters at Stanford University for psychology. A big goal in Abby's life is to travel around the world with her family. During her travels, she hopes to help out in different towns around the world, changing it little by little across the globe.

I Will Make a Difference
Lauren O'Malley

CHAPTER 5 – I Will Make a Difference

Swimming. To me it is like a heart beat. I can't live without it. It's something I do and something that is a living part of me. It is not easy and it is not something I just do on the side. It is what I love to do and what I motivate myself to do to become the best that I can be. Swimming is something that forms dreams in my head and makes me realize that if I work towards something there is a chance I can accomplish it. As a young person in this world, I think it's important to believe in yourself and know that you are destined to do something worthy of the person you are.

For me, I found swimming to be that thing to push me forward. I started doing the sport when I was six years old. From the beginning I was like a fish in the water. I was comfortable there, splashing around, holding my breath, and diving in headfirst. It was just something that made me happy and I loved doing it.

As I got older, the sport became a more serious thing. The question of if I wanted to put forth effort into this sport or another came up, and I was not sure what I wanted to do. I thought about it and realized that all I had ever really done with my life was swim. Before committing to it fully though, I wanted to try other things. My schedule became very full with all my new activities. I was on the cheer squad, played soccer, attended a tennis academy, and did some volleyball on the side. All my time and energy was consumed, but yet I still didn't feel like I had found my niche. Something was missing in my life, and I soon realized it was swimming.

After this epiphany, I begged my parents to let me join swim again. Them, being the loving and caring parents they are, were willing to let me do so. After joining the team again, my love for the sport was solidified. It wasn't just the sport itself that made me love it, but it was everything that came with it as well. I was taught life skills of discipline, honesty, loyalty, dedication, and respect. I was taught what it means to be a part of a team and support one another. I was taught what excellence really is, and most important I was taught how to set goals and dream big.

Having dreams and setting goals to reach your dreams is the essence of human life. It is the pursuit of excellence or personal excellence that propels us to greatness, and even through failure we are better and have learned skills to make the next pursuit attainable. I believe there is potential locked up inside of each and everyone of us, and it is our job is to unleash it! Pope John XXII once said, "Consult not your fears but your hopes and your dreams. Think not about your frustrations, but about your unfulfilled potential. Concern yourself not with what you tried and failed in, but with what it is still possible for you to do." The possibilities life has to offer are endless, and here is where we can help each other. We can motivate one another to set goals that push us towards excellence. We can inspire one another to dream dreams that are out of this world. And we can keep raising the bar for what is average in this world, so eventually average becomes the next extraordinary.

In my life, so far, I have seen too many people settle for mediocrity even though they have the potential to be greater than that. I want to make a difference in this world by setting a new trend for average. I want people to expect nothing less than excellence from themselves, and for them to stop at nothing to reach their goals. I want to create a ripple effect by helping people understand the underlying power of having dreams and setting goals, and for them to spread that knowledge. Here is where I will make my difference.

It is impossible to inspire people with empty words. "Do as I say" is an old and tired saying, implying "I know better than you." "Do as I do" is a much greater challenge. It requires dedication to ideals, sacrifice in deed and living a creed or motto, not just "hoping" to do it. Our lives are a body of work, a canvas that cannot fully be appreciated without perspective and time. Everything we do, the good, the bad, and the indifferent, is put into this work of art that leaves an everlasting effect on this Earth. In a generation that has grown accustomed to instant gratification, it is our challenge to persevere beyond that need for easy accolades and awards. We as a generation need to recognize that what we do with our lives does not just affect the here and the now, but also our future and the world's future. The ultimate perspective to live through is the big picture. Look for things far in the distance, and always act based on the question "How will this affect my future and the world as a whole?"

The most effective way to establish good habit patterns that lead to this kind of successful living is to work regularly toward short and long term goals. Having a dream and setting goals towards reaching a dream form a structure for your life. Some believe that we all have a destiny, designated for us at birth, to be fulfilled later. We cannot, however, fulfill anything we are destined to accomplish, or be, without putting forth the effort. Can you imagine a person with the talent to be a world-renowned concert pianist who never spent a day practicing? In my world, it would be sad to see a talented swimmer who failed to put forth the effort and missed qualifying for or winning the Olympics by one one-hundredth of a second. It happens.

When you work towards something and put forth an honest effort the rewards you receive in the end are so much greater than ones you would receive had you taken the easy way out. The pianist who puts their heart and nerve into their performance, regardless of the stage, will find great satisfaction in fulfilling their destiny. For me, sometimes friends will look at me as if I have two heads when I talk about getting up at 5:00 in the morning to dive into a pool in the middle of the winter. They joke about my obsessive need to understand and do well in all of my classes. Then I see them work a little harder, or find an outlet of their own to pursue with vigor. I can't help but become inspired myself. We can all be example figures in some aspect of life, so remember that when you do something there is always someone watching that you can inspire. Helen Keller once said, "True happiness is not gained through self-gratification, but through fidelity to a worthy purpose." The challenge I have is to live up to my own personal excellence, and to live it proudly and with enthusiasm. No one knows us better than ourselves, and in the end if you feel like you gave it all you got that is what counts and what will enhance your life and quite possibly the lives of those around you.

Deep inside we all want to live a life that is worthwhile and has some sort of impact. No one wants to be a person that went along for the ride of life and did not put anything into it or get anything out of it. We cannot merely be that tree that falls in the forest and no one hears it. We want, if nothing else, for the trees around us to be moved.

The dreams and goals we set do not need to be extraordinary or ones that will make us heroes in the world, but just ones that have the purpose to create some sort of positive difference in our own individual lives. Of course, there will be that group of people who desire to become heroes and make universal effects that alter everyone's lives, but do not be discouraged by their grandeur, thinking what you do will have no effect at all. We all affect one another with every action we take. For example, if I decide that I will take five minutes out of my day to empty the dishwasher instead of just letting all the dirty dishes pile up in the sink, I affect more people than just myself. My mom will not be angry with a full sink of dirty dishes, my siblings will be thankful that they did not have to do the chore, and I will be feel better about myself having done it. Our relationships with one another create a domino effect, and even the smallest decision made can alter the lives of all the people around us. The more positive actions we make, the more positive others will make too. We all have the power with each decision we make to build others up and make the world over all a better place. Sidney Sheldon once said, "Try to leave the Earth a better place than when you arrived." Imagine a world where each of us set this as a personal goal and lived it out day-by-day.

Each of the decisions we make all add up to define our lives and the kind of people we are. A great person is measured by his or her character, which is judged by what he or she does when no one is watching. Making the right decisions every day and doing all the little things right help us to become the best us we can be, which is the ultimate goal in life. It is always said, "Watch your thoughts, they become words. Watch your words, they become actions. Watch your actions, they become habits. Watch your habits, they become your character. Watch your character, it becomes your destiny." If we could take a mirror and reflect back on the person who we were, we would find that the person we have become was created by all the decisions and choices that that person was faced with.

This is where swimming has come into my life and has helped me. It unfolds truths and talents about myself that I never knew I had. It has made me realize the potential I have within me, and that if I just put forth the effort and believe in myself I can accomplish my goals. My goals have created structure for my life. They help me keep focus on what I believe is important. They help me to push myself and work through tough situations. They help me to learn life skills that go far beyond the lane lines.

What goals and dreams have done for me is what I want to share with others. Everyone can have dreams, but they need to set goals to reach their dreams. They also need to know they have the potential to do so. I want to make a difference in this world by helping people realize their own potential and the fact that they can make a difference in this world. I do this today by giving swimming and school my all. Tomorrow, my story will continue, but it will have the foundation that I have built today. Roger Babson said, "Let him who would enjoy a good future waste none of his present."

As I step up to the block before my biggest race of the day, one that will be done in minutes, I look back in the mirror to all of the moments that brought me here. It is the triumphs, the tragedies, the friends and foes, the moments of doubt and the moments that set my heart free. This is the culmination. As Rudyard Kipling said, "If you can fill the unforgiving minute with sixty seconds worth of distance run, then yours is the earth and all that is in it!" The starting horn blasts, and I am off. My earth, my moment, my victory!

Lauren O'Malley - Bio

Lauren came into the world with a roar in Chesapeake, Virginia in 1996 and never stopped to look back. Raised by two former Naval Aviators, Lauren learned early to shoot for and expect excellence, but it wasn't until she found her passion in the swimming pool that she really took ownership of that excellence. An NISC All-American in swimming, Lauren boast a perfect A average in school and is in the top 5% of her class. She stays involved in her community through school clubs, swimming, and Christeen, providing tutoring and mentoring throughout the year. Following behind her big sister Shannon, a swimmer for the National Champion Georgia Bulldogs could have been a daunting task. Instead Lauren looked at it as an opportunity and forged her own path, all the while being grateful to have a friend and confidant in her own sibling. Lauren also has a younger brother Luke, who originally stole her place as "baby" of the family, but later stole her heart as one of her biggest fans. Family and friends are a big part of Lauren's life and she enjoys having opportunities to spend time with both, not surprisingly, out on the water skiing, wakeboarding and boating. She loves her pump-up music and can usually be found rocking out after an eventful practice.

Lauren doesn't plan to use swimming to define herself but instead, hopes to allow it to help her develop all of her talents to their fullest. She might one day find the cure for cancer, design the first truly energy efficient car, or send a space ship to Mars. For now, she simply loves to give life her best and open up a world of endless opportunities.

A Change in Perspective
Nick Willett

CHAPTER 6 – A Change in Perspective

In our era of modernity, it is inarguable that communities- on a very large scale- are faced with many economic, ethnic, socio-cultural, and political problems that they must contend, and their denizens are left to feel the blowback from. Adults, the eternally-sagacious paragons of wisdom and experience, are the primary overseers of the contentions encircling these community-focused issues (which homeowners aren't paying their dues, where will the SPLOST funding go this year, whose children decided to knock over every mailbox on the corner of X street in Y neighborhood); while they are often better equipped to deal with such issues than "children" such as myself, this is not the absolute.

"Children" Are Not Children

True, "children" aren't trained in the ways of mortgage or financing or accounting, internal revenue, jargon, jargon, jargon, but it is often the case that they have quite the attunement to the goings on of their community. Prolific instances abound of proactive "children" (I use quotations here in a sarcastic manner as I do not find that term wholly fitting for those of an older persuasion, say, teenagers) making notable changes in their neighborhoods, towns, local politics, public works, etc. Many programs promoting such progress are often founded by "children" (usually supervised by adults, of course), such as ecological conservation programs, those promoting more active involvement in local politics, and so on. So with all of this in mind, how is it that I intend to make a difference?

Suburban Comforts

Well, to understand that, I must address a few particularities about my community. For one, it isn't exactly the tensest environment to live in, economically or socially; East Cobb and its surrounding areas are about as well-to-do and complacent as anywhere could be. Teenagers are generally a restrained bunch, the sort willing to tug on the leash of their overlords, but never ones to break that leash and sprint off into the middle of traffic. Kids are kids, not a lot of problems there. Some cultural/ ethnic diversity exists, but much of it is whitewashed to the point of being non-threatening to any of the more prolific groups. Faith is almost universally relegated to Christianity, and a general air of malaise hangs over any of those so daring as to have a momentary interest of politics, shortly to be abandoned in favor of watching the Falcons game.

A Maelstrom of Consternation

All snide commentary aside, not much can be done in this community for the time being, not unless something catastrophic were to happen, a sharp increase in poverty, perhaps. So, with nothing to be done on a local level, I am left to broaden my horizon, say to an entire metropolitan city. Atlanta, jewel of the South that it is, has certainly become smudged and tarnished over the past few decades, even after having crawled out of the economic ditch it had been wallowing in for about a century. Rampant vagrants, a high rate of violent crime, racial and ethnic tensions, economic stakes, and in all of this, a precociously nestled political presence. Quite the deadly concoction.

Putting a Stop to Violent Crime

A good place for some progress to wriggle in where it would yield the greatest effect would likely be in the violent crime sector. More often than not, such crime is attributable to the lower economic classes in the city doing what they feel is necessary to survive, this often being theft, carjacking, or murder. To that end, something must be done to put these people in a place where they need not feel that they must congregate together in gangs or groups and prey upon others just to ensure they can go another day, and an easy way to do this is by improving the situation of and attitude toward education. If you ever want to see true teenage apathy toward education, look no further. Teens in these low-income areas (the ghetto, the projects, you all know the names) are not inclined to learn and try to become educated, for whatever reason, often because they find no interest in being part of an institution, pursuing a career, or what have you, and as such, many avoid it altogether. To change that perception, I intend to make an effort to create an outreach program, one of significantly greater efficacy and scale than other such programs; cliché, perhaps, but it is the most viable solution. By bringing in a few members of their community, success stories who rose to prominence out of virtually nothing, some ground can be made, I feel. Consider, if you will, that much research has shown that, in general, it only takes a strong work ethic, a goal(s), and a modicum of self-discipline in order to achieve as highly as even the most intrinsically talented among us-something I can attest to and acknowledge. All that is needed is a hearty push in the right direction, a nudging toward some standard of achievement, and to build upon that.

Old Hatreds, Older Problems

Despite our best efforts, racial and ethnic problems continue to be a prevalent feature of the South, and greatly so in our state, in our diverse cities and townships. To stymie prejudice is an altogether unprecedented feat, one attempted many times throughout history and to no ultimate avail; people will always hate other people, for whatever inane reason they can formulate. But some good has been done in this area, some progress has been made. In an effort to expedite that progress, I intended to act as an intermediary between conflicting groups, an arbiter, to break down some of the barriers that have been forged by hundreds of years of distrust and unabashed anger. A challenge, undoubtedly, but all too plausible given the right environment for arbitrage, and a simple willingness by those prejudiced parties. People tend to fear or distrust difference and what they are either unwilling to or cannot practically understand, and both afflictions are easily cured if I can simply force a confrontation. So, I will establish a meeting place, perhaps at a residence or restaurant or the like, and coax conflicting groups into a confrontation with one another, to face what they have been avoiding head-on, and the work past old hatreds, let bygones be bygones, the like.

Invitation to the Bounty

I must confess this next area is where the adults have to take over, if for no other reason than I lack a firm understanding of the world of business and the politics of the greenback. Our economy is in a slump though, I can understand that, and businesses are firing-or, as they like "politely" put it, laying off- working class citizens in droves, I can see that. But I will take a proactive approach to better appreciate the situation of companies later; for now, I am concerned over how to help those most heavily impacted by the recession. I will create a survey system designed to approach the destitute and impoverished and gather data on what these people need the most in order to sustain themselves, items like blankets, clothes, gas, food, water, and the like. Of course the latter four are always objects of need, but I want to push past providing the necessities, and offer a bit of luxury as well, toys and books and games and the like for children, hobby items for the parents while they look for work or look to dredge themselves out of monetary hell. When someone like myself has such a bounty, it is only all too reasonable to extend it to others who do not, or had a taste of it before, or who have never had more than what they absolutely needed. Not to mention that such provisions will keep children in schools, keep them learning, so that they may at one point be given an opportunity to succeed as well.

A Personal Note

Unfortunately, all problems start at home, and I am all too familiar with this. Distance is a powerful ally to social recluses, those undesiring of the company of others, and I have extended this unkindness to my family. Yes, it is, indeed, personal now, steel yourself. I have historically failed to see myself as a member of a larger unit, concerned with my interests above all others. It has taken longer than it should have, but I have realized my error in this. One cannot hope to change family, nor can he or she hope to abandon them altogether, nor can they expect to be left be by these people who so brazenly intrude upon their intrapersonal self-absorption. Family is forever, unavoidable, inexorable. I will make a difference with my family, with my role in the grand scheme of kinship. I will open up more, about my problems and concerns, about my thoughts and ideas, about how my day was, mom, about how it was the same as every other, and how I wish you would stop asking that, but I appreciate that you do. Expression, respect, appreciation. That will be the effective checklist I mark off whenever I have any engagement with my family, what I will be looking to extend. "Children" and children (yes, there is a difference) alike tend to neglect such efforts in their adolescence, but I can change that, and I wholly intend to.

No Respect, No Respect at All

A pet peeve of mine that comes up often when I watch the interactions of teenagers and adults is the unerring disrespect. And I mean on behalf of both parties. Some respect has to be leveled at the teen in order for them to pay it back in kind; it's a cyclical process. Too often I find that children feel that they have been disrespected by a teacher or adult, and while this may sometimes be without a proper basis, it leads many to return that disrespect; again, cyclical. The only way I can really make a difference is to set an example. I try to offer respect without an expectation of receiving it in return, and much to no surprise, I eventually see the fruits of that labor. Teens need only follow such an example, and they can generate a positive cycle of respect, instead of the less-savory alternative.

A Much-Ignored Truth

My name is Average American, and I leave a carbon footprint. The environment is a fragile thing, we've all been taught this lesson over and over to the point where it just becomes inconvenient, but do any of us really care? Do any of us really consider just how fragile our planet really is? After all, the majority of ecological problems tend not to reach out here to the suburbs and cul-de-sacs and rural areas, aside from the occasional slightly-off temperature that keeps a few pondering for a time before writing it off as nothing big. Despite this, we all have a part to play in the ecosystem, whether we can acknowledge it or not, and the majority of us don't. The sheer number of cars in a middle class suburban area produce more air pollutants than we really think they do; families have two cars on average, due to the volume of families with two employed parents. It all piles up after a while, that choking effervescence that wafts about in the otherwise-fresh air of these deciduous neighborhoods. I will strive to reduce the carbon footprint embedded by those treading upon the natural gifts they are so fortunate to be surrounded with, to show the damage they are causing for their future generations, to have them consider that while "the future" is quite a long ways off, it will catch up with them eventually. Introducing local programs where tangible statistics are given to impress upon those who have not seen the power of a few metric tons of gaseous exhaust upon nature would be the best route. We like to hold aloft the idea that all this ecological drama will just come to a head "in the future", at a time where we will likely be dead and gone and the generations that follow us will be left to wallow in the mess we made for them, but what kind of an attitude is that? What sort of person does one become when they leave their progeny to the mercy of deathly smog clouds and dying forests and poisoned water and poisoned fish and dying livestock and draught and famine and a penultimate, painful, untimely, unwarranted, uncalled-for death? If for no other reason than that I should want my grandchildren to be able to play outside without a gas mask and hazardous materials suit, I will make a difference.

Making a Difference in Myself

It is not without a heavily-weighing understanding of my own faults and flaws that I should see where I can foment difference in a space outside of my own. No one can claim perfection, but it is significantly harder to admit imperfection, especially in such a wide format. I only say this because I am guilty of many of the errors that I have made mention of, that I have made clear my intentions and methods of changing. That paragraph about neglecting the import of family? I am most assuredly guilty of that, but I am guilty of prejudice, I am guilty of not minding my ecological impact, of my own willingness to forsake the future in the name of my comforts, of ignoring the destitute and unemployed because I live in more comfortable environs, outside of the realms of poverty, of expecting respect when I have warranted none at all, of acting like a child, instead of a "child". I find solace in that I can acknowledge these flaws, and can find in myself the will to correct mine, and then to fix the problems that they stem from. I have made progress within myself, so that I am able to make progress in my home, my school, my community, my state.

Closing Remarks and Thoughts

I will not only make a difference, but I will continue making a difference. I will make a difference in college, when I am left to my own devices to fend for myself, treated as an adult for the first time. I will make a difference in my work, where I will generate as great and positive an impact as possible upon everyone I encounter, upon everyone I work with, for, and whom work for me. I will make a difference upon the world, awash with problems the likes of which I could have never expected or foreseen, could have never been prepared for, that could only be experienced and adapted to, as only the worst of problems can. I will make a difference because I have learned what a difference means, what sort of effect it can have as it ripples outward, causing a chain reaction of other differences, just how far it can go before that ripple even begins to even out remotely. I will make a difference because I can, because I have been given the ability and opportunity to do so, because I can trigger that chain reaction, because I can help put a smile on the face of impoverished, because I can help the races and ethnicities of the world coincide and collaborate, because someone has to do it, and why should not I?

Nick Willett – Bio

Nicholas Willett is a seventeen-year-old purveyor of all things snarky, sarcastic, satirical, hammy, non-conformist, and astute (or so he thinks he is, but that point is debatable). Born in Savannah, Georgia, the young Mr. Willett has spent the better part of his young life striving toward a gambit of different goals, raising the bar in some cases and ambling on beneath it in others. He has been described- with great detail- as a "Pleasure to teach" and an "Excellent student." Growing up the youngest of three, Mr. Willett enjoyed the comforts of the middle-class, a doting mother, and a beautiful environment that sculpted much of his precipitating nostalgia. Being a child of many words but only a few of them spoken, and a disposition that kept him aloof from most of his peers, Mr. Willett was forced to turn to other outlets of attention. At a young age, he took an interest in literature and began a descent into the world of storytelling and media that has not stopped since, and has been at the epicenter of all goals set since his adolescence. He has heavily invested his personal time and effort into writing short stories and novellas to hone his skills, the chapter appearing in this being his first and thus far only published work, and continues to pursue his goals at becoming a successful author, continuing to write in his spare times and share his work with friends and family for review. A self-proclaimed social recluse, Mr. Willett has often found challenge and frustration in attempting to find a sense of belonging and acceptance among peers, often going to extreme measures to avoid being forced into social situations at school and other extra-curricular programs. In recent years, he has found the courage to move past these obstacles in the interest of bettering himself and creating lasting relationships. Currently, Mr. Willett lives at home with his soon-to-be-wed sister, doting mother, and inspiring yet distant father.

The Butterfly Effect
Rachel I. Cohn

CHAPTER 7 - The Butterfly Effect

"Human felicity is produc'd not so much by great pieces of good fortune that seldom happen, as by little advantages that occur every day."

--Benjamin Franklin

I Will Make a Difference

To have an impact on another's life is an achievable act that presents itself daily. When one encounters people, there exists a decision on how to act. Happiness occurs when one extends aid, advice, companionship, or any such action that will help. And if it becomes a custom of mine to think of what I can do to help or to think of how I can better at once my community and myself, then I can create a new luminosity to everyday deeds.

By pursuing this mentality in the various facets and passions of my life, I will make a difference.

Making a Difference through Education

I began tutoring her in the summer of 2013. She struggled in school and found little enjoyment in her studies, but her mind was open and excitement danced around her. Originally, I was told to help her with language arts, but as the school year approached and the challenges of middle school began to settle, I became a tutor for her in all areas.

To see her improvement brought such light to all. I recall one time when she came, her eyes beaming and her voice full of confidence. I started the lesson by asking her to tell me about her subjects and her recent and upcoming assignments. "I got a 93 on my social studies test, a 95 on my science test and a 100 on my math test…" She was ecstatic, and my heart leapt up in my chest. Not only was she achieving highly, but she was also excited about learning and doing well. She told me that she was going to get all A's that year, and she began to tell me in animated tones the way that the information she learned in school related to her own life.

The abilities she gained from the tutoring did not merely teach her a bare minimum of skills needed to pass a test, but rather it helped her to see that learning new ideas and gathering knowledge is enjoyable, and this message will have benefits throughout her education.

And I felt as if I was not doing anything…I was simply providing aid to someone who was willing to learn. One hour, sometimes two hours, per week–it seemed small in comparison. A small part of the day that led to large impact…

Making a Difference through Building Confidence

Similarly, a few months earlier, I had spent one hour with a woman studying for her GED, or high school diploma. She was a single mother of two and the type of amiable person that exudes righteousness. When she walked in the door, one could tell that her heart was golden. She sat down across the table from me, and nervously looked around as she pulled out her materials. We talked of fractions, greatest common factors, number lines, and probability.

Each problem that she solved correctly seemed to take her one step nearer to her future. Each accurate answer led to a smile and a subsequent determination to focus on the next problem. Her concentration was deep and her mind persistent. By the end, she was confident, and this confidence led her to continue studying. A few months later, she passed the GED and has since enrolled in college.

I spent one hour with this woman, yet every time I see her, she thanks me, and she attributes part of her success to me. I do not fully understand how sixty minutes merits such gratitude, yet I was nevertheless elated to help.

Making a Difference through Continuation

On a different note, I am a member of my high school's marching band. When I was a freshman, many aspects of the organization seemed unattainable. How was I to memorize music? How could one march and play at the same time while maintaining posture? How does one know where to march throughout the show? And how does one survive in high school?

Luckily, I had a newfound family to guide me. The euphonium section supported me, accepted me, and helped me to grow as a musician and as a person. The challenges I faced were not met alone, for I knew that my section was there for me.

As an upperclassman and part of the leadership, I realize that it is my duty to recreate this feeling of acceptance and assurance for the younger members of the band. Although we act as a unified front, the band is made up of individuals, and each individual can make a difference in the experiences of the other members. It does not take a large effort, but simply continued actions, albeit small ones. I feel as if I am merely doing what I should when I act properly during rehearsal, when I remind my section to count, when I stay an extra ten minutes after rehearsal to help a freshman memorize a stand tune, when I ask the younger members how school is going and if they need help in a class. Most of what I do takes little effort, but it lets the others know that I am there for them and reminds them that they are important members of the band.

By continuing the examples set forth by the alumni, I influence the environment of rehearsals and the mind-set of those around me. Of course it is not just me—it is the cumulative effort of everyone, every student putting forth his/her best to achieve a common goal of creating music at the highest level all the time. It does not take much to do this, but when everyone contributes, the results are astounding.

Making a Difference through Music

Music truly can change lives. A few years ago, I discovered an amazing charity called the Playing for Change Foundation. In their own words, the PFCF can be described as the following:

> "While traveling the world filming and recording musicians, the crew became intimately involved with the music and people of each community they visited. Although many of these communities had limited resources and a modest standard of living, the people in them were full of generosity, warmth, and above all they were connected to each other by a common thread: music.

> "Out of these discoveries, the Playing for Change Foundation was born and made its mission to ensure that anyone with the desire to receive a music education would have the opportunity to do so. The Playing for Change Foundation is dedicated to the fundamental idea that peace and change are possible through the universal language of music" (Source: playingforchange.org).

Aside from the annual donation around the holidays, I wanted to do something more. With the music honors society at my high school, I helped to organize a benefit concert to raise money for the PFCF's Stand by Me Scholarship, a program through which a person can donate money for one student's music education for an entire year at one of Playing for Change's music or music and dance schools. Small ensembles from the top music programs at the high school performed a variety of pieces, sharing the power of music and the capacity of music to sweep us away into another world. We raised enough money to sponsor two students, and at the next concert we hope to double the number.

There is something powerful about the language of music, and it has the ability to take away the troubles of life and replace them with a momentary yet resonating joy.

Making a Difference through Stories

To further exemplify how one can make a difference, small, sometimes routine actions can sometimes be much more when they directly affect the happiness of others. I write for the school newspaper, and it astonishes me how a couple hundred words written about someone can touch that person's life.

I enjoy writing features articles because I can depict the beauty of one person to an audience. One of my favourite articles was composed of short features on three "hidden heroes" at our high school: a cafeteria worker, a sign language coach, and a custodian.

There was such joy on their faces when I was interviewing them and when they told me of the experiences they have had at the high school. I did not expect to find the excitement and passion they each felt in their jobs and interactions with the students. One had been working at the school for over thirty years, and another kept the job as a part time job because she loved being there for the students every day. Their selflessness and willingness to bring happiness to the school taught me about simple daily exchanges and how, if happiness defines them, then they define the happiness of others.

Furthermore, when I went to interview the custodian, I had to ask a co-worker for directions. He started to reply, but could not find the word in English. I study Spanish at school, and repeated my question in that language. He face instantly lit up as he gave me instructions.

A few days later, he came in to clean the newspaper classroom when I was staying after school editing. We struck up a conversation, and I learned about his life, and he about mine. We speak in Spanish which helps me practice my skills, and our sporadic exchanges bring brightness to my day. He is a great family man, and whenever he speaks of his two children, he is proud and happy. Now, when I see him around the school, we exclaim the other's name and enjoy a pleasant conversation.

It makes me feel jubilant when I send a draft of the article before it is published to the person I am featuring, and they respond with such phrases as "I have always wanted to be in the newspaper," or "I never thought that I would see my words or my story shared." It is lovely to know that I can bring that joy to people by providing a means through which to share their story.

Making a Difference Through Volunteering

A final illustration is that of The Foundation for Hospital Art. The Foundation is a non-profit organization that provides painted murals of happy landscapes and animals to hospitals around the world in order to spread cheer to patients and families in hospitals.

One of the greatest ways to serve one's community is to sacrifice time to help others. Through a simple act of painting on a "paint-by-color" system, many people can transform the atmosphere of a place of struggle. Several high school students and I went to a homeless shelter for recovering addicts where we painted canvases with the men to donate to nearby hospitals. It was heart-warming to see these men giving time as well as to converse with them, for they had interesting stories to share.

We were open and candid in dialogue, and the connections we made between our lives, so different upon first glance, made the experience a mutual experience in which we could both find meaning. One man asked if I knew of a local highway, and was so excited when I said that I did, and he proceeded to tell me how he lived in a tent in the woods near that highway, foraging in a tent and living freely, (although hiding from the police) and caring for wounded animals. He wanted to express his story, and by connecting, even in a minute detail, he became happy.

Another man and I spoke for a while about the bonds of family. Although our backgrounds were completely different from one another, we both had a brother, and from this a tapestry of talk was sewn.

To spend time with the men while simultaneously giving back to a greater cause exhibited the ease of creating a positive influence.

How You Can Make a Difference

As shown in the previous examples, one can see how a small action can resonate within another person's life. It may seem a great task to make a difference in the world, but it is easy if you start with one person, and make helping those around you a habit. I have learned that the way to make a difference is by doing it, not just one whole step at a time, but in steps that are barely perceptible, so that when you look back, each step seems as if it were nothing at all, yet it holds a larger impact.

Listen when necessary; act when necessary. Start today, and establish a mentality of genuine empathy for others, and the effects will follow. As Mother Teresa guides, "Never worry about numbers. Help one person at a time and always start with the person nearest you."

Rachel I. Cohn – Bio

Rachel I. Cohn is a junior at Lassiter High School who enjoys writing, reading, and playing music. She is the Features Editor for the school newspaper, *The Laureate,* and this is her third year on staff. While a member of the high school marching and concert bands on euphonium, she also participates in the Atlanta Tuba and Euphonium Ensemble. *También, estudia el español y le gusta aprender los idiomas.* She volunteers at the Foundation for Hospital Art, babysits imaginative and adorable children, and tutors in academic subjects. Ms. Cohn enjoys studying language arts and hopes to pursue a degree in English. In her free time, she enjoys playing cribbage and mah jongg with her family, spending quality time talking, finding the obscure origins of punctuation marks, researching the United States Postal Service, and listening to Gerald Finzi. In additional free time that is oftentimes not so free, she reads as many Agatha Christie novels as possible, dabbles in fiction writing, reads the dictionary, and maintains pen pal relationships.

Dropping the Ball
Ryker Martin

CHAPTER 8 – Dropping the Ball

All You Need is Hard Work

Thud- another dropped pass. I scramble to pick up the ball that shouldn't have hit the ground and the head coach shouts, "Everyone drop and give me 15!" A dozen angry looks and remarks shoot my way from my teammates. After the push-ups, the assistant coach calls me over. I jog over to him, wishing I could change places with him. After all, he's really good at lacrosse. He is on the high school varsity team and has even played in a state championship! As I profusely apologize for my lack of skill, he says, "It's alright. This is just something that you have to work at. You're already better than me when I started." Shocked, I looked up and asked, "Really!?" What he says next has been something that I have lived by for the past five years of my life. "Not everyone starts with natural talent. Someone with natural talent, who doesn't put any effort into getting better, will eventually fall behind. What accelerates you to becoming exceptional is hard work. Not talent. Not equipment. Work."

His words rang true to me, and the more I contemplated the idea of hard work being as valuable as talent, my overall attitude and perspective started to change, opening a whole new world of possibilities. This high school lacrosse player probably has no idea how much his words have influenced me, but I have applied this idea to every aspect of my life and it has sent me on a journey towards becoming a well rounded adult. That assistant coach made a difference in my life.

Now I am him. I am the assistant lacrosse coach. I played on a team that went to a state championship, and I have worked hard. I'm even a certified youth lacrosse official. It's now my turn to influence and inspire. Rev. Billy Graham once said, "One coach will impact more people in a year than the average person does in a lifetime." I know Rev. Graham is right. From the moment that I started this job, I have tried to positively influence my players by being a good example to them and by trying to help them establish their own self-motivation. I push them to their limits on the field and encourage them to try harder in school. It is a great feeling to see someone take your advice to heart and I have become addicted to this feeling. I want to keep influencing people to work hard and be the best they can be, just like the high school lacrosse player did for me.

Hard Work at School

This notion of the importance of hard work had a major impact on my attitude regarding school. I was a good student in elementary school, but I was never challenged. Like many kids, I was more interested in recess and lunch than the core subjects. When I got to sixth grade, I tested into the accelerated track. It was a lot harder than anything I was used to, and I knew I couldn't just continue to coast through with little effort. Dropping down to the on-level track seemed like a more attractive option every day. This was around the time that my coach shared his take on hard work with me. With that in mind, I did what I needed to do to stay on course: I did all of my homework (something that was new to me), I worked harder on problems and asked plenty of questions when I was confused, and I got after school help. Because of my hard work, I was able to achieve good grades and stay on the accelerated track. I've been at the top of my class since sixth grade, and my mindset definitely changed. Instead of coasting and just doing enough to get by, I now search for ways to challenge myself and inspire other students.

Applying What I Learned To Help Others

I try to go above and beyond, both in the classroom and out, by taking all AP and honor classes to challenge and stimulate my mind and become more insightful, and by tutoring other students. I'm on virtually every volunteer student tutor list at school. As a tutor, I try to motivate kids to work hard in their classes. One of the easiest ways to accomplish this is by showing them how it feels to get good grades after a lot of hard work. Recently, I had the opportunity to tutor a student athlete, "Jay." Jay was really struggling in math. He was very frustrated and felt badly about himself and was worrying about his academic eligibility to play basketball. Jay sensed that there was just something he wasn't getting in class and it was keeping him from doing well in math. I agreed to help him and after just one session of tutoring, he made a 100 on his next math test! He was so happy and felt so much better about himself, and his mom was so grateful that she not only thanked me, but contacted my mom to thank her, too! I now get paid to tutor Jay whenever he needs help and Jay isn't worried about being academically eligible to play basketball. Jay has gained a valuable skill in the classroom: confidence. He now does much better on his own and doesn't need my help as often. I help a lot of athletes get their grades up in order to be eligible to participate in school sports, but I also want them to keep those grades up during their off season. One way to achieve this is to make sure their coach finds out about their better grades, giving the student a little more motivation. All my efforts in tutoring have landed me the spot as the official tutor of the lacrosse team, which presents me with a lot of opportunities to influence my teammate's perception of academics. I am making a difference.

Making Good Choices

Although being a coach can be a big influence, your peers may be your biggest influence. Everything you do is noticed by your peers. You can have a huge impact on your peers just by doing the right thing and setting a good example. Making good choices is a very effective way of making a difference both in school and out. Bad choices have just as much impact as good ones. Choosing to use drugs and alcohol, for example, can have a huge negative impact on you and your friends. When I was a freshman, the varsity lacrosse team had a bit of a drug problem. Despite the drug problem, there were a lot of very talented players on the team, but all that talent was wasted because of a really bad decision by one kid. He smuggled drugs in his bag to an out of state lacrosse tournament. Because of his bad decision, nearly half of the kids on that varsity squad got kicked off the team, killing their chances of winning a state championship. That player made a difference, but certainly not a favorable one. I work hard on making good choices.

Intrinsic Motivation

I believe that deep down everyone has some sort of internal motivation that comes hard-wired within us; it just takes some outside force to put it in motion. Once in motion, it should stay in motion (if Isaac Newton's law of motion is correct). Hard physical work was never a strong suit of mine. I would much rather lie down, eat chips, and play FIFA; however, once I began to play lacrosse, I needed to be in shape because it requires strength, agility, and endurance. I decided to develop a fitness routine to increase my endurance and become stronger and faster. It's a pretty tough training regiment consisting of a rotating cycle of running five miles one day, lifting weights for two hours on another day, and practicing lacrosse shooting for a couple hours the next. This is a continuous routine that I only break a few times a year for holidays and family. Without intrinsic motivation, it would be impossible to keep this up. It took me a while to get into the groove of working out hard (like 4 years), but I've experienced a huge payoff. I lost 30 pounds, move much faster, and I'm more agile, but it wasn't easy. Sometimes intrinsic motivation comes naturally to people, while other times it can be incredibly elusive. This hard work made a difference in my own life, and because of it, I am healthier and a better athlete.

Work Ethic and Determination

Encouraging teens to do for themselves is another way I try to make a difference. As the Chinese proverb goes, "Give a man a fish and you feed him for a day. *Teach* a man *to* fish and you feed him for a lifetime." One of the best things to do for someone is to teach and encourage them to become more determined and to develop a good work ethic. Your work ethic and determination have a much greater impact on your life than anything else; it can make or break you. But a little effort goes a long way. On my lacrosse team, I try to be encouraging when someone is struggling. I can't just make them better, but I can show them how to get better. I teach them things they can work on, but it is totally their call to work on it or not. If you push people too much they can become dependent on you, or resent your help. Another way I do this is to lead by example. Humans tend to like to try and mirror anything they admire: it's just a natural instinct. If you find yourself in any position of power, someone's goal may be to follow in your footsteps; if you continue to work hard, they will want to work hard, too. You have then given them the ability to become more determined and have a better work ethic. Hard work also yields some unexpected rewards. My hard work has made me more confident, positive, and passionate about my interests. People consider me to be responsible and self-disciplined, and I now see myself as ambitious and determined.

Hard Work Never Goes to Waste

In ninth grade, I participated in both marching band and lacrosse. That year, our band was chosen to march in the 2010 Macy's Thanksgiving Parade in New York City. After a lot of practice and hard work, I made drum line as a freshman and I was very excited to be marching first bass drum in the parade. The band got to see all the sights, attend a Broadway show and even see the famous Rockettes while we were in New York City. The parade crowd was tremendous and it was awesome to perform for a national television audience! Participating in such a grand event certainly made a difference in my life and hopefully inspired the kids watching to learn to play an instrument so they might someday march in a big parade. After ninth grade, I decided to concentrate solely on lacrosse and dropped out of band. I continued to enjoy percussion, but never got the opportunity to perform again. When my senior year began, I wanted to reconnect with my percussion ability in a different way to help cheer on our football team. I started taking a drum to the football games and creating different beats to rouse the senior student section. Every time I brought my drum to a game, our team won! If you believe in football superstition, my drum made a difference.

Final Thoughts

Everyone can make a difference. Every single day, you can make a difference. You don't have to be the Pope or Mother Teresa, or win a Nobel Prize or start a worthy charity to make a difference. Making a difference is easy if you are willing to share the best parts of yourself with others. Try to connect with those around you. Set good examples by working hard and making good choices. You never know who is watching, who is waiting to be inspired. Understand and accept that you may never know of the differences you make- large or small, just as I have never been able to thank that high school assistant coach for making a huge difference in my life. I have tried to pay it forward many times over through my efforts to inspire the youth that I have encountered. Now that I am heading into my new, college life, I wonder how my life will change, but I feel confident that I will meet any challenges head on. I am positive that I have made a difference and that I will continue to make a difference, not because of some special talent or recognition, but because I am willing to do the work. I know that I will encounter situations which will require a lot of hard work, different work than I am used to, but I am ready. I will welcome these life changing events. I want my college experience to be exceptional and hope that it leads to a career where I will continue to have a positive impact on the world. I will make a difference and I won't worry about dropping the ball, because I know sometimes great things happen when they're least expected!

Ryker Martin – Bio

Shawn "Ryker" Martin is a senior at Lassiter High School in Marietta, Georgia. He lives in East Cobb County with his mom and dad, and has a sister who attends The University of Georgia. Ryker continually maintains above a 4.0 GPA, is in the top 10% of his class, and has received Academic Letters each year in school. He has received an AP Scholar Award, participates in Lassiter's National Honor Society and Science National Honor Society, and is a successful math and science student tutor. In 2010, Ryker marched with the Lassiter High School Marching Band (percussion) in the Macy's Thanksgiving Parade in New York City, and received a Band Letter. Ryker is a varsity lacrosse captain, received Lassiter's Scholar Athlete Award, and holds the highest GPA on Lassiter's Lacrosse team. In 2012, Ryker was the captain of Lassiter's JV Lacrosse team and was awarded the Most Valuable Player Award. Ryker played four years with the select East Cobb Thunder Lacrosse travel team and he contributes to the larger lacrosse community by coaching middle school teams and by officiating youth lacrosse games and tournaments as a U.S. Lacrosse certified official. Ryker has also volunteered for many organizations, including Trojan Youth Lacrosse, AJ04 Lacrosse, Lars Tiffany Lacrosse Camp, and Must Ministries. Ryker enjoys spending his free time with friends, watching and playing sports, especially soccer, and playing with his dog and cat. Ryker plans to study engineering or business management in college and looks forward to opportunities in college that can expand his interests and community involvement, and lead to a rewarding career.

I Will Make a Difference

Hannah Sbaity

CHAPTER 9 - I Will Make a Difference

"Because I know about the Holy Land, I've taught lessons about the Holy Land all my life, and - but you can't bring peace to Israel without giving the Palestinian also peace. And Lebanon and Jordan and Syria as well."

~ Jimmy Carter

My Story

It's not every seven year old's dream to spend their summer hiding during a war. On the morning of July 12, 2006, Israel launched waves of air strikes on Lebanon, setting the start of a Second Lebanon war by the Israelis. I could see the first bomb go off since I was having breakfast on my grandparent's balcony. The balcony has a perfect view of the ocean, horizon, and Beirut and beyond. When the bomb went off, the whole building shook and my mama and Teta yelled for me to get down and crawl inside. We shut the shutters, locked the doors, and turned on the news. We sat in tears and fear while listening to the static sound of the television, trying to comprehend what they were saying, but all we could really hear were the war planes and bombs in the distance. When we calmed down enough to focus on the television, we could see disturbing pictures of those killed in the bombings. My parents told me, my 6 year old brother, and my 1 year old sister to sit in the bedroom so that we didn't see the terrible images being shown; however, one image was enough for me to see how scary it was out there. My family and I, including my grandparents, parents, siblings, aunts, uncles, and cousins went to a small hidden resort on the coast of Lebanon where we could be safe. We stayed there for a few days, and lucky enough the U.S. Navy came and rescued us. We had to leave all of our belongings behind and could only take one carry on per person while a boat took us from Cyprus, to many states in America, and finally back home to Georgia. My family was lucky enough that we were American citizens visiting in my parents' home country, but what about the other families left to die in terrible conditions?

After I returned safely back home from a rough journey, I wanted to make a difference for those that didn't have the same opportunity as I did; however I was only seven years old: what kind of difference could I make? I didn't erase the thought from my mind since I still pray every day thanking God for sending me brave troops that protected me and sent me back home. When Gary Martin Hays and Adam Weart came to Lassiter High School to give young aspiring writers a chance to write about something that they would like to make a difference in, I knew exactly what I was going to write about. I want to create a foundation called MEFF or the Middle Eastern Families Foundation.

The two main goals of the Middle Eastern Families Foundation (MEFF) are:

1. To rescue those families that may not be American citizens by teaming up with neighboring friendly countries and create refugee centers and
2. To create refugee centers within the countries themselves for those people as well.

All of these goals need huge funding and peaceful negotiations, and I believe if we collect the estimated amount needed to fund the goals and made connections with helpful organizations, the countries in the Middle East such as Lebanon, Syria, and Jordan with be inspired to cooperate with one another in order to ensure the safety of their own citizens. In order to raise the large amounts of money, there are seven different ways to spread the word.

"Online Advertising"

Posting ads on websites that receive heavy traffic is a good way to get the word out. Social networking sites such as Facebook, Instagram, Twitter, or Myspace are heavily trafficked sites that provide potential sums of money to donate to MEFF. These ads are also helpful because they only show up next to profiles that meet the specifications of the targeted market.

"Newspaper Ads"

Daily and weekly newspaper ads allow us to target specific geographic neighborhoods, which can be helpful by selecting those areas that are known to have people willing to donate to charities living there. This is a traditional form of advertising and it could possibly be the best way to start advertising MEFF.

"Radio Advertising"

Radio advertising is helpful because we can match the station with our target demographic that would most likely donate to this helpful cause. In order to reach adults aged 35 to 64, an adult contemporary station will work. An alternative or urban station is good to reach those aged from 18 to 24.

"Television Advertising"

Television ads are effective in this case because visuals are used. Once the audience sees the reason behind building the refugee centers, there is an emotional appeal to the cause and they would most likely donate.

"Event Sponsorship"

Advertising MEFF through event sponsorship can be helpful at charity venues. These venues contain people who will most likely donate to this cause. Some kind of auction may help people donate large sums towards MEFF.

"Word-of-Mouth Advertising"

Speaking in public places at events may be effective because it reaches out to different audiences. These large or small audiences have potential donors who may help MEFF raise a lot of money.

All of these ways of advertising may be helpful in raising money for MEFF, but teaming up with large organizations that can be handy in the refugee centers and advertise more widely will be in our favor. These organizations include:

- American Near East Refugee Aid (ANERA)
- International Rescue Committee (IRC)
- American Red Cross

However, before I can even think about getting the word out, there are several steps needed to be taken in order to officially obtain the status as a nonprofit organization. A nonprofit doesn't have to register internationally to operate on a global basis, but a nonprofit status insures that the organization is tax exempt in the state or country in which it operates.

Step 1

The first step is to form a Board of Directors which includes like-minded people who have an interest in the new nonprofit's goals and the population the organization will serve. The Board of Directors should include governmental, business and target-population representation and it is important that all board positions are voluntary with no profits. The board should consist of members, and should appoint a President, Vice-President, Treasurer and Secretary as administrators. Since MEFF is international, it is important to consider asking residents of those countries to serve as advisers to the Board of Directors.

Step 2

The second step is to define the nonprofit's mission, goals, target population, and area of outreach in writing. It is essential to research and define the target population and area of outreach, or the locations the nonprofit will provide service which will be necessary when filing application documents for 501(c)(3) nonprofit status and when seeking donors. All members and advisers of the Board of Directors must provide their resumes, list of affiliations, and contact information.

Step 3

The third step is to create a business in writing which should include: the organization's mission statement; a brief introduction describing the organization; an administrative chart showing the amount of responsibility; a needs statement that addresses the target population and an idea of services, programs and proposed projects; objectives and goals; marketing and fund raising strategies; and a detailed 3-to-5-year proposed budget. The budget should take into account the following: staffing; facility costs; contracted services; travel; staff and board training; office equipment and supplies; marketing expenses; postage and printing; and any other projected costs.

Step 4

The last step is to register the nonprofit business name with the national business registry and to file Articles of Incorporation in the state in which the nonprofit will be operating which will be Georgia in this case. The documents needed are generally available on the state government website, in the corporations division, requiring nominal fees to file both the business name with the national registry, and to file Articles of Incorporation. It is mandatory to file for the federal 501(c)(3) nonprofit status. File form SS-4 is available from the Internal Revenue Service (IRS) to obtain a Federal

Tax Identification number which is free. Another form that I must obtain is Form 1023, from the IRS as well, which must be completed and mailed with a $500 fee. I will be willing to get a job in order to get the foundation starting to pay for the fees that come along with creating MEFF. Receiving approval from the IRS for nonprofit status will take several months.

Final Word

It is in my deep interest to create Middle Eastern Families Foundation (MEFF). In order to create this foundation, I need funding, donations, partners, and cooperation. The funding and donations can come through advertising in the ways I talked about in this chapter. American Near East Refugee Aid, International Rescue Committee, and American Red Cross are only three of the many organizations that are potential partners in this operation. The cooperation I need in order to successfully create this foundation is on a large scale, including the Lebanese, Syrian, and Jordanian governments working with one another and the friendly neighboring countries in order to create refugee centers safe for their citizens in a time of crisis. In order to get started and get the word out, registration as a nonprofit foundation is crucial. This foundation not only needs those components but it needs understanding and devotion, and I have both of those qualities since I went through exactly what many are having to deal with now. Having a safe place to go during a war is what every family in these countries deserves. If we can't bring them to the United States of America, let's bring the United States of America to them by providing the safety that we Americans feel while living in the USA.

"The purpose of government is to enable the people of a nation to live in safety and happiness. Government exists for the interests of the governed, not for the governors."

~Thomas Jefferson

Hannah Sbaity - Bio

Hannah Sbaity is not only a hard working student attending Lassiter High School, but is compassionate for others and shows that when wanting to make a difference in the Middle East. She currently vacations in Lebanon, her parents' home country, every summer and lived through the Lebanese- Israeli War in 2006. She wants to make a difference in the way Lebanese, Syrian, and Jordanian citizens are sheltered in a time of crisis by creating MEFF (Middle Eastern Families Foundation). This type of commitment and interest is not new to someone like Hannah. She has a reputation of being involved in many clubs and organizations. Hannah is currently among the top students in her class rank and takes challenging classes while trying to balance her academics, Beta Club, Renaissance Team, Mock Trial, and Debate Team. She is interested in graduating from Harvard University and becoming a Criminal Justice Lawyer when she is older. Some of her greatest accomplishments include getting her poem published in The Reach of Song in 2009, placing first or second in the County Science Fair for the past two years, placing in the 2013 Blue Key Speech and Debate Tournament, winning third in the Art Reflections Competition, serving as a page in House of Representatives at the Georgia State Capitol, and many more smaller contests. Hannah is currently in the process of creating and organizing Lassiter High School's first ever international festival to open the students' eyes to different cultures and their customs and food. She is very passionate about learning about other cultures and even listens to foreign music which contributes to her ability to speak English and Arabic, and she is currently learning Spanish and French. Hannah hopes that her previous accomplishments, unique outlook on different cultures, and passion in helping others contribute to her creating her dream foundation and truly making a difference in this world.

Promoting Healthy Habits Throughout Schools

Adam Ward

CHAPTER 10 – Promoting Healthy Habits Throughout Schools

Healthy Habits Shoved Down My Throat

As a teenager, I can still vividly remember my mother cooking that frozen spinach that sat at the back of the freezer for months for me and my sister. The taste still stings in the back of my mouth, and I'm not sure if I'll be able to forget the lurid visual appearance of the wretched vegetable: a giant mountain of goo! However, over the years, I have realized something. My mother wasn't trying to torture me and my sister. She was instilling healthy eating habits in me from the get go. There actually was a reason for eating all of those vegetables and always going for after-school walks! I am truly thankful for the influence that my mother has had on me in making smart decisions pertaining to my health. To this day, I withhold my commitment to a healthy lifestyle by eating a simple sandwich and banana for lunch, running on the weekends, and, of course, eating that delicious frozen spinach one night a week! Unfortunately, many children are raised without healthy habits engrained in their everyday lifestyle, and these poor bodily decisions escalate during school years. And while many of us who are reading this book might be dedicated spinach eaters, it is important to remind ourselves why youth must be taught correctly from the start.

A Wake-Up Call

I never truly understood how important my health was until I became an adult. When I was a youth, it never really occurred to me that my body was that susceptible to my poor eating and sleeping habits. I thought I was invincible! Why couldn't I have just opened my eyes, looked around, and seen what poor health habits can do to one's life? No wonder I was cranky and irritable in the morning! No wonder I produced less than mediocrity in school! No wonder college was filled with more pain and not enough enjoyment! I hope that young people really think hard about the health-related choices that they make in their younger years, and that they will realize the lasting effects of such ill-advised decisions.

I was born with perfectly normal health 26 years ago. Growing up in a normal suburban home outside of the city, I was subject to the normal trials and tribulations of childhood. I would go to school, come home, and play outside for the rest of the day. Sounds typical doesn't it? Well, as a common American child, I also consumed my fair share of Fruit Roll-Ups, Mac n' Cheese, and tons of soda. It was delicious but not nutritious! Sounds familiar?

I was a kid! What better did I know? Everyone else's child was eating the exact same thing. Sugar, caffeine, saturated fats, and LOTS of carbohydrates were a way of life for me, an average American child. My younger years as a child were typical. Both of my parents worked and were viciously trying to make their way into the corporate world. We were a normal middle-class family that ate in only two or three nights of the week while the rest were spent flying from work to school or activity to activity with a quick McDonald's stop thrown into the mix. My parents were always whining to themselves about how unhealthy we ate. "Trying to juggle such a busy lifestyle and, at the same time, eat nutritious, hearty foods is such a struggle!" my mother would say.

By the time I was eleven, I was entering middle school. That meant more work and no more recess. Recess was a great time for me when I was in elementary school. Not only did it allow me to explore my personal abilities, but it simply gave me extra time to be an active child. That was out the window now! And with more work, and not to mention a drama-filled, peer pressure environment, I didn't know how I would find time to be active outside. I saw myself slowly fading from the active, happy child that I was to a bipolar, preoccupied tween. I always ate the same ole' school lunch that everyone else bought: Chicken tender basket with fries and chocolate milk. But hey! I was young and I wasn't hurting myself! At least I didn't think so...

High school came upon me in a blink of an eye. High school. One of the most important yet memorable parts of one's life! I wanted it to be a great four years, and my body was the least of my worries. The work was grueling with about four hours of homework each night. I was getting to bed around 12:30 and waking up at 6:00. After weeks of this unhealthy schedule, my body started to take a toll. I was always tired in class and my grades were dropping quickly. I was emotionally unstable, irritable, and was having mental breakdowns almost every week. Not to mention, I was eating complete junk food. I hardly ate breakfast and lived on fried chicken for lunch and Pop-Tarts and soda for snacks. I needed caffeine to stay awake from morning till dusk and it really only made me more irritable than anything. On top of this, I played soccer in the fall, basketball in the winter, and baseball in the spring. And of course, I would be offered the occasional liquor or pot at a party. Why not! Everyone else is doing it.

After four years of stress and poor decisions in high school, I was entering college. I felt terrible, I looked terrible, and my mediocre grades that I earned throughout high school landed me in a typical state school in the middle of nowhere. I would be so tired that I found myself almost falling asleep in class and at the wheel. I remember going to a party that one of my friends was throwing at his house. I was really very excited about the party and I now remember having a great time, but the night I returned home from the party, I was so exhausted and lightheaded that I couldn't even remember what had happened.

I continued to pursue sports in college. I actually got a partial scholarship to play soccer at my state college! Every day after school, I had practice for three hours. The practice consisted of two-mile runs, tackling drills, scrimmages, and weight training to maintain our shape. We always received the normal speech of good health and hydration. Though, no one ever listened. Money was always tight for me, and I was always looking for the best deals on foods to stock up on. I began the traditional college diet of coffee in the morning and Ramen Noodles for dinner. Yes, I was always tired, but I needed the money to pay my way through college. One day, my team and I were running a ten-mile practice for soccer. I had awakened that morning feeling unusually queasy and abnormally tired. My brain was moving extremely slowly that morning and my muscles were achy. I think I even remember myself taking as cold a shower as possible just to get my blood flowing and my brain working. A dreary and stale morning and early afternoon at my classes made for an even more exhausting afternoon. Before practice, I gulped down about an ounce of water and went on my run. By about the fifth mile, I was nauseous, queasy, and my eyes were about sealed shut. Before I knew it, I was laying in the cold grass unconscious.

This had never happened to me! I have always been able to run this far! What's happened to me? Why now? Am I sick? That was the end of the line! I was tired all the time, moody, always queasy... I needed to see a doctor!

I couldn't remember the last time I had gone to the doctor's office. Sure! I went when I was a kid and when I was in high school! I couldn't remember when I had gone during my college years though. I visited the doctor in town, and they ran some tests. My doctors came back with shocking news that I had been diagnosed with hypoglycemia. He said that my years of food deprivation, poor sleeping habits, and overactive lifestyle contributed to my disease. This really hit home for me and I knew that I needed to get back into a healthy lifestyle.

I am now older and wiser. I track my blood sugar throughout the day and make sure to eat balanced meals every day. I exercise often but with large levels of water intake beforehand and I am visiting my doctor as often as possible. Things are great! I feel great! Unfortunately, because of my poor health and eating habits as a youth and young adult, I will be living with this condition for the rest of my life. While it is totally manageable, I still feel as though I lost something as a young adult. Maybe if I had just taken better care of myself, I would have had more friends in high school, higher grades, and a much better college experience. I now truly understand how important it is to maintain your health even when you are young, and I hope that young people will learn from my mistakes and choose to live a healthy and beneficial lifestyle from the get go.

While this story is fictional, it certainly relates to many people in our world today. Everywhere we go, unhealthy habits are everywhere. At school, in the store, at the workplace, and even at home. And unfortunately, these poor health habits are influenced by poor parenting from the start. It is ultimately the parents' duty to teach their children strong health habits to last them throughout their life. As the famous singer songwriter Graham Nash once said, "Teach your children well."

"Did He Say 'Diet'?!"

And unfortunately, many students find themselves asking this question every day. And no, a diet isn't where you eat nothing except celery! Diet is the "healthy intake of nutrition." There are many aspects of health that students overlook while attending school that could negatively affect them in the long run. One predominate problem today is poor dietary behaviors. According to the CDC, over 11% of teens consume soda three or more times per day. Over 17% of students drink no milk for over a week! And 5.7% of students have not eaten any green vegetables or fruits for over a week. The University of Copenhagen led a study on how poor diet affects school behavior, and they came to the conclusion that students who consumed higher-calorie meals, sugar, and sugar-sweetened beverages were more prone to develop sleeping problems during school. This therefore affects the quality of work produced by the student and inhibits the student from doing his or her very best. I know I would do terrible in school if I didn't get enough sleep! Never-the-less falling asleep in class every day! So, it is very important for any active student to practice sensible dietary habits to not only get the nutrients that they need but to also prevent sleep deprivation.

According to the California Department of Education, over 1/3 of children are obese in the United States. Therefore, it is our responsibility to prevent these amazingly high numbers from getting any higher. A major role of the obesity epidemic is sugar-containing beverages such as Coca-Cola or Pepsi. There needs to be an emphasis on the drinking of water throughout schools! If every child drank a simple eight ounces of water at school every day, the student population would be much healthier and even prevent school illnesses, which can spread quickly.

How Can We Improve?

Schools have taken a step in the right direction by ridding of sugared beverages and replacing those with fruit juices and diet sodas. But, maybe we should take it a step even further. According to the US Library of Medicine, caffeinated beverages not only cause crashes after about four hours of consumption, but they also make some personalities irritable or negative. The ridding of caffeinated beverages all together from schools would dramatically change the amount of caffeine being consumed by students. I know that because at my high school, everyone runs on caffeine! The way that this would be done is by creating awareness of the negative effects of caffeine in schools across the nation. Creating school alliances supporting the consumption of non-caffeinated beverages would help bring attention across schools and to administration and school districts. Large groups of students, parents, and faculty would then propose a plan to rid the vending of caffeinated beverages on school property to the school board. By using large amounts of support and evidence of caffeine's negative effects on students, a hopeful change will be made! Don't get me wrong, sometimes I need some coffee, but if a student felt that they needed a jolt of energy, they can simply bring a caffeinated beverage from home. That way, everyone will be happier and healthier!

Lastly, a large and common problem that many of us see today is anorexia and lack of nutrition. According to Dr.

Lauren Muhlheim of Los Angeles, California, over 50% of girls ages 11 - 13 see themselves as overweight, and 80% of 13 year old girls have attempted to lose weight. Unfortunately, we live in a culture that glorifies slim, petite bodies that not everybody can have in reality. Students and adults are constantly feeling pressure around school, work, or in public for being in shape and looking thin. Eating disorders can starvation can often lead to poor attitude, lack of concentration, and extreme pressure from peers. This therefore makes school quite a struggle, not only physically but emotionally. Seeing this problem as evident in our schools today, a universal health and dietary habits class, I believe, should be a required class for all students to take in elementary, middle, and high school. This is alongside the already required health class that students take while in school. This class would last for only a week for the first week of school every year, reinforcing the tools that students need to make good healthy choices. Students should also be able to visit with their school counselor and should be able to talk about their dietary habits with their counselor. So, not only is the school counselor guiding your academic life, they can also aid a student in making healthy choices! These propositions for enriched health training could simply be brought to the administration. By carefully guiding the school staff through a plan where students can take these health classes and visit their counselor during the first five lunches of the school year, classes and counselor meetings could be made possible.

A Reminder for the Future

As we transition into a world that becomes increasingly competitive academically, it is our duty to remove all learning barriers that will inhibit a student from doing his or her best. While poor eating habits are almost inevitable due to the parents' influence over a child, schools can take part too in insuring both a successful and healthy future for a student. I know myself! And I know that if I did not eat my greens, consume protein, and drink A LOT of water, I would be a very cranky person, never-the-less, doing poorly in school. There are great ideas for health and dietary improvement that need to be heard, and the involvement of such programs and counseling would most certainly ensure a positive, exciting, and healthy future for all students across the nation.

Adam Ward - Bio

Adam J. Ward is a resident of Marietta and a native of Georgia. He attends Lassiter High School where he tackles many Honors and AP courses and is currently in the 10th grade. This is the first book that Adam has participated in writing, but has written many award-winning essays for the Daughters of the American Revolution, Sassafras Literary Exchange, and the Fleet Reserve Association. He also enjoys oratory, having won the 2010 Optimist Club International Oratorical Contest for the state of Georgia. Adam is an active student in his school, participating in the Lassiter High School Trojan Band, Model United Nations, Science National Honor Society, and the Student Leadership Team. In his spare time, he enjoys running, listening to music, watching the news, shopping at the mall, playing with his dogs Sandy and Luke, and relaxing with his sister Kendall, his mother Darlaine, and his father Andy.

The Gift of Soccer
Bailey Peacock

CHAPTER 11 - The Gift of Soccer

Sparking a Love For the Game

Everyone needs a dream, a passion, and a goal. Soccer is a game that has provided me with all three, and can do the same for so many more people all over our state. Children need something that they can turn to when they are having a rough time in school, with their friends, and at home. One might be skeptical, but a simple game like soccer can give children that special something. Once a passion for the game is ignited, children will work so hard and put so much effort into chasing their dreams and goals until they get everything that they want and more from the sport and form inseparable bonds with incredible people. That is why I will make a difference in a child's life by working in summer camps with young children to spark a strong love for the game of soccer and providing them with a dream to become the best soccer player that they can be.

The Start of A Journey

I began playing soccer when I was four. I started out in a recreational league in Alabama mostly because my older brother played and I wanted to do everything that he did. I played with boys and girls and had so much fun trying to chase the ball with the horde of other kids that were trying to score a goal. Eventually, a few years later, my family and I moved to Tennessee where I continued to play recreational soccer and learn a little bit more about the game as I went along. At this stage in my life, soccer was fun to me because I am a very competitive person, and like to play sports, board games, or anything where I'm involved in direct competition- especially with my brothers. My brothers, Bryndon and Bryce, and I would play in our backyard a lot and I always enjoyed the sweet little triumphs and victories that occasionally came with fierce competitions between my brothers and I. Even though it was just U8 recreational soccer, I lived for the weekends when I would be able to march onto the soccer field and play and score goals with my friends. A game that simply consists of trying to kick a ball in the back of a net gave me something to look forward to every weekend.

I moved to Georgia, right after winter break, when I was seven years old and in third grade. I still loved soccer and immediately started playing recreational soccer at North Atlanta Soccer Association, for whom I still play currently. Playing at NASA was great because even though it was rec, my coach still taught us the very basics of the game and how to use the correct techniques. Being a girl that had just moved to a new town and entered a new school in the middle of the year, it was pretty difficult to make new friends, initially. Even though I maybe didn't have as many friends as I would have liked, I still had a great family and a beautiful game to play twice a week and on the weekends. Soccer is a game that has always been a friend to me and has always been there for me to turn to.

The Journey Continues

After playing a year or so of rec at NASA, I tried out for the U10 Academy player pool at NASA. I was so nervous for my first real try-out. I was scared that I wouldn't make the team, but fortunately, I did. When I started out in the program, it was so overwhelming because it felt as if all the other girls in the pool were better than me. We did technical work almost every practice, which involves learning moves to beat other players 1v1. I started off not knowing any of the moves and was not nearly as proficient as the other girls that had already been in the pool for a year. I think that this feeling was ultimately a good thing for me because in trying really hard to be just as good or better than the other girls, I would focus more in practice and try my very hardest to master the moves. I made it a goal of mine to become better at every practice.

After I completed my days in the U10 academy, I moved on to the U11 academy and continued to improve little by little. I kept improving because soccer had already become my passion and something that I hoped that I would one day be great at. As I grew older, I continued to play soccer at the U12 academy level and progress greatly. When I finished my U12 season, it came time to try out for select, where there is no longer a pool of players, but the players are divided up into teams, based on skill level, that will remain the same for the rest of the year. When try outs rolled around, I made the Elite team and continued growth as a player because the level of play gets higher and higher as the player gets older, generally, and I really wanted to be one of the best players in my league, Athena A. The teams that we played in this league were a little tougher than the ones that we played the year before, which, again, motivated me to focus in practice and get touches on the ball outside of practices with my team, sometimes. I believe that having a passion for a sport is a really great thing for kids. It forces kids to exercise frequently. In fact, according to ussoccerplayers.com, the average soccer player runs seven miles in one game. It helps kids to stay out of trouble, and manage time well, also.

The Benefits

After my U13 year was over, I moved on to U14 with the Elite team at NASA. I played ODP, which stands for Olympic Development Program, which is run by US Youth Soccer, and ultimately provides girls and boys with the opportunity to be scouted by National Team staff and college coaches. In the summer, the state girls' ODP teams travel to Montevallo, Alabama to participate in Region Camp, where a pool of twenty-five to forty players are selected for the pool that can be invited to various events throughout the year. After making the region pool at camp the summer after U14, I was invited to go to Boca Raton, Florida for a tournament between the four regions of the United States. This event was an incredible opportunity for me to get scouted by lots of college coaches and National Team staff. Soon after that event, I was invited to travel to Costa Rica for an international tournament with the Region ODP team. While there, I will be able to play against great competition, visit a children's orphanage, and sightsee. This is truly a fantastic opportunity that I would not have if I did not play soccer. Soccer has given me so many opportunities from traveling afar, to maybe even getting a college scholarship to play soccer. I want to pass on my love for the game to another child so that more people can experience what I have and have even more chances to become a successful adult.

I plan on making this difference by working at kids' camps this summer at NASA and playing soccer with as many kids as I can and making it fun for them. The only way that anyone can get the most out of anything is to enjoy what they are doing and put their heart into it. Every young child wants to be like the bigger kids and by playing with children and having fun with them, I hope that they will begin to love soccer and take advantage of the opportunities that come with playing the game at any level. Not only will children have chances to become successful through soccer, but they will become great friends with incredible people along the way. They will form bonds with their teammates that can never be broken, and will meet new people in the different places to which they will travel. Also, playing soccer will give some kids a goal and a dream that they will chase constantly and will work hard to achieve. Having a goal in mind is such a good thing, especially for children, since most of them don't have one at young ages.

The End Result

All in all, children can benefit in so many ways from becoming committed to soccer. Endless opportunities come from having a love for the game and trying to chase a goal. Every child can have success from becoming dedicated to the game; all they need is a spark to start the fire of passion.

Bailey Peacock – Bio

Bailey Peacock is a current tenth grader at Lassiter High School who is currently taking two AP classes and is a member of the Varsity soccer team at Lassiter. She received an academic letter based on her ninth grade academic record, as well as a scholar athlete letter. Her favorite subjects in school are Spanish and literature. She is involved with club soccer at North Atlanta Soccer Association and US Youth Soccer Olympic Development Program and the Region three pool. This spring, she will be traveling to Costa Rica with this Region three team to play in a tournament against other teams from Costa Rica. She enjoys playing and watching sports, along with reading, and spending time with friends and family. She is part of a family of five and has two brothers: one older brother that is a senior at Lassiter, and one younger brother who is in sixth grade at Rocky Mount Elementary school.

Change the World
Shannon DeSantis

CHAPTER 12 - Change the World

When I was in elementary school and someone asked me what I wanted to be when I grew up, I answered with the typical "I want to be a surgeon" or "I think I could be a pretty good lawyer." And it was true then, too. We all had the idea that we were going to have these grandiose professions and take in large sums of money. However, once we became less naïve, most of us started to get a different perspective on what we wanted to do with our lives. The typical "I want to be a surgeon" turned into "I want to get married and have kids. I want to live in a house with a big yard bordered by a white picket fence." Throughout middle school, most people bought into this deception, including me, but as soon as my freshman year of high school came around, I finally started to think differently.

I can remember hanging out with a friend one day, and he asked me what I wanted to do when I grow up. After a few moments of silence as I tried to gather my thoughts, I finally knew what I wanted to do. At first, I laughed because I knew I was never going to respond to that question with the typical answer ever again. I looked at him and told him that I was going to change the world - I was going to make a difference. That definitely took him by surprise, but then he asked how I was going to do that. I looked at him and honestly told him that I had no idea.

Now, I embraced the thought of making a difference, but what would it look like to make a difference? After pondering this question for a long time, I became discouraged. What could *I* do to make a *difference*? Unfortunately, the discouragement overwhelmed me with the lie that I could never make a difference. And for awhile after, I believed that I couldn't make a difference. I didn't see how I could do anything that would make a difference, whether they were small or large acts. I didn't figure this out until one day when I was making a fire.

Big Fires Start with Small Embers

My dad is a big outdoorsman and raised me to have the same love for nature. We tend to camp a lot and spend a lot of time outside. With that being said, I was sitting outside by a large bonfire pit with virtually nothing in it. There was a log that had been part of last night's fire and a paper towel that another camper had thrown in. I turned over the log to find one small piece of the wood, about the size of a quarter, which had a small ember on it. Ready for a challenge, I took the paper towel and placed it next to the last ember. I blew at the log to try to light up the ember, and I did that for about five minutes. The only difference I made was that now the paper towel had a few burn marks from the heat, but I was not about to give up. I kept at it, and all of the sudden, the entire paper towel burst into a giant flame. I would be lying if I said that I didn't jump up into the air with excitement. Knowing that there was not enough wood to keep the fire going, I looked around and gathered some small twigs. After those caught on fire, I upgraded to branches. After the branches, I added in the final element – the logs. I stepped away and admired my masterpiece.

A few hours later, I returned to my fire and it was still burning strong. By now, it was nighttime. The only thing keeping me warm on the cold November night was the fire that I created out of scraps. I was so pleased with my creation, so I pulled up a lawn chair and enjoyed its warmth. There was no one else around, so naturally, I began to think. I stared at the dancing flames and realized something - this was how I was going to make a difference! No, I was not going to make fires for a living, but creating that fire was the solution to my discouragement.

I always thought that I had to do something extravagant to change the world, but recalling the fire, it was just the opposite. I realized that with one small ember and a little bit of effort, I could create a huge fire. Likewise, with even the smallest desire to make a difference and an eager heart to do so, I *could* make a difference.

Little Drops of Water in a Not So Big Ocean

My discovery and resurrected desire made me remember a quote by Mother Theresa. She once said, "We know only too well that what we are doing is nothing more than a drop in the ocean. But if the drop were not there, the ocean would be missing something." It occurred to me that I don't have to come up with some grand scheme to make a difference; I could just do the little things. Even though I would do small actions, they could add up into something bigger than I had ever dreamed of. Encouraged by Mother Theresa, I set out on my journey to act on this desire and make a difference.

Now, the next step was to figure out what small acts I could perform. I started by thinking of the little actions other people had done towards me that made a difference in my life. Soon after, I remembered a friend who left me speechless.

In between two class periods, this friend and I walked from one class to another. Even though we weren't in the same class, we came from the same hall and went to the history hall together every day. But one day was different. We made our way to the history hall and stayed outside of the classrooms to finish our conversation before we went our different ways. Towards the end of the conversation, I commented on her necklace. It was a blue cross – the most beautiful cross necklace I had ever had the pleasure of seeing. This wasn't anything new, though. I commented on how beautiful it was all the time because each time I saw it, its beauty took my breath away. But this time, she took it off her neck and placed it in my hand. I stared town at the blue necklace, speechless. I looked up at her in disbelief that she would give anything that beautiful away. But she just smiled at me and told me that it was just a necklace, and then she disappeared into her classroom.

It was hard for me to concentrate in class because I was so surprised at what had just happened. Then, I realized that it was that simple. The act of selflessly giving a necklace to a person who saw so much beauty and value in it was enough to make a difference.

Live to Serve

Now, it was my turn. On a normal Sunday, I went off to church. I came home and felt that the Lord had placed something on my heart. I kept feeling the urge to live to serve. I let that sink in for awhile and knew that that was another way I could make a difference. *Live to Serve*. So now, continuing on this journey, living to serve would be my next step.

Soon after, I went on a mission trip to Costa Rica. Yes, it was an amazing experience that I could go on and on about it, but there was one thing I learned more than anything: I didn't have to leave the country and go on a mission trip to serve. I could serve my family, friends, neighbors, and community without spending a dime. I'm not saying that mission trips are a waste of time or money by any means. I love them, and I even plan to go on two more by the time I finish high school. But, I now felt challenged to serve those around me. So I did just that.

I was at a restaurant with a group of girls that I didn't know too well at the time. We were all eating our food and my water glass became close to empty, so I stood up to go refill my water. Before leaving the table, I looked at the cups of the girls surrounding me, and sure enough, someone else's was getting pretty low, too. I got her attention and asked if I could get more water for her. The stare I received from her made me feel like I said something wrong; I was sure that I had done something wrong. But, after a second or two, I realized that the stare came from her astonishment that I would ask such a question. She was amazed that I would go out of my way and do something for someone other than myself. That, in itself, shocked *me*. She handed over her cup, and said the sincerest thank you with such disbelief that I even offered. That's when I knew that I could make a difference.

I learned to serve everyone around me by going out of my way to do the simplest things for them. Whether it was at school, with friends, or with my soccer team, I tried to put others before myself. I learned that this is a way anyone can make a difference. When we grow up, the world teaches us to be selfish, but what do you think would happen if the world became self*less?*

By being selfless, we can all make a difference. If we make it a goal to be selfless, we start to act on compassion. And if we act on compassion - or even just see people compassionately - we start seeing through the facades that people tend to hide behind.

Seeing with Eyes of Compassion to Make a Difference

We can see people compassionately by making ourselves curious enough to try and *truly* see them. For example, have you ever been at a red light in rush hour traffic and looked at all the people in the cars around you? Probably not. At that time of day, we are usually so caught up in our own world that we would never even give them a glance. Now, have you sat in that same scenario and wondered where these people are coming from or where they are going? Have you ever been curious about the burdens that have weighed them down or the obstacles they have overcome? Probably not. But when we start thinking about who a person really is – not just the person behind the horn – we can become compassionate.

I think that I have started to understand the ways that I could make a difference, but the truth is, by doing these simple things, we can *all* make a difference. It may seem like a cumbersome task or an impossible endeavor, but it can be done. Even though the smallest actions may seem like a drop in the ocean, Mother Theresa made it clear that with that drop, we just made a difference. With multiple drops, we can all start adding to that ocean. Likewise, by serving others, we are putting others before ourselves. When we serve others, we become more and more selfless. And if you ask me, the world could use more selfless people.

I now know that a small desire, with some effort, can create a great fire. I now know that I can add even the smallest drop to the ocean. I now know that serving others and acting compassionately towards them can make a difference. So that is what I will do. I will make a difference by doing the little things. I will make a difference by putting others before myself. I will make a difference by living to serve. And even then, I pray that I make a difference. The way I see it, if I impact just one person's life positively, my life will have been worth living and I will have made that difference.

Shannon DeSantis - Bio

Shannon DeSantis was born and raised in Marietta, Georgia, where she received her preliminary education. She attended elementary school at Wood Acres Country Day School. After that, she moved on to Mabry Middle School, and later, finished her high school education at Lassiter High School.

Ms. DeSantis has always enjoyed getting involved in her church and school. Starting in middle school, Shannon was eager to attend any retreat or mission trip she had the opportunity to attend. At school, she enjoyed becoming a part of the leadership programs they offered. Starting in 8th grade, Shannon was elected as class president. She continued this leadership role for five years and was again reelected to finish off as the senior class president. Shannon was also involved in other leadership and service clubs including National Honor Society, Pay It Forward, Renaissance, DECA, and FCA leadership. Not only was she involved in extracurricular activities, but she was also involved in spirit and pride. In the 11th grade, Shannon enjoyed being a mascot during the football season, as well as, being the MC for pep rallies in 12th grade.

Although Shannon enjoyed participating in school activities, her true passion was soccer. Ever since her father signed her up as a little girl, she fell in love with the sport. Ms. DeSantis followed this passion for many years, playing at different clubs and levels. During high school, Shannon played on the varsity soccer team for three years as the goalkeeper. During the latter years of her high school experience, she got opportunities to play with nationally ranked club teams. After playing for so long and experiencing these new levels, she decided that she wanted to continue playing the sport at the collegiate level. With that being said, Shannon has committed to play soccer at Lander University. There she will be majoring in Business Administration and minoring in Spanish.

I Will Make a Difference

Katelyn Balevic

CHAPTER 13 – I Will Make a Difference

Intro

"You've changed so much since you found out about Texas!" he yelled. It made me flinch hearing him raise his voice like that. He'd never done that to me before.

"I know but... But I thought you said that when there are problems in a relationship, you try and fix them, " I said defensively. I hated how weak I sounded.

"That's for marriage, Katelyn," he said harshly. "And I just can't see myself marrying you. I don't..." He faltered then continued. "I don't love you the way you love me."

All I heard were the words, "I don't love you." They seemed to jump out more than the rest of the sentence, landing yet another well-placed punch to my gut.

"That's a lie. That's not you speaking, that's your sis-"

"We're fifteen, Katelyn! We don't even know what love is!" He yelled even louder than he did last time. People were starting to look at us.

I couldn't believe what I was hearing. It seemed surreal. I felt so broken that it was as if I couldn't feel anything at all. Everything I'd known was finally torn apart. Now my old life was nothing. There was nothing left unbroken - my family, my reputation, and now my relationship. It was all over, just like that. And in that moment, I gave up.

"I'm sorry it has to be this way," I could hear him say, but instead of looking at him, I looked up.

"Is this it, then?" I asked, as if anyone up there was even listening. "Is this how it ends for me, your beloved child?" I sneered, spitting out the last few words. I knew God had abandoned me long ago.

The boy in front of me looked confused. I didn't pay him any attention. After all, he had just said he was done paying me his.

"You know what?" I demanded, still glaring upward. "Two minutes. One hundred and twenty seconds. That's all it will take for me to cross that parking lot!" I yelled, taking slow steps backwards towards the student parking lot. "Two minutes," I repeated, "and we can talk about this face to face."

I turned away from the boy I thought I knew, away from the band room, away from my so-called friends who stood there and watched, gossiping amongst themselves. I turned towards the parking lot, towards Shallowford Road, towards the last thing that I was ever going to know from this world.

"Katelyn, what are you..." I heard my boyfriend - now ex-boyfriend - trail off behind me as I picked up the pace. This was it. I always knew it would end like this for me eventually. I wasn't strong enough. Life had always seemed like it was too much for me to handle. I never felt good enough.

The light had just turned green. It was rush hour and people were trying to get home. I counted backwards in my head.

One-hundred-and-twenty. I wiped the tears from my eyes so that I could finish my life with dignity. I hated the fact that I had given him the satisfaction of making me cry.

One-hundred-and-ten. I was so done. I didn't want a long, "happy" life. I wanted to be done now. No more for me.

One hundred. It was finally going to end. All of my torment, my misery, the feeling that I was constantly trapped and trying to free myself. Feeling like I was never good enough.

Ninety. All of the nights that I spent up late working tirelessly for something that didn't even matter, stressing to the point of tears over school, my family, my relationship, my friends who didn't understand.

Eighty. This was good. No more stress. No more misery. No more tears. It would just be over.

Seventy. "I'm sorry it has to be this way," he had said. Yeah, right. He wanted it to be this way. I was too tough a case, not even my great saint of a boyfriend, the boy who got pats on the back just for putting up with me for so long, could fix me. And I knew now that he didn't want to.

Sixty. It probably wasn't even that. I had problems. I was frustrated. I was sad. I guess somewhere along the line he decided I wasn't worth his time anymore. I wasn't worth the effort.

Fifty. My family felt the same way, and I knew it. I was a burden. I was the mentally disturbed daughter who only added to an already stressful situation.

Forty. It probably wouldn't take them that much time to get over me anyway. They were all tired of me and my never-ending sadness.

Thirty. My friends might be sad. Maybe the band will do something special for me. Maybe my English teacher can explain it all to the other students in the simple, matter-of-fact way that he always explains things. Maybe they'll tell stories about me. Are there even stories about me to tell?

Twenty. The street was close. I could hear people yelling my name, but I would already have taken care of my business by the time they reached me.

Ten. This is it. This is all that will be left of Katelyn Balevic. Memories of a sad, broken girl.

Five. There. That's the car. That's the one.

Four. This is it.

Three. This is how it ends.

Two. Say goodnight, Katie.

One.

My Story

That is the product of anxiety and depression. I'm not going to try and talk about it as if I know everything about it because I don't. However, I have experienced it firsthand, and I know the damages it can cause. Believe me when I tell you that they can be very destructive and even deadly.

The night before this happened, I had given up. I felt defeated and hopeless to the point where I had decided that I was done with life. I told my siblings where they would find my body. I instructed them on which dress I would like to be buried in. I had considered suicide before, but this felt real. Very real.

Then, twelve hours after I was persuaded that I am loved and valued and needed, my boyfriend dumped me. That was the icing on a really gross cake that was my life. It was all caused by a series of unfortunate events. Some might call it bad luck or divine retribution. I don't know what to call it. I just know that I really didn't enjoy it.

During the summer before sophomore year, I found out that my family would be moving to Texas after the school year concluded because my dad got a promotion. Being a girl with good friends, a fantastic boyfriend (whom I did end up getting back together with), teachers I loved, and many leadership opportunities ahead of me, this came as quite a blow. The school year started, and I didn't tell any of my friends what was going on. My dad had already moved to Texas and begun his new, well-earned job. I thought maybe if nobody knew, I could pretend it wasn't happening for a little while.

Of course, that didn't work. Trying to battle this impending change on my own - which in my mind, was an impending doom - added a lot of stress to my life, and people started to notice. I ended up telling my boyfriend in order to explain how I'd been acting. My friends found out not long after.

But it didn't end there. It's not like everyone found out my little secret and then all of the stress ended. If anything, it only increased. Grades dropped. I pushed away friends and family. I stopped caring about things that were once important to me. Eventually, it felt like I cared about nothing at all - including myself. I lost the will to live. It seemed useless to try and do well in school or be a part of my family or reach out to my old friends because I felt like no matter what I did, it was never good enough.

That's the way a lot of people feel - not good enough. I know that compared to many, I don't even know what pain is. I know that there are people who are struggling to keep food on the table or trying to keep a family together or don't even have a family at all. I know that there is death and disease and things so much worse that what I've ever had to handle. But pain is pain. No matter what reason you feel it for, you're still feeling it. And it's not easy to make it go away.

The Facts About Depression

Depression is defined as a mood disorder in which feelings of sadness, loss, anger, or frustration interfere with everyday life for weeks or longer[1]. In 2012, depression affected 1 in 10 Americans at one point or another. Around the world, it's estimated that 121 million people are affected by some form of depression[2].

A few of its symptoms include[3]:

- Fatigue and decreased energy
- Feelings of guilt, worthlessness, and helplessness
- Loss of interest in activities or hobbies that were once enjoyable
- Overeating or appetite loss
- Irritability, restlessness
- Thoughts of suicide and suicide attempts

The Facts About Anxiety

Anxiety is defined as stress that can come from any event or thought that makes one feel frustrated, angry or nervous. It is a feeling of fear, unease, and worry[4]. This stress is something that everyone feels at some point or another. An anxiety disorder is when a person lives in constant fear and worry, and it interferes with a person's ability to live their life. There is more than one type of anxiety disorder, and each refers to a different set of symptoms.

Some general symptoms for an anxiety disorder include[5]:

- Feelings of panic, fear, and uneasiness
- Repeated thoughts or flashbacks of traumatic experiences

- Uncontrollable, obsessive thoughts
- Nightmares
- Sleeping problems

What I Want To Do

Pain is complicated because many times, the people who want to ease your pain don't really know what you're going through. No matter what they say, if they haven't experienced the situation themselves, they really won't know what it feels like to be you. This also makes it easy for them to forget what you're going through. Their sympathy wears down because it's not directly affecting them, so they don't constantly feel the presence of the burden that you're carrying.

That's where I want to help. I was told a while back that the intro to this chapter reads like a novel. That gave me an idea. I've always wanted to be an author. Writing has been something that I've always enjoyed doing and something that I've always been sure I wanted to pursue as a career. So why not let that be the difference that I make?

I always love reading a story that I can identify with. It doesn't have to be something that I have experienced necessarily, but if I can relate to how a character is feeling, it makes the book a worthwhile read. You can learn something from that character's story and how he/she goes about handling it. This can be very helpful in handling your own situations because it puts things in perspective. It's so easy to get lost in the things that are dominant in our lives. Sometimes I forget that while I'm frustrated with this move, at least I have a nice home to move into, and I'll be there with my family. Some people have neither of those things.

My hope is that I can write books that encourage someone to choose something better than standing in front of a moving car. I want to give someone hope. Even if its just one person, it would be worth it. That's one more person who has someone to look up to, even if that person is just a character from a book. I want to give someone a better mindset than one that says, "Give up," because no one deserves to feel hopeless and defeated. There is always hope.

If You Are Experiencing Depression and/or Anxiety

- Don't be ashamed to tell someone what's going on. It's easy to feel like nobody cares about your problems and what you're feeling; that's not true. There's *always* someone who cares. And even if there's no immediate way to fix the problem, sometimes just venting to someone can make you feel a little bit better. Getting things off of your chest can help. Don't be afraid to just let it out.

- If there's nobody you already know that you want to talk to, it might be smart to look for a therapist. These people won't judge you for what's going on, and everything you say to them is confidential. Going to therapy doesn't make you crazy or unlovable. It just means that there are things on your plate that you can't handle alone, and that's okay. It is perfectly okay to not be okay. Despite what it might seem, a lot of people aren't.

- At all costs, *please avoid self-destructive thoughts and actions.* You are valuable. You are important. Many times, it's easy to let the careless things that people say make you think otherwise, but do not listen. If you ever feel like self-harm is the only way to fix something, talk to someone. Or go for a run. Or bake some cookies. Or do anything that brings you joy or can at least take your mind off of the situation at hand until you get your feelings in check.

If Someone You Know Is Experiencing Depression and/or Anxiety

- If someone opens up to you about something that's going on in his or her life, you need to take him/her seriously. The best thing to do is to listen. Whatever he/she says to you, there's no way to know exactly what's going on in his/her head. Saying something rude or making a joke out of it could affect that person in horrible ways that you could end up regretting for a lifetime. There's nothing more frustrating than someone telling you to get over it or let it go. That is something that needs to be done at an individual's own pace, not when commanded to do so.

- Be someone that can be trusted. If somebody confides in you, the worst thing that you can do is spread it around or use it as means of embarrassment. Be trustworthy and dependable. Tell this person that you can be there for him/her whenever you are needed, and stay true to your word.

- In some situations, the best thing to do is tell someone else. It might just be a heads-up to an adult that you're worried about what's going through somebody's head and you think the situation is bigger than something you can help him/her with. However, if you're concerned about the immediate well being of a person and convinced that the situation is an emergency, tell an adult and call 9-1-1.

Final Word

Depression and anxiety are serious issues that need to be handled accordingly. It is always important to know that you are never alone. Ever. You are valuable and important and loved, and nothing can ever change that. Don't give up because it takes someone who has experienced true pain to fully experience true happiness. There will be better days ahead.

---

[1] National Library of Medicine

[2] Healthline

[3] WebMD

[4] National Library of Medicine

[5] WebMD

Katelyn Balevic – Bio

Katelyn Balevic is an aspiring writer and lover of photography. Her other interests include reading, waterskiing, and swimming. She marched in the Rose Parade on January 1st, 2013 with the Lassiter band. She loves spending time at her grandparents' lake house on Lake Chautauqua in New York with her family and close family friends. She plans on attending college in the northeast, possibly in New York City. She currently lives in Atlanta with her mother, an older brother, a younger sister, and two golden retrievers. She has an amazing father living in Texas and a brilliant older sister attending Cornell University. She wrote this chapter because it helped her through her experiences with depression and anxiety, and she hopes that it can help others, too. She would like to say thank you to her friends for making her time in Georgia something that she will always remember and cherish. She would also like to thank two very special teachers who constantly encouraged her and taught her more about life than any teachers she has ever had. Their support reminded her on bad days that there is always someone who cares. She would like to thank each of her family members, particularly her mother and her brother for believing in her and being proud of her when she felt like there was nothing to be proud of. Finally, she would like to remind herself as well as others that when times of trouble arise, you can give up on God, but He will never give up on you.

Global Cultural and Religious Education

Robert Longyear

CHAPTER 14 – Global Cultural and Religious Education

A Common Experience

My life has been filled with scenes of evil, oppression, and hatred. I have grown up hearing about the never ending turmoil in the Middle East, Asia, and Africa. I have seen the footage of death, seen reports of the hatred, the abuse, and the suffering of people around the world. Even as I drive to school in the morning with the radio on, or turn the tv on to relax at home, the evils of this world are still ever present. I have seen the pictures of the refugees, the homeless, the nationless, and the hopeless. I have seen the pain on the faces of the oppressed and the dejected. I have felt sadness that could not even come close to that of which these people have endured. Even as I write this, there is a people without a home, or a belonging. I can see them, though I sit in a comfortable life with many luxuries; nothing I feel can compare to them.The conflicts of the world follow me around each day, be it the Middle East or Africa. Conflicts that could be prevented. Not just prevented, but the conflicts could be changed into cooperation and hope for people that have none. Not just overt conflict, but general feelings of hatred. Hatred that is expressed in so many ways, hatred that could be prevented.This is not about the usual be more loving or compassionate like the past paragraph may suggest, but this is about a solution. A real solution.

Let me explain something to you, I am not a well-renowned college professor or political columnist. I am a high school student. A high school student who is not influenced by money, getting re-elected, aligning my views with the majority, or my professional reputation. Rather, I am impartial.These issues are all too visible throughout the world, I have noticed that something needs to be done.. The motives for the wars halfway around the world will eventually become ever closer to my home and yours. It has already been seen with terrorism becoming an ever present threat around the world. The issues will be the roots of conflict and death for the next generations, that would be, your children and grandchildren. These political, social, and dangerous problems could be reduced or even prevented through one simple concept. In this,I represent the next generation, the ones who will be affected by the issues that are forming today. Issues that are otherwise ignored, or if they are noticed, are not solved due to petty partisan politics,or the selfish greed of world leaders. This is not to be a preaching editorial about how you should change the world or how you should act, but simply information that is neglected due to the possibility of unpopularity. I am no expert, but what I tell you is true and it needs to be said. This is about Education.

A New World Problem

Currently around the world there is a growing problem. The problem is complicated due to a number of reasons, be it political, or economic. The fact is that there are millions of people around the world who are not being educated on the world around them. Not just the world around them, but the people around them, the cultures around them, and the differences between themselves and those that are foreign to them. Our world is becoming an evermore globally connected web of interaction. People are exposed to so many things that they have never even imagined, and therefore cultures they have never imagined could exist. Cultures that they know almost nothing about, that might as well be from outer space. This is the root of the problem, as these people can be corrupted by the lies and blind unreasonable hatred of those around them. Those leaders who they look to for guidance , and the information that is corrupting these uneducated people with supposed facts that are fabricated, untrue, and that serve the purposes of those who wish to cause damage, pain, and hatred. Demagogues and so called leaders, who hold power and only spread propaganda as education to those that they govern are responsible for this problem, as is the rest of the world for not addressing it. Unfortunately these people that they govern truly believe the lies and propaganda, as they have no other sources of information or education on the truth.

    The statistics do not tell the full story, no matter how believable your local news, or reliable your website. Physical conflict between countries is on the decline, in favor of using words instead, imagine that? The hatred most dangerous is that from or towards an entire ethnic group, or organization. The conflict that arises from this is not stoppable by countries, or a single voice. It can only be stopped by individuals; the Taliban has nothing without their new members. Al-Qaeda has nothing without their willing members. Guerrilla warfare is non-existent without guerrillas, just as terrorism has no foothold without terrorists. If everyone refuses to fight, where is the war? This is accomplished through true facts. Truth that must reach those who are most susceptible to the false messages of these groups or leaders. Membership must be attacked, education is the weapon.

A Well-Known Issue: Israel and Palestine

Let us use the Israeli and Palestinian situation, that many are familiar with, as an example. Whether you favor the Palestinian or the Israeli argument, there are facts that cannot be ignored. The fact is, that there are 1.2 million, yes million, registered Palestinian refugees in camps in Jordan, Lebanon, and Syria. It can only be assumed that at least a third of these refugees are children. Children who have grown up in camps, surrounded by people who despise the Israelis and the western powers who back them. These children are raised on one concept, hatred for those who allegedly took away their homeland. The problem as a political issue is one thing, but it has turned into hatred of a culture, and specifically a religion. This view is shared throughout the region, and must be changed. The point is, that these Palestinian children are learning to hate the Jews. This is where education is needed. If these children were taught about other cultures, in this case the Jewish religion, maybe this hatred could be curbed. Unfortunately, this view of the Jews is shared throughout many Middle Eastern nations, many times for no good reason, or simply because it is the norm. The blind hatred for another religion may be prevented through truth. In many cases, the suicide bombing and the terrorism that is a daily threat for the Israelis is carried out by the young people who have grown up in this tense and hate filled environment.

In my own life, education has completely changed my view of the world and the many different attitudes in it. I was almost five when the tragedy of the attacks on the World Trade Center occurred. Now that I am much older, I know of the changes that occurred in the world after the events on the 11th of September 2001. All that anyone hears about now is the airport security, and the post- 9/11 steps that have been taken to amp up security. Due to the messages spread by the news, my peers, and even adults I have come into contact with; I came to view the religion of Islam with nothing but contempt. That's where my education changed me. After being educated on a few rudimentary details of the Islamic religion, and later much more comprehensive studies, my views have changed. All it took to change my attitude, was a little truth in education, and meeting new Muslim friends. I would like to add here, that neither one of these cost me anything, in fact it gave me something, a new correct perspective.

Hatred of a religion, or culture without a complete understanding is like taking a test on a subject you don't know. Education can change perspective, and it is clear what must be done. People must be educated, not in math, or science, or literature, but in the world around them. Global cultural, and religious education must be carried out, at least for the next generation, and truth must prevail. The lies and rumors that cause unfounded hatred must be abolished through truth.

A Problem Through the Ages

Out of all the aspects of culture, religion, race, and ethnicity are the most utilized to manipulate people.

Ethnicity is a term used to describe the association of a person with a group who share particular cultural traditions or a homeland, whereas race is used to describe the association of a person with a group who share a common biological ancestor. Historically utilization of religion is evident in the Holocaust, ethnicity in the tragedy of the Rwandan genocide, and race in South African apartheid. In each of these situations, the people of the nations are not to blame, but the governments and organizations that are in control. The spread of manipulated information provides scapegoats for economic or political problems. The only way that large scale oppression can take place is if the people believe the propaganda. Education can prevent this. Had the German people been taught about how the Jewish people are no different, the results could have been different. Similarly, had all people in South Africa during apartheid been educated about the other races and that they are all human beings that situation may have been different as well. The power to prevent hatred and evil lies in the availability of education to the masses and the courage to stand up against the propaganda and the lies.

The Solution

Education does not have to be carried out in formal schools with classes, textbooks, homework, and grades. While this would be ideal to have in all locations around the world, it is a bit of a long shot to try and attain this. The point is that if even simple education can be provided to the people who have no source of information on other cultures or religion, it would be extremely beneficial to the world. Just as multilingualism is looked upon as a benefit in the business world, knowledge of the cultures of the world should be looked upon as a favorable trait. Not only could it benefit the world in keeping conflict at bay, but it would open opportunities for groups of people who may not have very many. Mathematics, and science education is important, but the benefits of cultural education far outweigh any other subjects because it makes way for cooperation, which opens up doors all around the world. Educating people on the world around them is essential for a peaceful, cooperative, and connected world for future generations.

This concept is all great in theory and seems like a very attainable and worthwhile cause, but as of now a serious global effort has not been attempted. The leaders of the world need to understand and get behind the idea that the world will continue to exist after they are gone. It is time to start looking towards the future and making the world a safer and more peaceful place to live for the generations to come. Global cultural education is a first step and a necessity, as the technology of today allows for people to reach new places and new people on a daily basis. The global economic system relies on an interconnected system or nations consisting of different religions, cultures, and races. Education about our differences can only make the bonds and the benefits stronger and more profound.

I propose an organization that will see to this. A global education initiative that is an international force of teachers, students, and volunteers that are dedicated to the future of cooperation on this planet. Teachers and college students from many different racial, religious, and national backgrounds would allow for excellent cultural and religious education. The international nature of such an organization would provide volunteers from many different backgrounds; which would make for unique educating capabilities, and the new interactions that can help foster new mindsets.

This organization, speculative as it is, would need to have a relatively large amount of capital to create the infrastructure needed to achieve this mission at the start; fundraising would then need to be continued. A central headquarters would need to be established as an administrative center. This headquarters would be the central part of an organization that would have many smaller staging hubs throughout the world. These would serve as regional hubs that would send out the teachers and volunteers to the target area. It would be beneficial to have certified teachers hired full time to serve as field management, and then utilize college student volunteers, and teacher volunteers as the brunt of the educating force.

A Final Word

The next generation of this planet is growing up in a world riddled with constant security; with fear being ingrained into the minds of children that is aimed at a specific group. Fear or anger, while not unfounded, focused on an entire group of people due to the actions of a few is the cause of so much bad in this world. A culturally and worldly-wise educated global population is a necessary step towards a peaceful world. In the areas of the world that are plagued by oppression and war so much is taken away from the dejected masses that live there, but education is the one thing that can never be taken away from them. I won't let my future be filled with hatred and war becoming an everyday event. As inhabitants on this planet, it is our duty to leave it a better place than when we entered it, I intend to do just that. While one person is capable of making a difference, an entire population or people that are motivated to provide for the future is unstoppable. Any education is power, but education on the world around us can light a spark that can change everything, a certain degree of world peace is possible if all the minds of the world can join together to make a safer world for us all.

Robert Longyear – Bio

Robert Longyear is an 11th grade student at Lassiter High School in Marietta, Georgia . Robert was born and raised in Marietta, Georgia. Robert lives with his parents and younger sister. In his free time , he enjoys acrylic painting , woodwork and the outdoors ; he is also involved with his high school chorus, volunteering through his church, and community. He hopes to be able to do as much for the world around him as possible throughout his life. Robert enjoys biology most of all subjects in school, but holds his education in all subject areas as an important part of life. After high school , Robert plans to attend a prestigious college and aspires to go on to medical school. Robert hopes that his point will be understood and through his writing he hopes to make a profound impact on the world around him.

Called to Serve
Julia Miller

CHAPTER 15 – Called to Serve

Overcoming the Odds

Growing up in this world isn't easy. You feel as if you are constantly being judged by every step you take and every word you say. As a child, school was never easy for me. I learned differently than other kids, and some people thought that I was the weirdest child ever. I was diagnosed with ADD at a very young age, and many people made fun of me because of it. Learning to read and write was very difficult for me. In fact, I was told I would never be able to read. Imagine being six years old, in first grade, and your doctor telling you that you will never learn to read. Would I ever overcome it? And if I did, would it be easy?

Near the end of my first grade year, my parents got a call home from my first grade teacher saying that I wasn't going to pass first grade in a few months because I couldn't read; they took immediate action. Running me to dozens of specialists and tutors over the next few months, they never gave up, and neither did I! I spent hours a week with a specialist trying to help me to read by using different teaching methods. After many months of working hard and striving to reach a goal, I went from not being able to read at my level to being able to read beyond my grade level. My teacher didn't know how I was doing it: that was the best part- seeing her jaw drop when she called on me to read in class and I could. Much to my teacher's astonishment, I passed that year and proved her and my doctor wrong. No, it wasn't easy, but I never gave up. As I grew much older, that same work ethic directed my actions not just in school, but also throughout my life.

Answering the Call

I grew up loving the sport of soccer and started playing at a very young age. I began playing at my church and then moved on to play select soccer at the YMCA. The last year I played soccer competitively was in eighth grade. At that point I was on both the A and B select teams at the YMCA for my age group. But in that year, I felt a different calling- a calling that would change my life forever. Each year my church holds a weekend long event called Disciple Now. That weekend, God told me He had a plan for my life but that soccer was in the way. Confused as to why this was happening to me, I was a little taken back. Soccer was my whole world at that point in my life and imagining my life without it was very difficult. Yet, I promised God I would do it. I talked to my parents the night I got home from that weekend, and they looked at me as if I was crazy, but they understood. They had me call my coach and ask to set up a meeting. Later that week when meeting with my coach, he said he understood and told me to take a month off to decide what I wanted to do. After a month of prayer, I called my coach to tell him my decision. He didn't answer, so I left a message. "Hey coach, it's Julia. I just wanted to thank you very much for being the amazing coach you are and for giving me so many wonderful opportunities. I've taken this month very seriously in trying to make my decision. I believe the best thing is for me to quit. Please call me back. I'd like to talk to you." Since that day he has never called me back.

Holy Water

A few months passed, and God still hadn't told me what He wanted me to do with my life. I was getting frustrated and wanted to return to soccer more than anything. That summer after eighth grade, I went to a Christian camp called Camp Glisson with my best friends, Lindsey and Jenna. The day we arrived, I had told our counselors my story and how I was waiting for answers. They prayed that God would reveal those answers that week, and he did. One day, while we were kayaking, our counselors told us to go off on our own and pray and talk to God. I paddled off and prayed God would show me what he wanted me to do with my life. I opened my eyes and gazed at the water: God said to me very clearly that He wanted me to help people with no water. My eyes began to fill with tears as I was surrounded by water. After many months God had finally told me His plan. We paddled back with our group, and our leaders asked if anyone wanted to share what they prayed about. Without even raising my hand, my counselors asked me if I wanted to share. Filled with excitement, I, of course, said yes. I told them everything and they became filled with joy too. The minute we got back to our cabin, we knew we had to do something. We decided the best thing to do was to start a non-profit. That day, we came up with the name "Holy Water."

I came home from camp and told my parents the news. They looked at me with a weird expression and said, "but you're only fourteen." Yes, I was only fourteen, but I wanted to make a huge difference in the world. I'm pretty sure my parents thought this was just a phase I was going through, but it wasn't. The next week at church, I shared my story with my youth pastor at the time, Jason Scott. Jason and many of the other youth staff have helped me get Holy Water off the ground and has helped make it become what it is today. The youth staff at my church had many ideas to help build the foundation. We started small, but then got bigger. Many people underestimated me because I was so young, but I was never doing this on my own. I had many friends and family to support me.

Before Holy Water was created, I hated public speaking, and would do anything to avoid it. With Holy Water, I was forced into speaking publicly. The first time I spoke publicly was in February of 2012. My new youth pastor, Justin, asked me to speak at our annual Disciple Now in front of 500 people about Holy Water. That got rid of my fear for public speaking immediately. That weekend we raised $3000, and from then on Holy Water took off. In October of 2012, Holy Water filled for non-profit status.

Goals of Holy Water:

When you're a teenager, school seems like a never ending cycle. There's never a dull moment in my life. I'm always helping at school or church, but most importantly just helping people in general. Holy Water sometimes gets put on the back burner, which is not what I like, but unfortunately happens. Although, even in those times of stress and the non-stop chaos of life, I still know what I intend on Holy Water to become.

At Holy Water, our goals are to provide people anywhere in the world with clean water through wells, filters, and other water filtration devices. Our motto is simply, "Water 4 the World." Those words may seem so simple, but yet they mean so much more. Many people think this motto may seem like a dream that will never be obtainable, but you never know if you don't try. When we say water 4 the world, we literally mean the whole world. Many times when people think of places that need water they only think of places in Africa, but Africa is not the only place in need. There are places all over the world dying to get clean water. People are in such a need that they will go as far as stealing water from little kids.

Back when I spoke at my church's Disciple Now, we were fundraising money to build a well in Maralal, Kenya at a children's orphanage called Springs of Hope. I had first heard about this orphanage through one of my youth ministers Gaylen, who pointed me in this orphanage's direction. We had raised all the money we needed in just one weekend, but then we got some unfortunate news. The orphanage had once had a well to provide for the orphans, but the orphanage didn't own the land. The landlord found out that they had gotten a water supply and built a fence around the well so that the orphanage could no longer access it. They were scared that if Holy Water tried to build another well, that the same thing would happen. These children got hope, and then it was brutally taken away from them. That orphanage is the reason why Holy Water strives to provide people with water, because people are that desperate to the point where they steal from children. Even though they got their water taken away from them, they knew someone was watching out for them. Holy Water wants to be that person watching out for people. We also want to provide hope to communities and make lasting impacts on lives.

As of right now, Holy Water is still in search for their first out-of-country water project, but for now, Holy Water plans to do small mission projects in the United States. Holy

Water will be doing projects such as: passing out water bottles to the homeless in downtown Atlanta, going on a trip to West Virginia to help satisfy needs, and so much more. Holy Water has already become so much more than I could have ever imagined, and I'm so grateful for the support of my community. This foundation has become something I love to share with the community. We all work together, we all fundraise together, we all change lives together.

Water?

Why water? Doesn't everyone have water? These were the questions I had too. When God told me He wanted me to help people with no water, I didn't understand that not everyone has water. I knew people were poor, but I didn't know water was something that many people lacked. I'm not the only one to ever believe this, and that's why I believe it's my job to educate people on this issue, not only educate, but give back to people. Some people may feel that helping people is too hard, or it's not their job to give back. Others think that they can't make a difference in this world because of many various excuses. The truth is giving back and making a difference doesn't take skill; it just takes passion! Who says you're too young to make a difference? Who says you're not good enough to make an impact in someone's life? We as humans are our biggest enemies at times. We are scared of failure so we never try new things. Did we ever think that an occasional failure may be a good lesson? Probably not, because society says that if we fail in an effort we fail as a person. I believe society is wrong. I'd like to meet a person who hasn't failed one time in his life. I believe this nation's youth is taught that they can't be of any significance in this world until they grow up. And when they grow up, they often believe that their efforts won't make a change either and that someone else will take care of the job instead of them. So when people ask me why I take on such a big task as solving the world water problem, I tell them it's because I'm not scared of failure.

One of the most widely used websites for worldwide water information is called water.org. Their vision is to provide safe water and the dignity of a toilet for all in their lifetime. They also educate the public on just how bad the world water crisis is with heartbreaking statistics. At least 780 million people lack access to clean water. In fact, the world water crisis claims more lives through disease than any war claims through guns. If those facts don't shock you, then maybe this one hits home for you: every twenty-one seconds, a child dies a water-related illness, an innocent child! Any water website would tell you these facts, and many more. The other thing people don't know is that most of these people can find water sources, unclean water sources, but water sources none the less. Children are forced to skip school to walk miles and miles a day to get to this water source for their family. When the water source is brought home, it is most likely ridden with disease which causes many deaths. People have asked how providing clean water will help people. First off, just providing them with clean water is a blessing within itself. Secondly, clean water will enhance education. Last, it opens for them a future full of opportunities. Like I said before, children skip school many times to go get water, diseased water, and don't get an education. By offering them with clean water, you give the children an opportunity to go back to school and get an education, instead of them worrying about their family not having water that day. Many times we take education for granted when we shouldn't. We should use our education to change the world. To quote Nelson Mandela, "Education is the most powerful weapon which you can use to change the world." Every child deserves this opportunity.

Become aware and become active

Too frequently, people often misunderstand that this water crisis can even be happening in our backyard without us recognizing it. No, I don't mean literally our backyard, but in our cities, towns, state, nation. Many times we believe that the only people who deal with problems like these don't live in the United States. Therefore, people believe it is not their duty to help. Yet in many cases, these people are also very wrong. For those living in our Country, this false belief is often times all too true. West Virginia would be one of those states. My church used to go on mission trips to West Virginia to help some of the poorest people there. Not all, but many people there, don't have clean water or any water at all for many different reasons. I've never been on the mission trip myself, but I have been told stories of the problems seen there. In the 2010 census, West Virginia was ranked 49th out of 50 states for lowest household income and lowest per capita income. We need to realize that this issue is right here in our very own country. We would like to think our country has no issues at all when it comes to common necessities, but we would be greatly mistaken. It's our job to become more aware of these issues and be willing to step up.

When I was younger, all I wanted to do was travel to a foreign country to help people. Then a friend told me something that changed my view forever. "You don't have to cross the sea to be a missionary; you just have to see the cross." There are daily mission fields right in our own towns, but we just have to be willing to help. so how can you help solve this water crisis? There are many ways- some big, some small. One of the best ways to help is to get educated on the subject first. The second effort you can make is to help educate others on the subject. These may seem simple, but yet they can make a world of a difference. Some of the major choices you can make are to donate to a non-profit or a water crisis website which helps fund a water project. Donations can either be big or small, but no matter what they will still make an impact. To me, one of the coolest clean water inventions is water purifying filters. These filters are small, and many are inexpensive but can do so much for a community. This filter does not require much: an example, some filters are in straw form, from which a person can drink from the straw and by the time the water hits his mouth it is purified. Other filters may be more complicated and not be as small. These filters can purify whole buckets of water and containers of that sort. Some of the bigger and more expensive projects you can contribute to are projects such as wells. The cost of the well depends on the location of the town that needs the well. A company will dig deep down into land until they hit fresh water. Sometimes a well will require miles of land to find fresh water, which is why the cost is so major. These wells usually provide for a whole community instead of a few families like filters often do. There are many things you can do to help, but you have to be willing.

We take water for granted. Besides contributing to water products, there are choices we can make in our daily lives to help this worldwide issue. We all know that taking a thirty minute shower can be the most refreshing experience in the world, but we really only need to be taking a five to ten minute shower. We have all at some point in our lifetime bought a water bottle, taken one sip, and thrown it away. We need to be more aware of how much of a waste it is and try to conserve. If you don't want the water bottle anymore, give it to a friend, put it in your dog's water bowl, or water a plant: don't just throw it away. Turn off your faucet while you are brushing your teeth because leaving the water running is such a big waste. There are many ways you can monitor how much water you use. If anything, saving water will cost you less on your water bill, and that should be motivation within itself.

Y-O-U can make a difference

Sometimes stepping outside of our comfort zone can be hard. Being only 14, and starting a non-profit, I was kind of the odd one out. Most teenagers that age want to watch TV, sleep all day, eat food, and always try to prove their parents wrong. But I was a kid who wouldn't watch the world suffer and not do anything about it. Many times we say we are going to do something to make a difference because we gain a passion for it, and then give up on it a few months later. I've noticed that society has placed a stereotype on my generation as being irresponsible and not trustworthy. Unfortunately many of my piers have started believing this stereotype. Many times teenagers are too scared to do something radical because society is always watching them. They feel as if a leash is constantly holding them back to the point where the can no longer dream the dream they once had as a child. They don't want to stand out because society tells them the best thing to do is act ordinary and blend in. Our generation could be a generation on fire for what we are passionate for if only people knew that it is ok to be different. So I'm telling you, it's ok to be different. Many times I have gotten ridiculed for what I am trying to accomplish, but I have never given up, and neither should you. Stand up for what you believe in, because you might be the only person to make a difference. One day you will make a difference in the world whether society likes it or not. Change won't start until you make a choice to make a stand.

    If there's one thing I've learned throughout this whole experience, is that you're never too young, or too old to make a difference. There are many things that this world is in need of. Maybe you're the one to start making the difference. I believe everyone has the potential to make a difference in the world if he or she follows a dream. You can always achieve a goal as long as you never give up, no matter how silly the dream may be. One of my ambitions is to change the world, while another is to be on the Ellen show one day. These may seem too big or too unrealistic, but who is to tell you that you can never achieve your dreams. You are never too young or too old to dream big!

I believe we use the word impossible to often, and that has led generations to think many goals are impossible. Maybe if we start looking at the impossible as a challenge, the impossible won't be so impossible after all. When I was little, I never thought in a million years I would be where I am today. I wanted to grow up, play soccer, and become a lawyer, but sometimes the way we have our life planned out just isn't supposed to happen. Looking back on my life then, I laugh because I could never see myself becoming a lawyer. People have come in my way and tried to crush my dreams, but it only made me stronger. I've been told I can't too many times, but I've also proved people wrong that many times. In the end, I believe that people should be satisfied with the life they live. If they aren't then there's always time to change. I want to inspire the youth of the nation to rise above mediocrity and help them become extraordinary. This world has too many ordinary people, and I want to be the one to change that. I want to one day look back on life and say I did the best I could to make this world a better place. Sometimes when we get a calling, we need to stop asking questions and just take a leap of faith. You may not always understand, but that's the beauty of it. Although we try so hard to fit in with society, we should stop listening to society and listen to our hearts. Holy Water may be slow going sometimes, but I plan to accomplish great outcomes with it one day. Society will tell you to give up many times, but no one said society was ever right. So live each day as if you were on a mission to change the world, and who knows what will result from it. One day you will make a difference. One day you will change the in world. One day.

Julia Miller - Bio

Julia Miller founded the non-profit organization, Holy Water, in 2009 at age 14. She has spoken at many youth conferences encouraging kids to make an impact in the society they live in. She does many service projects in her community, including one of her favorites- serving the homeless in Atlanta. Julia attended the 2013 Georgia Girls State and was elected as state Supreme Court Justice by her piers. She is the 2013-2014 school year Lassiter High School Fellowship of Christian Athletes president. Julia also loves to write poetry. She also earned her bronze award as a Girl Scout, and is a recipient of the silver President's Education Award. She is a member of the Lassiter High School Marching Band, who participated in the 2010 Macy's Thanksgiving Day Parade, and the 2013 Rose Bowl Parade. She is also a member of the Spanish National Honors Society. Her future plans are to inspire others to make a difference in the world through her story and actions.

To learn more about Julia and her story, visit her website at www.holywaterfoundation.com or her blog at www.watergirl11.blog.com

What's Your Dream?

Catherine Olivia Sicard

CHAPTER 16 – What's Your Dream?

A dream is something you must work hard to achieve and it can be anything. You can dream to go to college. Dream to go to the moon. Dream to fight cancer. Dream to have a friend. Dream to not be bullied. Dream to be accepted. Dream to see your kids happy and healthy. Dream to live to see tomorrow. A dream can be a grand one or a simple one, yet it is still a dream. Everyone has a dream, from a young age, of what they want to do and who we want to become. As time goes on our dreams change, we start to find more simple dreams. Still, only a few people have enough dedication to pursue their dreams. With help from others, our dreams can come true, sometimes we just need a little push. Dreams do not come easy. If they did, they would not be dreams.

Is anything impossible?

From a young age, we are taught to set goals. These goals are made to accomplish task and to challenge our minds. As goals become greater, they become tougher to complete and require more effort to finish. *Impossible* is the word that comes to mind when we give up on the goals we are trying to reach. But nothing really is impossible, everything can be achieved. Yes, it might be a banal saying, but think about it. Everything can and has been accomplished not just once, but numerous times. It just cannot be achieved easily; it takes hard work, inspiration, passion, dedication, and a determined mind to complete all things in life. Every accomplishment in life comes with many trials and some trials will not be successful. Do not let that stop you, life is full of fails we all face them and we get right back up and try again. Thomas Edison failed many times before he accomplished the light bulb and he never gave up, where would the world be without this invention? Those failures should give you the power deep inside you, the determination, and a reason not to give up. Prove to those who doubt you that you can do it and let that power drive you. Your goals do not come easy. They require years of determination. You must work until the wave holding you back is the reason you are a superior and confident ship.

The climb of struggling

For some, the work needed to achieve a goal will not take as much effort as it will for others. Everyone is different and we all work and learn at different rates. Twenty in every one thousand people suffer from a learning disability. Some people never overcome the nightmare of their disadvantage. Learning disabilities place a giant hold on your life, it holds you back from succeeding and it breaks your confidence down to dust. Always being stricken with the sigma "*dumb*" is hard to overcome, it always haunts you with every failure and accomplishment. It feels like a sinking ship, but you get over it and the ship stabilizes, yet the cruel words keep pouring in until you realizes it is skinning again and it is a long way to the bottom. The sigma of learning disabilities from a young age, the confidence, that keeps everyone else motivated, is destroyed.

Learning disabilities can be vast and they can be minor, yet they still place a challenge on you no matter the size. A learning disability is a condition that makes it difficult to acquire knowledge and the skills expected from others of the same age. It makes it harder to retain the information given. A student suffering from learning disabilities will work twice as hard, if not more, than the average student. The simple things that come easy for an average student, do not come easy for a student with a learning disability.

My dream of striving

I had a dream, it was to prove to people I was not "*dumb*". I was done being told I could not be in the regular classes because I would not be able to keep up with the average work load. The stares and whispers of the stigma of *dumb, stupid, retard*, and the segregation of small group classes made me determined to prove to everyone I was not who they thought I was. I just did not know how I was going to that. *Determination*: was the only thing I had to push me forward and allow me to overcome my greatest challenge. I had sunk well below the bottom before taking action. My confidence was gone, there was nothing to encourage me to strive, except the motto "I think it. I believe it. I can do it." My father badgered it into my head every chance he received. Yet, I still did not think, believe, or do anything, till the stares and whispers made me start to think. I was tired of always feeling like an outcast, worthless, and depressed. It was time I took action.

After years of not doing anything and just pretending the cruel words that haunted me night and day were not offending me, I decided it was time to take action. Walking through the halls day after day feeling *dumb* made me determined to leave the stigma *dumb* behind me in elementary school. Middle school brought a new change and a new me. I was no longer in small group classes, yet I did not feel any change. I still felt as if I was *stupid* and the personal teachers, placed in my classes just for me, did not make me feel any better. I was not going to let anyone or anything get in my way of proving I was not *dumb*. I began to rebel against the parapro teachers. I refused their help, *study* guides, extra time on assignments and test, and extra notes. To the teacher's dismay, I would openly throw away all extra materials. I refused any extra time on any test or assignments; I completed everything in the time given with all the other students. I spent every waking hour studying, waking early before school just to review my notes. I studied more than anyone could imagine. I worked alone and without help, allowing only encouragement from my teachers and peers. By the end of seventh grade I'd maintained honor roll all year by myself. For the first time ever, I looked forward to returning to school.

I had been recommended for higher level classes, which I was pleased to accept and felt and my excitement soar, maybe all too fast. My confidence was at an all new high only to be broken down once again for I was being told by so called educational professionals, who did not know me, that I would not be able to handle the work load. This was the last straw. My parents took action and went to the school's principle to get me placed in higher classes. The meeting was successful and I was permitted to take the classes I'd worked so hard attain. When the year ended, I had all A's and excelled in every class. I had proven everyone wrong and achieved my goal. Now, I have the mindset, confidence and determination to excel at anything life throws at me.

Accomplishing the Impossible

Overcoming what I thought was my greatest challenge was not an easy task. I still face problems every single day, especially when I have trouble or believe I cannot complete a duty. These challenges will never go away, but I will never let them stop me again. I have learned to face my problems head on and that has given me confidence I take with me everywhere. I still must study more than most, but now I know it pays off. There are many times I feel as though I have reached my breaking point, like everything is coming to an end and I am worthless, but with every failure, I am more determined than ever to complete the assignment at hand. I had never felt as if I had truly overcome my learning disability until I was awarded with an academic award of Highest Average in Honors Literature. Literature has always been my greatest struggle, so this award gave me the confidence I needed to prove I could do anything. This award meant more to me than anyone could imagine. It was not just an award, it was my life's triumph. I overcame the hardest part of my struggle with learning disabilities. Learning disabilities stay with you forever, but now I can mask it because I made my point. Although the voices from my past still haunt me, I realize now that I have excelled beyond most those voices. I would not take back having my constant struggle because it has given me the greatest gift I could ever ask for: the confidence and determination that I can do anything I set my mind to.

The Spark

I achieved my goals with tremendous help from many people. Without them I would not have the mindset I have today. The feeling you get when you succeed on what you worked so hard to get is incredible, it is like no other feeling in the world. Words cannot describe it, but you feel it with everything you do after.

Now I plan to inspire others to achieve their goals and dreams so more people can feel the way I feel. Everything is in the mind, if you think you can achieve something, you will achieve it. Just keep telling yourself "you can do it". You just cannot give up on the first challenge that gets in your way. Allow it to encourage you to reach your goals quicker. It is never too late to try and accomplish a goal, just take the initiative and do it step by step. Everyone can use a little encouragement. Do not let others get you down with their negative feedback. Rise up! Show that you are better than they think you are.

First, you must write down what you wish to accomplish. Place it somewhere where you will see it every day. This will allow you to always know what you want. Then, take action and make a plan. This plan should be a step by step plan on how you will accomplish your goal or dreams. Make it a check list, so you get a burst of accomplishment every time you achieve something and it places you one step closer to the finish line.

The Purpose of Life

Every life has a purpose, but what is that purpose? We wake up every day not knowing what lies ahead of us or what to make of ourselves. We don't even know where we will be tomorrow, yet we still wake up. We do this on the quest to find our purpose with only a few guidelines to lead us. "The purpose of life is to contribute in some way to making things better" for your life and for someone else's life (Robert F. Kennedy). We set goals all the time, but do we actually achieve them? You can think all you want about making a difference, but what is the point if you do not actually pursue your goals? What really is making a difference? Making a difference is not about trying to change the world, or doing something grand; it is about making an impact on one single person in the world. There are seven- billion people in the world and all you have to do it help, inspire, or encourage one of them. You have the power to change someone's life.

What does your Future Hold?

Where do you see yourself in ten years? That is your dream of where you wish to be. There are many challenges you will face to get there. It will not be easy to accomplish your dreams, but it will be worth it in the end. The first step on your journey to pursue your dreams is to not give up no matter what. Everything you do to accomplish your dreams puts you one step forward to living your dreams. How many times have you given up on something you were working on? We all do because we get frustrated, tired, or we do not see the point and have no dedication or inspiration to finish. Dreams work the same way, many people never have their dreams come true, leaving an empty spot in their mind and a "what if..." on their thoughts. They will never know what they could have become, but you still can and you can encourage others to do the same thing, not just helping accomplishing their dreams, but helping them not give up when they believe their ship is going to sink. By being their last spark of energy you can change their whole world, might even save their life.

Think it, believe it, and do it!

Do not let something go unfinished or let a dreams turn into regrets from not pursuing it. Get up! Start making plans to make the right changes in your life. Go and make them happen. It is all in the mind you must: Think it, believe it, and do it.

Catherine Olivia Sicard – Bio

Catherine Olivia Sicard is a high school junior attending Lassiter High School in Marietta, Georgia. Her passion for animals has provided the ambition and industrious study habit to apply for and enter the University of Georgia's or Clemson's Veterinarian or Law program. She is known as the girl with eggs, because she personally takes care of ten chickens of various heritage and two ducks. She is constantly bringing home and fostering animals in need. Since she is an accomplished snow skier and boarder, she jumps at any chance to head to the snowy mountains. She heads straight for the harder trails, as she does in every day life. She currently works as an intern for the Karen Handel's Georgia Senate campaign. One of job duties is to make cold calls to inform voters about Karen Handel. Since she often times is told not so nice things or is cut off by a dial tone, she tells everyone she knows to please be nice to telemarketers and listen to what they have to say.

Although, at first look and looking at Catherine's grade you would never know she suffers from learning disabilities. Until now she has kept it private and hidden, but now she hopes to help and inspire other people to place the things that hold them back behind them. Catherine's struggles with learning disabilities began in Kindergarten. Her learning disability ignited a fire that inspired persistence and an unbelievable work and study ethic and she was removed from the learning disabled program in the eighth grade. Her self-motivation and determination has provided numerous school excellence awards, acceptance into both Honors and AP classes, and the pinnacle award this year by receiving the Lassiter Letter Award for a grade point average higher than 4.0. She understands firsthand the struggles students face and has devoted her time to support and mentor students in need.

Catherine has placed her learning disabilities behind her. She continues to strive allowing everything she learned from overcoming many struggles to help her every day. She now truly believes nothing can stop her from doing what she wishes to do. She is fueled by the underlying motto: Think It! Believe It! Yes I can!

Second Chance to Life
Lucy Singer

CHAPTER 17 – Second Chance to Life

She sits in her room, music blasting in her ears; the bitter-sweet melodies moving her with them. She sits alone with her mind, drowning in her own pain. Nobody is there. Nobody is ever there.

What has happened to her beautiful, innocent mind? She muses. She grew up. That is what happened. She has turned into the broken girl she never thought she would become. She dies every day, over and over again, her memories reminding her of how useless she feels. She sits in class, staring at the boy who will never love her back. She looks at her grades and remembers when she was a straight A student. She wonders why she thinks such dark thoughts. She cannot be that girl anymore, not with the pain that lives within her. All she thinks about is what the world would be like without her. Who would care anyway? Everyone would care, but she just denies this thought and makes herself think otherwise.

She walks into her house, fakes a smile and says her day was great. When she hears her mother's relaxed laughter during a phone conversation, she becomes overwhelmed with conflicted between feeling happiness for her mom's joy and the increasing emptiness at her inability to feel the same in herself. Her brother is doing homework at the kitchen table. He is the smartest kid in his fifth grade class and that makes her feel dumb. Dumb that she is no longer achieving the same honors than she was once able to accomplish. She pictures her father in his basement office, sacrificing his time to provide for his family's future, but she does not want to live that long. She makes it to her room and sinks deeper into her depression. She writes the note, opens her special wooden box that hides her secret pills and opens the plastic lid. Numb to all emotions, she swallows the bottle's contents without a second thought. She feels at peace as she pictures the beautiful landscape where she will exist when she dies. She thinks to herself about how happy her soul will be when it is no longer on this horrible earth! The pills take effect and the room goes fuzzy. Then it goes black.

Her mom yells up to her to come down for dinner, only to be answered with the simple sound of silence. She yells again, knowing that her daughter usually answers the second time. But, once again, the absence of her child's voice fills the house. Concern and frustration take over. As she walks upstairs to lecture her daughter, she hears nothing whatsoever. Maybe she snuck out? She reaches her teenager's room and sees a lifeless body. She runs over and takes her daughter's hand into her own. Feeling the weakest pulse, tears start streaming down her cheeks. She sees the empty bottle of pills and the note. She screams to her husband and son to come quickly. Her voice is shaky. They run into the room to see the terrifying scene of the almost dead teenage girl.

Now, her family is gathered around her, bawling. Her father calls the ambulance and a raspy voice answers. Soon enough, the ambulance gets to the house, ear shattering sirens wailing. The paramedics run into the house and put her on a gurney as gently as possible. They rush her into the ambulance vehicle and speed to the hospital. When they reach the hospital she is hurried into the emergency room behind a closed curtain. The doctors come running in to start their work. It is their job to drain the poison from her body, the poison she ingested through the pills she swallowed earlier that evening.

After the task of stabilizing her, a doctor walks into the waiting room to talk with her exhausted parents. He reports that she is going to physically heal, but the medical team found many scars and cuts on their daughter from her self-harming actions. The doctor advises the family to admit her to a mental health hospital for observation and treatment. They look at the doctor, mouths hanging open in shock. They never thought that their daughter was in so much emotional pain. They never imagined she would cause such extensive harm to herself. They thought she was a happy girl, but they were wrong. They agree that is wise to follow the medical advice they have just received. The doctor gives them the name of a facility that specializes in treating issues of troubled teens. They call the center to set up her admission. It is decided they will bring her there when she is released from this hospital. They will take her home to pack so she will have some comforts of her own while she is in treatment.

They walk into the hospital room as she is waking out of her slumber. She looks around. Is this heaven, or perhaps hell? She realizes that she is still alive and starts to sob. They tell her that everything is going to be okay but she says that is not why she is crying. Through her sobs, she tells her family that she wanted to die. It is the first time through today's crisis they allow the events to sink into their heart and soul. Their daughter actually attempted to kill herself

After a day of making sure she has physically recovered from her injuries she is released from the hospital. Her family takes her home to pack before driving to the mental health center. They pull into the driveway and walk into the house. Quietly sulking, she retreats up to her room and shuts her door. She is in a frenzied state. However she is quiet so not to allow anyone to know what she is doing. She searches her dresser drawers for her last resort, hidden rope. As she is completing the final knot, hanging it from the ceiling fan, her father walks in. He pulls her out of her room, forces her into the car and starts driving. In between cries, she asks where they are going. He replies that they are going to the hospital where she will get help. Her breathing quickens and she begins to panic. She screams that she is fine and does not need help. When they get there, she refuses to get out of the car. She throws a temper tantrum causing several counselors to forcibly remove her from the car.

Her dad completes the admission paperwork and they find her a room. She will not stop kicking and screaming. The nurses try to coax her to calm down but due to her manic state and heightened emotions it takes a sedative to lull her to sleep. Her dad and the professional team are confident she will sleep quietly for several hours. However they will monitor her closely over the next several days as she adjusts to her treatment plan. Their first objective is to keep her safe so she can begin her journey towards healing: mentally, spiritually and emotionally.

Her dad watches his daughter sleep. She looks so peaceful but he knows she is not. He finally walks out and as quietly and as gently as possible, he closes the door.

He sits in the waiting room exhausted, contemplating the events of the day. When her mom and brother arrive at the hospital he runs to give them a hug, and they embrace as a family searching for comfort. He explains what has happened over the past several hours and that she is finally resting. Her parents finally have the opportunity to sit with the team of professionals. They beg the counselors and psychiatrists to make their daughter better. They explain that it is their job to work with her and the family to provide the tools she will need to recover and cope with her emotions in the future.

Many weeks later

She is home! Her parents are so ecstatic. Her brother cries out of joy. When they look at her, it is obvious that she is happy and peaceful. She has more color to her face. Her voice is more cheerful and lively.

She tells them what made her attempt suicide; everyone is in tears. She is better and that is what matters.

She explains what it was like over the past several weeks in the hospital. She says that is was horrible for the first few days, and she hated everyone. After a few days she got used to the many things that she initially resisted. She eventually made some friends. She tells how she connected with some amazing people with interesting backgrounds. Every day she spent time with a therapist, and at first she did not want to do this. At first she did not want to get better. By the end of the first week, she realized that people actually do love her and she wanted to recover. After that, everything went uphill. She stopped having urges to cut herself. The recording in her head that keep playing the same message of how much of a disappointment she was went away.

She hugs her father, mother and brother, and thanks them for sending her to get help. She says that from now on she is going to help make a difference in the world. She is going to help people with depression to make sure they do not get as far off track as she did. She is going to save as many lives as she can. She needs to be a person her friends can turn too when they are unsure what to do with sad feelings. She needs to know that as a teenager she cannot handle everything. Most importantly, she needs to know that she should always tell a trusted adult when she or a friend is in trouble. She realizes that confiding in others who can provide help is not defying trust. She knows she would rather have a friend be angry with her for seeking help if it means getting help. She knows that prior to this transformation she would have felt betrayed if a friend had told another about her pain, even if that person was looking for answers about what to do. Now she knows that action can save a friend's life.

Many days later, she goes back to school. As she walks through the doors, everyone claps and cheers. People hand her notes and flowers and hug her. She asks what all of this is for and her classmates tell her that she is a survivor. She attempted suicide, failed, and got help. She is a special case of someone with depression, for she has gotten better.

A wide smile crosses her face and tears of joy run down her cheeks. She thanks everyone. She wonders to herself how she could have ever thought people didn't care if she died. Even people she didn't know are happy she is here, alive.

-fin-

My name is Lucy Singer, and the dangers of self-harm and suicide are very prevalent issues in my life. Some of my close friends suffer from depression leading them to self-harm and suicidal thoughts. Writing this story has been therapeutic for me since I too suffer from depression. I hope that this story will help people of all ages realize there are better options than ending their lives. It is hard to grow up in a world that gets more complex each day. Society tells teenagers that we must strive to be perfect for people to like us. At other times we hear the messages saying that no matter what, you are perfect and be yourself. These two totally different ideas confuse teens and mess with our minds. The media tells teens (though sometimes indirectly) that they need to be perfect so people will notice us or like us. Honestly, you just need to accept yourself. And yes, improving yourself is always a good thing, as long as you don't take it too the extreme by doing things that harm your health both physically and emotionally.

In the past few years, several people and families I know have been affected by suicide, either attempted or committed. This made me realize that suicide isn't just some selfish act but often the only solution individuals can think of to get rid of their problems. It is not a solution. Counseling therapy, medicine, or even just telling a close friend how you are feeling are ways to recovery. To keep teenagers, pre-teens, and even adults from taking their own life I wrote a fictional story that was inspired by real life events. If you know anybody who self-harms or is suicidal, tell an adult immediately. You can prevent it from becoming an extreme situation with irreversible consequences. By one simple action of seeking help, you can save a life.

If you are in immediate need of help call the National Suicide Prevention Lifeline at

1-800-273-8255

Selected Resources

- American Foundation for Suicide Prevention - *www.afsp.org*
- JED Foundation - www.jedfoundation.org
    Promote emotional health and prevent suicide among college and university students.
- National Organization for People of Color Against Suicide - www.nopcas.com
- Suicide Awareness Voices of Education (SAVE) – www.save.org
- The Trevor Project - www.thetrevorproject.org
     Crisis intervention and suicide prevention services to lesbian, gay, bisexual, transgender and questioning (LGBTQ) young people ages 13-24.
- Yellow Ribbon Suicide Prevention Program - www.yellowribbon.org

Lucy Singer – Bio

Lucy Jayne Singer is an aspiring young author and musician. She took the challenge to participate in this group of Lassiter High School group to write a book about making a difference. Lucy is an 8th grader, who began writing stories by dictating her tales to her father when she was in preschool. She hopes to someday become an accomplished author of teen fiction. In addition she has been studying classical piano since 5 years old and began percussion in the middle school band. She is completing her Girl Scout Silver Award and plans to continue her membership through high school. She spends her summers at URJ Camp Coleman in Cleveland, GA. Lucy has expressed the desire to follow many different dreams from being a genetic scientist, a food critic, a composer on Broadway, to being US Congresswoman. She is excited to start Lassiter High School in the fall of 2014. Her goals for her years at LHS include being in the marching band and becoming a Drum Major, joining the debate team, and being active in the Jewish Student Union. Lucy looks forward to connecting with teens in the NFTY (North America Federation of Temple Youth) youth organization. Besides staying focused on her academics and extracurricular activities Lucy always finds time for episodes of Dr. Who, Fairy Tail Anime, her dogs, listening to music, and hanging out with her family. A lover of visiting New York City, she also loves camping in the woods and sleeping in tents. Lucy hopes to Make a Difference in the world.

Finding My Niche
Samantha Sanderford

CHAPTER 18 - Finding My Niche

"Some people are filled by compassion and a desire to do good, and some simply don't think anything's going to make a difference." The beginning portion of this quote by Meryl Streep applies to me. I try to do as much as I can to make the world a better place and set an example for younger generations as well as generations to come. I want to make a difference and continue making the differences I already make. I have grown up in a household that teaches that it is best to help people who are less fortunate than you, whether it be helping monetarily or with your time. Although I do think that people can still help with multiple organizations and causes, I think everyone has a niche in which they are best suited to help make the world a better place. I think that I am lucky and have found my niche and the dominant way that I can help the world and set an example at an early age. I dream that I will make a difference by promoting and working with various programs that support special needs people and their families and pursue an occupation that works with the special needs community.

The Current and Revised Definition of Special Needs

The definition of special needs is mental, emotional, or physical problems in a person that require a special setting for education. Education in this sense does not necessarily mean a classroom setting. People are educated all throughout their day by having new experiences and information and learning how to respond and react to each new thing they may encounter. So, a revised version of that definition may be that the special needs are a group of people where each person has a unique way of responding and reacting to new experiences and information due to mental, emotional, and physical disorders. These ailments include Autism, Attention Deficit/Hyperactivity Disorder (AD/HD), Cerebral Palsy, Down Syndrome, Spina Bifida, and several other disorders. There are spectrums within each disorder, going from full independence to total dependence. The disorders just affect the view as well as the way a person may see or do something at different degrees.

Why I Want to Help the Special Needs Community

Now, one might wonder why I would like to venture into the world of special needs care. There are several reasons for this, however, and these are just a few. First of all, I enjoy helping people. I have always felt that it is my personal responsibility to work with people who might not be capable of taking care of themselves, whether it is children, the elderly, or people with special needs. I particularly enjoy working with people who have special needs because they show true appreciation and love. Even if the person in question does not show those feelings the entire time that you help them, the moments that they do smile or do laugh can make a person's week. A second reason I want to continue helping the special needs is that it is in my personal belief that it is the right thing to do. The right thing to do is to make a difference and help others whenever they may need help. Special needs individuals do need some help and I have an unshakable certainty that you help others. People should also do unto others what they want others to do unto them. If I needed assistance, I would want help and people to be with and trust my wellbeing with.

A final reason why I want to help the special needs community is because of a handful of people that have touched me. In my life, through the various programs/organizations I have worked with, there have been several individuals who have influenced the way I want to make a difference the most. One of the individuals is a twenty something year old with whom I swam at practice and in a Georgia Special Olympics meet. This boy could not talk or communicate due to his disorder and had several anger problems. He would refuse to get in the water and then, once he got in, he would refuse to get out. He also had a tendency to not stay in his lane and go swim in other swimmers' lanes. At the meet, he exhibited all of these tendencies and three people had to help get him back in his lane and, at the end, out of the water. However, when he went to the podium to receive his medal, he turned to me, smiled, and gave me a hug. He had never smiled at me before or given any sign of a positive feeling. His caretaker had told me that he did not like to touch other people as well. That brief moment of affection made me realize how proud of him I was, and how happy I felt helping him.

How I am Currently Making a Difference

The moment of pride that I felt was also the moment when I realized that my niche involved the special needs. I have found several organizations where I can make a difference in the special needs community. I have worked with programs that help people with multiple disorders. Some programs that I have helped with are Special

Olympics, KSU Play, and a program that allows the volunteer to read with special needs preschoolers. These programs allow people to make a difference in the special needs community. These organizations allow special needs people to react and respond in a safe environment where other people can help or even just spend time with them.

    I am currently making a difference today by participating in a number of organizations that fit some of the descriptions below. Several organizations have emerged over the years to help the special needs function in society and do normal activities such as theatre, sports, or school. Although each organization varies in terms of location, employees, etc., each organization has the same goal to accomplish. Each organization wants to help make a difference in the lives of the special needs individuals and their families. Some organizations watch children or adults while the rest of their family can go do an activity together, or just have time at home when they do not have to worry about the safety or concerns of the member of the family with the special needs. Another type of organization creates a safe environment where a select few activities or one significant activity can be taught and practiced such as a sport or fine arts program. Some organizations are specialized learning environments for the special needs. These organizations generally teach skills such as laundry, making canned soup, or something similar to that. The things learned at these programs help a person be somewhat independent and depending where the person falls on the spectrum of their disability, can even allow them to live independently. There are also generally local organizations that let younger children interact and play with special needs children so the special needs children can interact with people their own age.

Who Can Make a Difference within the Special Needs Community?

Many different types of people can donate their time to work with the special needs in these organizations. Almost every age can find on organization or way to help. Young people are able to interact with special needs children within the public education system by reading to the special needs children or even just talking to them. Adults can help more extensively through committing time through organizations and gaining qualifications to further advance the activities they can do with a special needs person. An example qualification is that a person must be a lifeguard to do swim with people who have certain riskier disorders. There are usually age requirements when working with organizations, but they vary between each separate group. Also, there are several different places a person can make a difference with the special needs. They can make a difference within their neighborhood, community, or even beyond that. Organizations vary between local organizations to worldwide organizations. An example of a local organization is KSU Play, founded and carried out in Kennesaw, GA. On the other hand, an example of a worldwide organization that helps the special needs is Special Olympics. However in both circumstances people can help by giving time or money to an organization that works with the special needs. Both currencies are in high demand and will continue to be in high demand as time proceeds. People can commit as much time as they want or as little time as they want and depending on the activity and program, the time to volunteer is seasonal and does not necessarily happen year round.

My Future with the Special Needs

I have plans to pursue an occupation to help the special needs community. The job options range from medical research to occupational therapy. I want to help special needs individuals daily. However, no matter what I most certainly want to continue working with the organizations that I work with now. I want to continue giving myself to special needs individuals who need someone to put their trust in. I would also like to find more opportunities to expand the types of programs I work with. I want to give time to as many helpful organizations as I can. As I continue to grow older, I want to contribute money to organizations that help the special needs globally whether the help is in finding a cure or in helping accommodate present day needs. My life will always have at least some dedicated time towards the special needs. I hope, however, that my future occupation and continuation of helping organizations will help me devote a great deal of my life towards the special needs.

Final Thoughts

I want to better the lives of as many individuals as I can. I want to let them feel comfortable and safe and fearless in terms of showing who they are and all that they can do. I want to continue being involved in programs that will help better the individuals altogether, including the way they behave and the way they think or emotionally feel about themselves. I am proud of what I am doing now to make a difference and am so delighted that throughout the years I have been shown ways that I can help. However, I just feel that I need to make even more of a difference and help even more people. I am proud of the accomplishments I have witnessed, the hurdles I have seen jumped, and the fears I have seen overcome. I have a spot in my heart for this group of people that have a unique way of responding and reacting to new experiences and information due to mental, emotional, and physical disorders. They bring insight and knowledge to me that I might not have ever thought about or learned. I cannot think of a better way and blessing to have that will have leaded me to make a difference. I have, am, and will make a difference in the special needs community.

Samantha Sanderford - Bio

Samantha Sanderford currently lives in Marietta, GA with her parents and younger brother. She currently attends Lassiter High School where she is enrolled as a sophomore. Samantha works as a part time lifeguard and summer league swim coach while she also coaches a Special Olympics team. She involves herself in several clubs including school chorus, church high school choir, several small groups, and Study Buddies which promotes individuals in high school to tutor younger kids. In her free time, she enjoys kayaking, reading, watching movies, and spending time with family and friends. Samantha hopes to later graduate high school and continue her education. She would like to receive a Master's degree in occupational therapy to continue working with the special needs.

The Music in Everyone
Anna Wang

CHAPTER 19 – The Music in Everyone

How I Fell in Love with an Art

I consider myself a friend, sister, student, and most importantly, a musician. When I was five years old, my mother brought me to a quaint music shop down our street. The owner sat me down beside him on the piano bench while he played a sonata, the first of many sonatas I would come to learn and love. That afternoon, I had my first piano lesson and after I knew that music would forevermore be a significant part of my life.

Eventually, I obtained an official teacher. She was a native Brazilian and seemed to always be telling me stories: the time her dog destroyed all the furniture, how her son broke his leg for the fourth time, and even stories about her own piano teacher. Each new lesson was not only an opportunity for me to grow as a musician but also one for me to learn life lessons: "one always makes mistakes when rushing through things", "never leave something to the last minute", and "live life to its fullest." Every time I made a mistake she would exclaim, "Mozart is rolling around in his grave!" and I would proceed to play the section once more.

Still I loved playing the piano. The music was challenging enough to keep me interested, yet still contained the beautiful melodic passages. Ultimately, I went on to explore more than just the classical piano works of the baroque era. My iPod was filled with songs by Green Day, Coldplay, and Maroon 5. I started playing rock songs on the piano, purely for my entertainment. I remember leaving the theater after seeing Harry Potter and the Deathly Hallows

Part 2 with chills from the mesmerizing film score. To this day, I still enjoy singing along to *Hakuna Matata* and *Be Our Guest* along with all the other beloved Disney songs. And after seeing Mary Poppins for the first time on Broadway, I promptly downloaded the entire album and fell in love with music theatre. Music meant the world to me.

It wasn't until I was in fourth grade when I joined my school's chorus and started making music with my classmates. Only then did I realize that I was one of a few that had been exposed to this part of culture. I was shocked. Up until that point I believed music education was something that everyone had access to. Unfortunately, that was far from being the truth. The thing that had meant the absolute most to me, something I portrayed as a universal idea, was not so universal after all.

What is Music?

A scientific definition of music is simply "a pattern of structured sound wave frequencies." However, music is obviously much more. Music affects people in ways that nothing else can. A wedding or a graduation ceremony can be made memorable through even one special song that speaks to someone. Music, as a version of poetry, can tell stories, describe events, and bring people together. Everyone should have the chance to experience the beauty of song.

Music is one of two art forms that cannot be tangible (the other being writing). Yes, there are countless stacks of sheet music; however, it is simply more than ink on a page and notes on a staff that create *music*. The Lassiter Chorus motto *"After the notes, the music begins"* is a subtle message, which explains how only after one manages to learn the pitches and rhythms can he or she truly start creating something meaningful. Music can be created with as little as one voice with a message.

How Music is Beneficial

Technical Aspects

Music, while a form of expression, can also foster education in young minds. Music theory focuses on the structure of music. These patterns such as harmony, melody, and chord progression can enhance the brain to work in a more technical way.

A study published in the *Psychology of Music* showed that children exposed to music training in rhythm, pitch, harmony, and melody demonstrated superior cognitive performance when compared with peers who had not been exposed to music education. The experimenters separated second-graders with similar demographics and no musical experience into two groups: one whose members received formal piano education for three years and another who members received no formal music education. The results showed that children in the former group displayed significantly better scores in verbal sequencing and vocabulary. However, the critical reading scores remained rather consistent within both groups. The researchers concluded that the absence of music instruction (due to the holiday break) reversed any earlier temporary cortical reorganization experienced by students. This proves that music education should not only be exposed to students but also be consistently administered on a fixed interval schedule.

Piano instruction is extremely effective when it comes to enhancing the brain. Children who specifically received keyboard instruction displayed advanced levels of vocabulary and verbal skills as opposed to children who did not receive the same kind of tuition. Piano lessons engage both sides of the brain and force the student to reading numerous lines of music at once. As the strength between the two halves of the brain increase, so do the individual nerve cells within the brain and especially the temporal lobes. This improves both memory and the ability to distinguish sounds and pitches. The level of technicality in playing the piano nourishes parts of the brain responsible for sensory integration, attention, critical thinking, emotional maturity, and motor capacities. A musician also has to access different areas of the brain simultaneously, as they use their ears, eyes, and muscles to create music. Learning the piano strengthens multi-tasking abilities and spatial reasoning, which in turn, benefit logical thinking and especially skills in mathematics. A study was conducted where college students were given ten minutes to listen to a piano sonata before taking an assessment. The assessment involved finding patterns in numbers and objects. The study was also conducted with preschoolers. Both groups showed superior scores than those that did not listen to the music. The USDoE showed that piano students scored considerably higher on standardized tests such as the SAT and ACT and further explained how music education can further increase a student's socioeconomic status. Clearly, there is a strong, positive correlation to music education and skill level in mathematics and language.

Cultural Aspects

Not only is music beneficial to the technical mind, it also influences the cultural aspects of one's life. Students who have admitted to considering dropping out of high school cite their decision to stay due to their membership in a music program. Music organizations such as band, orchestra, and chorus positively motivate students to strive for success and also provide a friendly atmosphere for learning and social bonding to occur. Also, students who have musical experience tend to take more pride and success with them as they have a newfound talent. Studies have also shown that musical students are less of a disciplinary issue. Musicians are also more likely to empathize with others more easily. The development of compassion and empathy early on in a child's life can form a bridge across the cultural chasm that leads to a decrease in racism. Music also increases teamwork and corporation. In order for a musical organization to function, one must function as part of a team rather than an individual. It shows students to perform and take action rather than observe.

Music also helps students through difficult times. A student from Olympic High School in Santa Monica, CA was battling depression, substance abuse, defying the law, and dealing with the absence of his father. Fortunately, a grant through the VH1 Save the Music Foundation provided him with instruments and lessons which turned his life around. A child with autism from Paul I. Miller Elementary School was able to finally feel a part of the class. Several teachers recount tales of students who are able to overcome their behavioral issues simply by starting to play an instrument. These students are also able to grow socially and academically while also prompted to make better life decisions. Music can foster creativity out of troubled kids and incite them to express their emotions through something healthy.

How to Increase Music Education

To Benefit the Mind

The most efficient way we can increase music education is by targeting the schools themselves. Every child in elementary school should start by singing a diverse repertoire of music. This further exposes their mind to other cultures and other ways of thinking. The child is now able to think for himself and start to create and improvise on his own. At third grade, students should start to play the recorder. The recorder is an inexpensive instrument and provides many of the same basic music theory skills developed in piano lessons. By fourth grade, every child should be strongly encouraged to participate in a school ensemble, whether it is the band, orchestra, or chorus. Once a child is put into an ensemble, he or she is enticed to build relationships with other members of the ensemble as well as become a more independent musician and student.

Music can also be involved in academic classrooms. By putting information into a song, students can easily associate the song with the curriculum. The more interesting or dramatic of a connotation that is formed will result in a stronger chance of the student remembering the information. Songs, chants, poems, and raps will improve memory of content facts and details. Instead of simply encoding information and putting into short term storage (also known as cramming), students will actually put it into long term storage where it is retrievable. Music from the baroque era also centers around 50-80 bpm (beats per minute) which provide a stable environment for students to focus in the alpha brain wave state. Different tones and styles of music can adjust the environment into a place where students can be calm, concentrated, and focused. Depending on the mood of the music, one can change the atmosphere of the room into something suitable for work. Music will, once again, provide a positive environment for students to work together and build teamwork skills.

To Benefit the Heart

Music should be used as a way for everyone to express themselves healthily. It is the doorway to our true emotions, thoughts, and perceptions. Music is a way to tell stories, describe events, and portray characters. Playing background music such as solo piano or classical contemporary can calm oneself to the point of reflection, where one can truly see where he or she is emotionally. One study has even shown that students who write with music tend to write twice as more than without. Writing songs can help students channel inner emotions (and sometimes trauma) into something understandable to others. Students can also create tracks or mixes filled with songs of their choice that reflect their viewpoints on their own life and issues in today's society. Grow with Music is a foundation that focuses on this aspect of music. It involves kids from birth to 5 years, thus targeting kids with music at a young age. The creator, Joan H. Pappas, focuses on introducing folk music as it is repetitive, easy to learn, and functional. She also incorporates as many as 15 instruments in order to allow the kids more expression and creativity. This organization is one of many that emphasizes on introducing music to kids early on.

Perhaps the easiest way to help increase music education is by simply helping out organizations that focus on spreading their love of music. The Fender Music Foundation, founded in 2005, has reached over 187,000 people with grants of musical instruments to schools, music ensembles, and music therapy groups. Their primary focus, however, is to advocate the importance and beauty of music to the general public. They wish to make the gift of music available to everyone, whether it is through a grant of music instruments or lessons. Regardless of age, the Fender Music Foundation wishes to spread their passion to everyone who is unable to experience it firsthand. VH1-Save the Music is another foundation that focuses on granting instruments to students who are unable to afford them. They have shown that the benefits of music are astounding and believe that music education can affect students in a positive way. The simplest way to help their goal of bringing music education to those who cannot afford it is by donating or helping out at a local event. They believe that even the smallest amounts of help can bring an experience of a lifetime for a child to learn from and remember.

How I Will Make a Difference

I hope to make a difference in the world of music. I first want to start out by continuing to encourage music within my own community. I have already started prompting many of my classmates to pick up a musical instrument or join a music program, not only because it is loads of fun, but also because it is beneficial. Fortunately, my community is very involved with its chorus, orchestra, and band; however, other areas are not. I will strive to establish music programs in these schools (especially primary schools) to give all students an opportunity to learn about music. I also wish to volunteer at schools, to give performances or simply free lessons to children who don't have the opportunity. I believe every child should be able to learn to express him/herself through song.

Most importantly, I will continue to make music, not only for my own enjoyment, but for the world to hear as well. Every song I am a part of, every note I play is another piece of music that I give to the world. I wish to share my love and express my passion of making music with others. I hope that one day, my music will either inspire someone to follow the path I have grown to love or prompt someone to also make a difference.

A Musical Future

Music has certainly touched me in ways that I cannot describe. It is a way for me to escape reality and see the world in a way that I want to, a world where everyone has the same opportunity I was given 10 years ago. I have seen firsthand how music can affect people, and it is truly something beautiful. As I sit here writing my last words to you (listening to Florence and the Machine's *Shake it Out*) I hope that you and I can make a difference with something that is clearly more than just an art.

Anna Wang – Bio

Anna Wang is currently a sophomore at Lassiter High School. She enjoys reading, spending time with her friends, and pondering the mysteries of the universe. Although her favorite subject is math, she has a strong affinity towards biology and writing. She has earned the Freshmen Mathematics Department Award and is a 2013-2014 GHP Semi-finalist in Mathematics. At the top of her class, she is set to graduate from Lassiter High School in 2016 and has high ambitions for her future.

Anna (mezzo-soprano) has been actively involved in the music world since she was 5 years old and has gained over 10 years of vocal and piano experience. She is not only a member of the prestigious Lassiter Choraliers, but also the 2013-2014 Women's Chamber Chorale Co-President. Anna has also been involved with the Greater Atlanta Girls' Choir, as a member of the choir and a pianist at concerts. She has passed the GMEA All-State Chorus audition numerous times and is a strong contender for the title of a Six-Year Senior. Anna enjoys all genres of music including alternative rock, classical, and film score. Her favorite artists include Debussy, Chopin, and Coldplay.

The Story of a Victim
Erica Copenhaver

CHAPTER 20 – The Story of a Victim

Intro: The Story of a Victim

In the beginning, I was like any other young boy. I was born prematurely in a small town in western Montana in which everyone knew everyone. Growing up, I had the best friends anyone could ask for and the most loving parents on the face of the Earth. Despite having a minor speech impediment and a body that was and always would be smaller and scrawnier than the other kids my age, I led a fairly normal, carefree life. Until it started.
On my twelfth birthday, instead of getting the standard Nerf guns, video games, or sports gear that any "normal" kid my age would have received, I was blessed by my parents to be put into acting lessons. From an early age, I had always been very animated, and I loved to be creative and play the imaginative games such as pretending to be grown and run my own household or acting as a strong superhero coming to save the day. Always I would put on a new façade in order to mimic the strength that I had always seen but would never have. Eventually, acting became my number one priority. I was teased quite a bit from the time my friends found out about the lessons and later told some other kids at school, but it started off pretty light; my parents thought nothing of it, assuming that they were just 'kids being kids' and that a little bit of teasing was a rite of passage for pre-teens and could only 'make me stronger'. After a while, the amount of teasing skyrocketed, often with newfound ferocity, and it soon evolved into much more than teasing when I performed in the first school play of the year. I was being harassed in the halls and threatened both in and

outside of school because 'boys aren't supposed to be actors.'

Immediately after the show, a group of kids whom I had grown up with and had even considered to be friends approached me and began attacking me both physically and verbally. I was chased into the school gym where another group of so-called "friends" was waiting for me so they could beat me further. As I lay helplessly on the ground, chants of "queer" and "homo" and faggot" rang in my ears and echoed through my brain. A never-ending sequence of kicks, slaps, and punches began and did not cease until I had blacked out from the pain. When the principal finally found me writhing on the ground, he alerted my parents and I was sent home. I vaguely remember being carried up by my father and laid on his bed. Through thin walls I heard my mother's sobs and father's reassuring voice attempting to soothe her. After a while, the shouting began. I overheard my father's thoughts on moving me to a new school or even homeschooling me on top of my mother's accusations that if he had not started me in acting this whole mess could have been avoided. Their voices grew more and more hostile, and I couldn't take it any longer and tried to block out the noise with the peace of sleep.

I drifted in and out of consciousness for a few hours before coming to and I belatedly began to feel the weight of what had occurred and the physical and emotional pain that lay in its wake. The sudden tone of my cell phone snapped me out of my stupor. Every text sent a chill through my body as I read them. "Walter's a fag!" "Kill yourself you flaming homo, no one wants you here!" "You'd be doing us all a favor to just get rid of yourself, we don't accept gays here." "Hold on, why are you still alive?" The more I read them the more they started to feel like the truth. Never had I believed my passion to be something that would cause so much turmoil in my life. I started to realize that maybe being different really was wrong, and I considered helping everyone out and removing myself from this world.

The more I thought about it, the deeper I fell into the gaping hole of despair that had engulfed my life in an instant. Everything that I knew was crumbling to pieces before me. I couldn't bear the thought that I was causing my parents so much trouble or that everyone whom I thought was on my side actually hated me for who I was. I made my decision. Limping and wincing, I hobbled over to my parent's closet where I knew my future lay. In a dusty shoebox under a coat I found my father's pistol that had never been used. Step by step I left the room and the house and ventured into my favorite place in the woods: a tree house that my dad and I had built a few years back. The overwhelming, cumbersome pressure of the hatred was pushing me into the ground, but I continued up the ladder and settled myself inside. With the blade that I had brought I carved some last thoughts into the wood structure. 'Go on without me, you'll be fine. Pretend I was never here...you don't need me anyway. Even if you don't feel the same, I love every one of you. Goodbye.' Then I loaded the gun.

As I held the loaded pistol to my sweat-slick forehead, I imagined the body that they would eventually find. What a sad thought it is to picture yourself dead. At least for me I knew that this would be the release. After this there would be no more pain. I would be free. Free from all of the insults, the abuse, the hatred, whether it be that of my enemies or *my own self-loathing, it's all the same. None of it will matter. I pulled the trigger.*

Though this story was fictional, there are hundreds of thousands of others like it that occur every year in the U.S. alone among countless others worldwide. This needs to change. It is my hope and my dream that we can spread awareness of this heinous crime called bullying and eliminate it altogether. With a lot of patience and a lot of support, we can help save the lives of kids and teens like Walter and put and end to the hatred. I have faith that if only I can affect just one person who reads this that he or she will pass the message of love and acceptance and someone's life may be saved.

Define: Bullying

What may be the most important thing about bullying that people need to understand is that it comes in many different forms. In general, bullying is defined as behavior that physically or emotionally harms a person. There may be an imbalance of power, whether the bully is physically larger than the victim or the bully is socially or emotionally intimidating such as being considered more "popular" or having a higher social status than that of the victim, though this is not always the case. Some definitions include that, "The behavior can be overt, with physical behaviors, such as fighting, hitting or name calling, or it can be covert, with emotional-social interactions, such as gossiping or leaving someone out on purpose." The three main categories of bullying include physical bullying, verbal bullying, and cyber bullying. Physical bullying includes, but is not limited to, punching, kicking, slapping, pushing, or otherwise causing physical harm to one or one's possessions. Verbal bullying may be defined as using words or language to threaten, discourage, or emotionally harm a victim. Recently, with all of the new technologies that are being introduced in this new "online era", teens have a new medium through which they can bully others: cyber bullying. Cyber bullying is using technology such as online websites, chat groups, social media pages, email, or text messaging to insult, embarrass, spread rumors or unflattering photographs of, or otherwise cause emotional damage to a victim. Unfortunately, where physical bullying typically only exists at school or during school hours, cyber bullying is not limited and may occur anywhere at any time, making the victim feel even more helpless. In many cases, a combination of different types of bullying is inflicted on the victim, so it is vital to learn about the signs of all of them and how to possibly prevent them.

Effects of Bullying

Bullying affects everyone differently, but in almost all cases the victim suffers from physical, emotional, or social damage that may have lasting effects on him or her. Some lasting effects of bullying include, "depression and anxiety, increased feelings of sadness and loneliness, changes in sleep and eating patterns, and loss of interest in activities they used to enjoy. These issues may persist into adulthood." This psychological damage may cause a victim to act out in violent ways. In the 1990's, twelve out of fifteen school shootings were led by someone who had been bullied before.[2] Also, a student's academic achievement might suffer as a result of bullying, and oftentimes teens that are bullied are more likely to skip or drop out of school. A bully can make a victim feel sad, alone, unwanted, or even unworthy of life. Article 3 of the Universal Declaration of Human Rights states that, "Everyone has the right to life, liberty and security of person." Bullying can make one feel as though all three of those things have been taken from him or her, or that he or she does not deserve those three essential factors of life. Bullying can also have long lasting effects on bullies, victims, and bully-victims (those who have both bullied others and been bullied by others). A study conducted by psychological scientists Dieter Wolke of the University of Warwick and William E. Copeland of Duke University Medical Center shows the effects of bullying on different aspects of life on four different groups (bullies, victims, bully-victims, and those not involved in bullying). The results are discussed in an article entitled "Impact of Bullying in Childhood on Adult Health, Wealth, Crime, and Social Outcomes" that was published in Psychological Science. From the article, one figure shows the relationship between the role of the child in bullying and the outcome as a young-adult.

Victims and bully-victims are also more likely to experience depression, panic disorder, or agoraphobia, an anxiety disorder, and bully-victims are more likely to experience suicidal thoughts or actions. Suicide is the third leading cause of death for young people (ages 10-24) behind accidents and homicide respectively, and on average, a suicide occurs every seventeen minutes in the United States.

Bullying can also affect students academically. The National Education Association estimates that 160,000 students every day miss school because they are afraid of being helplessly victimized or bullied by their peers, and for every ten students who drop out of school, one of them does so because of repeated bullying. Also, 90% of students grade 4-8 reported that they have been victim to bullying. Instead of being an institution in which students can feel safe and protected, many schools and their administrative teams are having issues controlling bullying. Up to 71% of students claim that bullying is an issue at their school, and over two-thirds of students feel that the issue of bullying is addressed poorly at their schools and administrative assistance is "infrequent and ineffective." This needs to change.

What Can We Do?

In 49 of the 50 US states, laws have been established in an attempt to prevent bullying, especially in schools. Though there are federal laws against harassment, as of right now there are no federal laws against bullying. Some federal laws should be established against bullying because bullying can, in fact, be against civil rights when the bullying is based on race, gender, nationality, age, or religion. Many state laws that are already administered require schools to take action against bullying if it is reported within the school, yet still students do not feel as though the matter is being dealt with entirely. Within a school, students could consider forming counselor-sponsored support groups in which victims can feel safe to speak up about their experiences and trust that action will be taken by the adult sponsor to prevent further bullying incidents. Such action may include consulting with the students one-on-one and notifying the parents of the bully and those of the victim about the situation. Students can also help to spread awareness of bullying and the fact that it no longer can be dealt with as something of little importance. Students or administrative personnel could give presentations during announcements or school rallies speaking out against bullying and discussing the effects that it can have on both the victim and the bully. Bystanders, or witnesses of bullying incidents, are encouraged to intervene because close to 50% of bullying incidents stop when the bully is confronted by a third party. Parents are encouraged to maintain open relationships with their children in order to allow their children to feel safe enough to talk about bullying. They could also teach their children about safety when using technology such as advising them to set social media accounts to private settings and to only disclose passwords to sites to parents as opposed to peers. Parents could discourage their children from posting intimate, private, or provocative photographs or statements online for their own protection. They should model respectfulness and kindness and advocate peace among peers from an early age and teach their children that bullying is wrong. The quickest way to stop a misconception is to spread true knowledge about it. Therefore, schools should develop programs or presentations beginning in primary schools and continuing on through middle school and high school that enlighten students on the effects of bullying and that bullying is only harmful and should not be considered a rite of passage.

A Personal Point: My Story

Something we all can do to keep our heads held high is to pursue what we love. For me, that love is poetry. Whether is deep and emotional, strong and beautiful, or even quirky and silly, poetry always manages to affect me. Every time I read a poem, I feel as if a part of myself has been unlocked and exposed to the world. At first this feeling was terrifying, but I learned to take solace in that exposure and started to channel my energy into writing poems of my own. Poetry got me through many difficult times in my life and always managed to put my situation into perspective. Since poetry has such a way of saving me, I know that it can do the same for someone else. Everyone needs at least one thing to which he can look forward and in which he can find solace and happiness to get him through the hard days. Though I would sometimes hear someone else's story and be audacious enough to deem their problems petty, I eventually came to know that all pain is relative, and that is the only way we can accept it. In terms of bullying, while one person might be going through teasing and name-calling and another through beatings and abuse, each person may be affected equally as vividly. In the same way, each person will seek to find a way to cope with that pain, and each of them deserves to discover it. Fortunately, when I was in need of consolation, I found it almost instantly. One day when I was on the hunt for a new poem to add to my mental inventory, I stumbled upon a work by Shane Koyczan entitled "To This Day." Interestingly enough, instead of being brought to a website on which I could read this poem or, if I were lucky, to see a picture to accompany it, I was sent to Youtube. I was intrigued. What I had found was something that would light the fuse for my future inspiration: spoken word poetry.

    This particular poem was about the author's experiences and thoughts on bullying, and I was mesmerized. His voice was captivating and his words powerful, and I could not get enough. I had found my ultimate escape. Immediately I delved deeper into the world of spoken word and with each new poem I read, a newfound interest developed inside of me. I had finally found the perfect way for me to express myself. I was particularly inspired by a poet by the name of Sarah Kay when I heard her poem "If I Should Have a Daughter" and her personal journey on the path toward spoken word. She talked about how she was encouraged to pursue her interest in spoken word poetry and how she eventually started a program bringing it to people all over the world. I was so excited by that idea that it got me thinking: what if I could spread my joy and my love and maybe help other people find their own?

    It is this thought that motivates me to one day start a program of my own in an attempt to give to others what poetry gives to me—happiness. My goal is to create a group in which members are free to express themselves in any way they choose. In this group, members will be encouraged to grow comfortable with revealing their true feelings and with the fact that they are not alone—neither in feeling that way nor in life. I want people to know that when asked the common question of, "How are you?" that it is okay to break away from the social rule that dictates that one must answer with, "I'm okay." I want people to know that sometimes, not everything will be "okay," and that they have every right to say so.

Though this group may start small, I want to invite every dreamer and believer as well as those who might not always see eye-to-eye with life. Hopefully, some day soon it will be filled with people who simply want to be happy and want to share that happiness with the world. Everyone is welcome to come and share what makes his or her heart beat like poetry, music, art, or what have you, for everyone deserves to be happy.

I will spread my testimony to everyone I meet in the hopes that he or she will learn from it and grow from it and maybe even share it with others. The more that people know about bullying, the better equipped they will be recognize it and stop it. In the mean time, I plan to provide refuge for those who seek it and to let them know that there is always someone who cares about them and that they are worth it. I will reach out to anyone, bullies and victims alike, and try to bring him or her to find what he or she loves and to devote his or her energy to that as opposed to wasting it on negative things that will only bring him or her down. We will campaign against bullying and spread our encouragements to pursue the joys in life through the means of social media such as Facebook, Twitter, and others. We will make announcements throughout school and hold public meetings to which everyone is invited to learn and to share his or her stories. Inspired by Thomas Jefferson when he declared that, "We hold these truths to be self-evident: that all men are created equal; that they are endowed by their Creator with certain unalienable rights;

that among these are life, liberty, and the pursuit of happiness," this club will be called the Pursuit. In this club, we will be free.

Final Word: What the Future Can Look Like

The more that students expand their horizons and the more that they are willing to accept the differences between themselves and their peers, the easier it will be to eradicate bullying. Everyone is born equal and therefore should be treated thusly. If bullying can be eliminated, there would be no more stories like Walter's, no more unnecessary anxiety or sadness or deaths, and no more hatred. When the world can accept that being different is not only all right but also vital in order to create an interesting and functional society. I hope everyone who reads this will learn at least one thing about bullying and be inspired to join the battle against it. In the meantime, I encourage you all to go out and do what you love and inspire others to do the same. In everything you do, be kind. You may just save someone's life.

Erica Copenhaver – Bio

Erica Copenhaver is a sophomore at Lassiter High School in the class of 2016. She is a 2014 Governor's Honors Program Nominee in the subject of Communicative Arts and has made the Principal's Honor Roll for three consecutive semesters. After school, Erica participates in many extracurricular activities such as Model United Nations and the Lassiter Math Team. She is also an active member of the Lassiter Trojan Marching Band and the Track and Field team. She commits herself to helping her community in as many ways as she can; this includes volunteering with the school shelter club and with the Interact service club. When she is not surfing the Internet, Erica spends her time reading novels, writing poetry, or painting. She and her friends love to go on adventures such as creek hiking or camping in the great outdoors. Her long-term goals include studying psychology or engineering in order to do her favorite thing in the world: help people.

The Precious Gift of Life
Paige Walsh

CHAPTER 21 – The Precious Gift of Life

My Story

As soon as I was born, I looked into my birth mother's eyes for the first time, not knowing I was never going to see her again. For reasons unknown, my biological mother decided she did not want to raise me. She wanted to give me up for adoption. Right away, I was put into an orphanage with many other babies who had no mother or father. My parents had always wanted to adopt a baby, and so they went through the long and challenging process of adoption. After many signatures and stacks of paperwork and background checks, I was adopted from Russia at only nine months old. At that very moment, my life was changed forever.

After spending some time in Russia with other families that adopted babies too, it was time to go home to my new life. After a ten hour plane ride, I was welcomed home to strangers I would soon learn to call my Family. My mom always tells me how happy and excited everyone was to meet me. I can only imagine how precious that moment was for my family. I remember looking at an old photo album of the quick, compact week my parents spent when they first adopted me. I remember a picture of a banner that said, "welcome home Paige" that was plastered on the garage to our house. It's nice to look back to that photo album every so often to remind me of how fortunate I am. Early on, my parents let me know that I was adopted, and that I should be proud of it, not ashamed. Because my biological mother loved me, she made the burdensome decision to let me go, to allow me to live a life she was not able to provide for me. I cannot be more thankful for her choice. Because of my birthmother's view on adoption, I now live with parents that would do anything for me, and I have a brother who encourages me to stand up for myself. I am able to go to school and make decisions for myself. I am able to go to college. I am able to make a life for myself.

I strongly believe in adoption. I was given the precious gift of life. I would not even be where I am today if I was not adopted. Every day I think of how thankful I am to have the life that I do. I was always taught to embrace my background story because that is what makes me...me and unique.

DNA Does Not Make a Family

When I was younger, my mom framed a poem for me so that I could understand that "DNA does not make a family, love does." It is called "Legacy of an Adopted Child." "Once there were two women who never knew each other, one you do not remember, the other you call mother. Two different lives shaped to make yours, one became your guiding star, the other became your sun. The first gave you life, and the second taught you to live in it. The first gave you a need for love and the second was there to give it. One gave you nationality; the other gave you a name. One gave you the seed of talent; the other gave you an aim. One gave you emotions; the other calmed your fears. One saw your first sweet smile; the other dried your tears. One gave you up- that's all she could do. The other prayed for a child and God led her straight to you. Now you ask through all the tears the age-old question unanswered through the years; Heredity or environment- which are you a product of?

Neither, my darling-neither- just two different kinds of love" (unknown author). Two different kinds of love that will forever be in my heart. I believe in adoption.

    I strongly believe adoption changes the world in a way most people will never understand. By adopting a baby, you are giving that baby a life to make for themselves. That's a big step to take. Just like any other parent, always wondering if their parenting is good enough. There is also a spark in the brain that makes you want to strive to be the best parent you can be. You want to make sure that you are giving this baby a better life than someone else might have given to them.

Well Known Adopted People

    Did you know that Marilyn Monroe, Babe Ruth, John Lennon, Angelina Jolie, and Oprah Winfrey were all adopted? Imagine how different the world would be today if some of these influential people were never born. Maybe Babe Ruth was the reason Chipper Jones or Freddie Freeman started baseball in the first place. Imagine if John Lennon never spread his love for happiness and equality. Angelina Jolie even believes strongly in adoption. She adopted three children! I never really think much of Angelina Jolie, but it really makes me happy that she adopted children. Words cannot describe how amazing adoption is. My whole point in bringing up these world-known people is to prove that adopted kids can make a difference in the world. Many people look up to these people. In my opinion, I think the world revolves around the people you meet and the people you look up to. Your heroes push you, whether you know it or not, to keep going and to try harder. This being said, we need to view adoption as a life changing experience.

And Now for the Rest of the Story

Every kid remembers constantly nagging their parents for a puppy. You tell them how you will be the responsible now and how you will feed it and take it on walks. Most of the time, the endless begging isn't convincing to your parents, but for some reason, my dad said yes.

I was eight years old and in the fourth grade when my dad and I went to Lake Lanier Island to look at Golden Retriever puppies. I was so excited! I remember being taken aback once we got there because the house was dirty, small, and smelled awful. The breeder took us out back to look at the dogs and told us which one we could have. I was under the impression that I got to choose from several, but no, there was only one that was available. The puppy that we could have was not the one I wanted at all. She was wet from playing in the bushes and she didn't have the bright, bubble gum pink nail polish on like all the other puppies, but we took her anyways. It didn't take long for me to grow attached to the once not wanted puppy. Holding her in the car made me realize how much I really loved her. She was so cute. She was like a fuzz ball that shed everywhere and on anything!

I decided to name my puppy Roxy. I have no idea how I came up with that name because most eight year olds name their pets and stuffed animals the dumbest names. The first night with Roxy was pretty unbearable. She would not stop crying and making a raucous. But lucky for me, I was a pretty deep sleeper, once I actually fell asleep. The next day I just hung around the house with Roxy. She slept most of the day, but every once and a while she would run around. I would say both of us became very close with each other. I never wanted to leave her, but I had to go back home since my parents were divorced. But going home made me that much more excited to come back.

Over time, days became weeks, and weeks became years. Those years with Roxy were filled with laughter and so many fun memories. I remember this one time; Roxy wouldn't stop jumping up on my friend. So, my dad yelled at her saying, "Do you understand me?" The funny thing is that Roxy actually nodded her head, like she understood my dad. That memory will always come up in conversation every once and a while because it was just so funny at the time. Another time, or let me say, a few times, Roxy jumped up on the counter and ate a chocolate cake, meat sandwiches, more cake, and more cake. I was always pretty impressed because she never once got sick. Even though she did bad things, it was always so hard for me to stay mad at her. She had the cutest face and made those puppy dog eyes that just make you melt right there and then.

She really was the best dog any one could have ever asked for. Whenever I was sad, she just laid there with me with her head propped up on my stomach. She always knew how to make me feel better. She was also a pretty smart dog too. She would always be there at the front door waiting for me to come home from school. I always wondered how she knew the time. I guess dogs just know. Whenever I went outside to play with my friends, Roxy would stand at the door and cry and cry and cry. The crying was so bad that I just had to let her come out too. I guess you could say that we were inseparable. All my friends knew how obsessed I was with Roxy. My entire camera roll on my phone was literally, always filled with pictures of Roxy. I couldn't help that she was model material. She really was my best friend. Roxy was always there for me when others weren't. Most people never understood the bond I had with her. I mean, she was only a dog, but that dog was my best friend. You would never understand the relationship between a human and a dog if you weren't a dog person. You would never know.

When I was a junior in high school, my life felt like it was falling apart. Roxy, at only six years old, got Lymphoma, which is a cancer. My best friend was dying right in front of me. One day, she wouldn't eat her food and she couldn't walk. She was struggling just to get up from the floor to her feet. At that moment, I knew the cancer had overtaken her. It was time. It was September 7th, 12:17pm when Roxy passed away.

My mom always said that it was ok to cry, but I never wanted to. I knew that Roxy would have wanted me to be strong and look at her passing as a way to remind myself that I had a wonderful life filled with memories that I would never forget. Roxy taught me to look at the positive side of things and to give people a chance. She never judged people based on their looks or how much money they had; she loved you for who you were and how much love you gave her. That's why I love dogs so much; because "a dog is the only thing on earth that loves you more than he loves himself." Roxy was the second best thing that ever happened to me. Throughout my life, I learned so many life lessons from her that I will never forget.

My older brother, Jason, told me that something good will come out of this. He told me that unfortunately life is full of losses and that these losses are meant to gear you up for bigger ones in life. But I think that Roxy was a way to show me how to live life happily. She was always happy, even when it was time to put her down. She was still smiling in the room. I think that she knew what was about to happen, but she continued to smile because she knew that her job was done. She gave me the best life ever.

How I Will Make a Difference

Because of Roxy and how much of an impact she left on me, I want to do the same with other dogs out in the world. There are so many dogs today that are abused by their owners or left to die on the streets. They are then taken to the pound to sit in a cage, waiting to die. Dogs are not meant to be abused. They are here in the world to show us what life means. When I grow up, I want to be able to foster dogs or work with the Humane Society so I can help dogs in need. Everyone deserves a life to live. Roxy allowed me to realize what's important in life, so I want to show her respect and do the same for other people. Somebody out there in the world deserves a dog to make them happy and to be able to feel the joy of just living and breathing. The Humane Society fights for the protection of all animals through advocacy, education, and hands-on programs. To adopt a dog or any other animal, you are making a difference in that poor animal's life. You are giving that animal the precious gift of life, and maybe even saving your own life. I want to stop all cruelty to animals. No one deserves to be abused or neglected. Pet adoption is just the beginning to making the world a better place. If everyone could get up and do something good for someone else, the world would be in the progress of transforming the publics' perspective on life. Let us all think positively. Let us all live with focus on others.

Paige Walsh – Bio

Paige Sveta Shuler Walsh was adopted from Ekaterinburg Russia when she was nine months old by Art and Vicki Walsh. She grew up in Roswell Georgia with her older brother Jason. Paige is a junior at Lassiter High School. She played softball for 6 years, 2 on the high school team. She is in the process of beginning her college search and plans to major in the areas of communications or journalism. She enjoys reading, listening to music and spending time with her friends.

To Change the World
Galilah Woubshet

CHAPTER 22 – To Change the World

This Feeling Inside

"The purpose of life is not to be happy. It is to be useful, to be honorable, to be compassionate, to have it make some difference that you have lived and lived well," stated Ralph Emerson. No matter what the age, you can make a difference, from volunteering at a shelter, to curing cancer; every little thing counts. I have always had this feeling inside of me that gives me a rush after helping someone. By seeing so many disabled and ill people, I know that many will surely benefit from my desire to help them.

Starting from the age of seven, I began volunteering at my gymnastics center to teach; I would help the disabled students in tumbling, bar, beam, and rhythmic. Although it was such a simple task to give up my play dates on Mondays, Wednesdays, and Saturdays for them, at the time, it meant much more for them then it did for me; I had impacted their life without even realizing it. My volunteering at Chattooga Gymnastics & Dance resulted in a life changing experience. It brought me closer to them and gave me a sight of interest into researching my future into the medical field. I was there from the end of my school to 8pm, purely because I loved it. Anything I was able to do to benefit their enjoyment, I accepted and worked for it to be fulfilled to the best of my ability. I spent great amounts of time with them teaching balance, control, and dance; their happiness provided me with a love for helping others.

I have a strong desire to impact the world because I have experienced many breath-taking situations in my life thus far. In an organization, known as UIC-GOD, I work as a volunteer to benefit the people that are not as provided as me. There are about 40 youth members that are apart of this organization set up by my church, and we all travel to different third world countries to offer them relative stability. I have given up four years of my summer breaks to travel with this non-profit organization to build homes, dig wells, and supply food to those without it. Visiting areas in which the people are not as fortunate as me gives me a glimpse of my future and how I hope to save lives. To those who can afford the costs of surgery and to those who cannot afford it, I will travel the world to benefit them by helping them get back on their feet after going through surgeries or dealing with severe illnesses. I hope to have a large impact on this world by the time I leave it; I hope that I can provide happiness to many people, as they have and will to me.

Family Crisis

Imagine being told that your own father has had cancer for seven years and is going to be having a transplant that may or may not save his life. In the fourth grade, I was the child being told that about her father. Then, at the age of ten, I was unsure on what kind of affect that would have on me. My mother and father were telling my sister and I that his life was in danger, and he has been taking chemotherapy for seven years. The disease, leukemia, was destroying him. There were months after he had his transplant where his hair would fall out in chunks and his skin would peel. The only way I got through it was with the strength of my family's love and our faith in the one and only God. Seeing our lives broken, shattered into millions of pieces, and gradually put back together of the span of three years, my life was yet again, evolved from that of a child to that of an adult. My mindset was completely different from that of my peers; I put on a happy face at school to cover up the pain and avoid questions. Knowing what many people around the world have or are going through, I was influenced into founding a stronger basis on my understanding of medical terms and knowledge. In the future I hope to save many lives and see the faces of children and parents shine from their tears of happiness rather than emotional pain.

In the seventh grade, my father having just been recovered, I was thinking that that would be the end of my suffering as a child; life quickly flipped itself around. One of my uncles came to visit us all from Ethiopia. The first few days started out so beautifully, as they grew on, so did the unknown tumor in his brain. My aunt had first noticed a difference in his speech, and that it seemed lagging. His friend noticed that he unknowingly drooled. My mother, being a part of the medical field, was not one to wait for things to get worse, so suggested for him to go to a hospital. After his visit, he was told that there was a tumor growing in his brain interfering with his speech and control of his saliva. Soon enough the tumor was growing, and his hair was not. His hair fell out, he would loose his balance and it took time for him to stand up from sitting due to the lack of blood flow to his brain in time. In a time period of 9 months, he was gone. Just like that, no time for surgery because of the rapid growth of the tumor, no time for proper goodbyes. My sweetest uncle's life was taken by a ruthless tumor that could not provide a thirteen-year old child the happiness of visiting her uncle in his later years and giving him happiness. Because of this tragic loss, I saw things normal teens did not; I felt things that normal teens did not. I went through a lot of miserable times to bring me to a fulfilling decision in where I want to be in my future. Helping several thousands of people with similar problems that my own uncle dealt with; neurological problems, I want to be the one to cure someone of the despair I went through. Help them; provide them with happiness, hope, and faith that there is one above that will always look in your interest.

My Future in Medicine

My future in medicine is a sight that I am looking forward to day and night, twenty-four seven. This upcoming summer I am volunteering at a hospital and shadowing a doctor. The summer after I will volunteer at the Georgia Brain and Spine Center, and I will shadow a neurosurgeon. Just by thinking of my future I receive such sudden chills; it is as if some very generous person is offering a three-year-old wannabe Cinderella the chance to put on the blue gown and hold the fairy godmother's hand. My happiness rapidly accelerates after helping anyone with anything; when there is a smile on a person's face that I have benefited, there is a smile on mine.

The plan I have set for my future is fully thought out over the period of time I have urged to become a neurosurgeon. When I receive my degree for finishing college, I plan to go into an accredited medical school. Once I finish four years in medical school, receiving my doctorate degree, I will attend a residency in neurosurgery. After I receive a fellowship in neurosurgery, I hope to be able to secure my own clinic and work a few years in that area. Then I plan to pursue my true aspirations of participating in *Medecins Sans Frontieres* (Doctors Without Borders). Within this program I look forward to having the opportunity to help those who are in under developed regions of the world, and who cannot afford the high scale services that are available to those in first world countries. Because my parents were born and raised in the third world country of Ethiopia, I have always felt an ambition inside of me for the duty to return to my country and help the people who long to be treated by someone of their own culture.

Changing the world is not something that happens in one day, or overnight. It is something that happens to people who dream of it day and night from their childhood. Mahatma Gandhi once said, "Be the change that you want to see in the world." As a teenager, although my opportunities are limited, they are not invisible. I hope to use the knowledge that I attain, the experiences I go through, and everything that I learn to influence the people around me and those that will make the generation to come. There are many young people of this generation who are easily influenced by what is new and popular, and this shows many detrimental effects in the society of today. It is necessary to have strong-minded and motivated people to lead the next generation of young people. Within the past few decades, the overwhelming amount of younger children who know too much than they should is increasing. It is also causing the formation of a generation of people who are confused in terms of priorities in life, despite what their parents and older guardians advise them. There is always going to be a large necessity for people who have the ability to positively influence the younger generation. This is also a large reason for why I enjoy volunteering at elementary and middle schools while I am in high school.

"Many men go fishing all of their lives without knowing it is not fish they are after." Henry David Thoreau advises us to live life for the experience, to find our purpose and fulfill it. Some say you don't know your purpose until you retire; others say you'll never get it right. I may not be right on the money, but I feel relatively confident in knowing why I was put on this planet. Through everything I do, every service, every activity, I realize that my fundamental ambition lies in helping humanity. I do not view suffering as a foreign thing, because of the obstacles I face with regard to my father's illness. However, instead of seeing those as solely miserable factors, I view those experiences as points that strengthen me and keep me aware of life's unexpected plans. I gain endurance from my battles and fight harder for what I want to achieve during my life.

Looking in her tired eyes as she accepts the plate of food with a weak "Thank you." Because I live so close to the heart of Atlanta, it is not easy to forget the reality of poverty that so many people experience. My church youth group frequently feeds the homeless and each time is a different experience for me. The most influential time was when we fed mothers and children at Perfect Heart's Shelter. I was told that the mothers were there with their children largely because of domestic abuse and in most cases, the fathers of the children would severely hurt them if they found them on the streets. I knew that this happened in parts of the world and I obviously acknowledged that it was bound to happen near me; but it was different when I looked into each of those mothers' weaknesses, almost absorbing their pain.

Overcome with emotion, I hugged each mother as she passed through the food line. Though it broke my heart to understand their daily situation, it inflicted a sense of enormous gratitude and a sense of responsibility in my personality. I also realized then that helping others really is the most gratifying experience.

Every summer since eighth grade, I have volunteered as an intern at the Meridian Health and Physical Therapy Center. I have helped the office with organizing of all sorts, and I have provided ultrasound treatment, with supervision, for the patients who needed it. These were the first chances for me to sneak a somewhat fuzzy peek into what I wanted for my future. Before these opportunities, I saw myself becoming a practicing surgeon in neurology. I currently see myself enthusiastically battling brain tumors and diseases overseas every day of my life. Being in the medical environment and working professionally in a medical atmosphere at such a young age not only firmly solidified my future plans, but it lit a burning fire of passion deep in my heart to want to become more than just a clinical surgeon. I see myself as a surgeon without boundaries, lacking gates or fences, and reaching out to humanity everywhere. I wish to be a part of the Society of International Humanitarian Surgeons' Surgeons Over Seas (SOS), primarily helping the impoverished and diseased people of my own culture in Ethiopia, but also going further to West Africa and Asia. My determination to fulfill my desires strikes a need for great achievement, and what drives me to succeed academically is precisely the avid yearning I have for helping humanity to the best of my ability.

Though I confidently know who I desire to become in the future, that does not mean that I know where life will take me. I believe that I am carefully looking for the experiences and benefits of life every day that I am given the chance to wake up and the opportunity to live. I would not know if I were wrongly after fish my entire life, but with my strong faith in God and my modest trust in his grace, I believe that helping others is my calling. How is it possible to know if we are fishing with the wrong mentality? Thoreau has recognized that we all aim for our desires, but it is important to focus not solely on the achievement, but more on what we experience as we reach them. On my road to becoming a superhero, I will live wholeheartedly in each day as I finally drape on my white cape and save the world, one neurologically impaired patient at a time.

Galilah Woubshet – Bio

Galilah Woubshet, a sophomore at Lassiter High School, is an outgoing, respectable, intelligent, and considerate female. She has a personality that glows with happiness; her joy shines on others and can quickly brighten their day. Galilah has been a dancer and a gymnast for twelve out of the sixteen years she has lived. She enjoys performing, but always provides time for her studies. Ms. Woubshet makes sure that she has her priorities straight; because of her urge to go into the medical field and become a neurosurgeon, she makes time for her education. Galilah is a straight A student that works and will work incredibly hard to reach her overall goal of becoming a neurosurgeon. All in all, Galilah Woubshet is a kind young lady with the potential and desire to help and provide happiness and health to those without it.

Make a Difference

Kelsey Freshour

CHAPTER 23 – Make a Difference

Health is a topic that lays heavy on the hearts of Americans and is not an issue to be taken lightly.

"If it's important, you'll find a way. If it isn't, you'll find an excuse."

My Grandfather

Friday February 4, 2011 is a day engrained in my family and I's memory until the day we will die. This is the date that marks my grandfather's passing. He was the victim of a lung infection, but he also previously suffered a heart attack, four clogged arteries, neuropathy, high blood pressure and heart disease, and he lived with the burden of type two diabetes. The saddest part is all of these issues could have been avoided. For years he was forced to be concerned with keeping track of and taking multiple pills a day. In addition, he also had to remember to inject himself with his daily dose of insulin. All of these health issues and annoying requirements to battle his conditions were results of his poor diet and lack of exercise. Like most people, he loved food; unfortunately, he had no will power to resist consuming it. He constantly ate out and ordered the option that contained an excess of fat, cholesterol, calories, and a lack of nutritional value. His choices led to his early demise and, while he was alive, a lesser quality of life. My Poppy could have lived a prolonged life with greater mobility, energy and fewer worries if he had maintained good health.

Karen Carpenter

On the opposing end of the spectrum is the story of Karen Carpenter. Singer of the number one hit *Close to You*, she was one of the all-time great musical sensations of the 70's. Despite her enormous fame, fortune, and success, she was convinced she was never thin enough. She refused to stop losing weight, and when she finally came to her senses, the damage she had done to her body was permanent. Sadly she died in 1983, at the age of 32, due to the effects of her anorexia.

Both of these stories demonstrate the devastating and ultimate consequence of poor health, a life severed shorter than necessary. Whether someone's lifestyle reflects the decisions of my grandfather or of Karen Carpenter, both are scenarios of unhealthy lifestyles. Even though health is a hot topic in America, two epidemics are still felt throughout our nation--obesity and eating disorders. Limitless efforts are being made to lower both, and I would like to be part of these efforts. Death is inevitable, but people unintentionally erase years off their lives.

Statistics- Can't Argue with Facts

According to the OECD, America still holds the place as the fattest country in the world. One third of USA's adults are obese. Seventeen percent of children two through nineteen are obese. Obesity leads to heart disease, stroke, type 2 diabetes, certain types of cancer, of these cancers some are leading causes of preventable death. An estimated 300,000 deaths per year in America are attributed to excess weight. These deaths are premature and not necessary. People leave behind grieving families and a life that they could have done more with. Eating disorders are another form of avoidable death. An estimated 8 million people in America have an eating disorder, 7 million women and 1 million men. Within the lines of these daunting statistics, I see a clear opportunity to make a difference. I feel that everyone is capable of fighting against obesity and eating disorders. My dream is to live in a healthy America, among people who have no excuse to not change, and to eliminate preconceived notions of what beauty is. If people were offered help in every area that they desired, and given a clear opportunity to succeed, then maybe the saddest form of death could be eliminated and messages of positive body image and healthy living could be spread across borders.

3 Key Components to Health

The three main contributing factors to both obesity and eating disorders are *food*, *people*, and *exercise*. I feel that if people understand these three topics, they can make a major difference in their life immediately as opposed to waiting for someone to come along.

Food

Most Americans, including myself, love all things greasy, salty, and sweet. Unfortunately, the majority of the foods that fit these criteria are not beneficial to our health. Therefore, most of the problem is in the kitchen. Fortunately, there are currently several cooking shows that instruct people on how to cook delicious and healthy meals. There are also many books and other sources of media that give insight on good replacements to peoples favorite unhealthy foods and meals. We should also monitor our portion sizes, eat when you are hungry, but do not eat after you are full just because you like or were taught to clear your plate. Even if we know what to eat and how to cook at our homes, we will still want to occasionally go out to eat. In almost, if not every, restaurant there are healthy options available, even in fast food. We just have to force ourselves to order the better option. In addition, grocery stores can be overwhelming and full of all the foods we crave but shouldn't consume a lot. However, there are all health stores you can shop at and tips to make you say no to the junk food. It is true that the healthier options can be more expensive, but if you search for coupons and look for sales then you make it more affordable. Can we even put a budget on your health and well-being? It is important that people can distinguish the better choice and have the will power to select it. To live a healthy life you have to morph your mind into thinking about the consequences of your impulsive actions. After you repeat something so many times, it becomes a natural habit. Moreover, the more you eat healthy, the easier it will be to curtail your cravings and develop a healthy mentality. However, we all need to indulge and give in to are cravings every once and a while— one meal will not make you unhealthy or obese, just as one meal won't make you healthy either.

Benefits:

Eating healthy has some obvious benefits such as looking and feeling better, but it also has some life altering effects.

- Reduces medical bills.

- Reduces the risk for heart disease, heart attack, and stroke.
- Protect against cancer.
- Lowers blood pressure, the risk of getting kidney stones and helps lower bone loss.

Exercise

Of course there are thousands of gyms and classes that are offered across the country, but money is a vital factor. Luckily, there are thousands of YouTube videos and free programs and articles on the internet that give you a free workout that you can do from the comfort of your own home. You don't need fancy equipment or contraptions to lose weight and feel great. You also do not need to devote hours a day in the gym. Working-out in constant and small increments every day is a minuscule sliver of time for something as important as changing or improving your life. Keep in mind any time is better than none at all, but once people fall into a slump of no exercise, it is very challenging to rectify your previous workout routine. I know many people view working out as a dreaded task, but that is also subject to change. For instance, you can get your whole family involved and strive for a common goal together by signing up for a color run, triathlon, warrior race, or anything else you take interest in. Just remember to make it fun-- walk with your dog, take a bike ride, hike a mountain, or even go swimming. Anything to stay active will prove beneficial.

Benefits:

- Reduces depression and relieves stress by releasing feel-good brain chemicals, reducing immune system chemicals, and by increasing your body temperature.
- Has many psychological and emotional benefits like gaining confidence, take your mind of taxing issues, becoming involved in more social interaction, and coping in a healthy way.

People

People need people. Find or create a support group. Get involved with networks of people dealing with the same issues and who can talk and motivate you. Also, listen to realistic testimonies. The biggest loser depicts incredible weight loss and is no doubt motivation and an amazing feat to see, but most people can't escape the struggles of work and home to go personally train with a Julian Michaels or Bob Harper. Real life stories of people in a more realistic scenario identical to yours are more relatable and can inspire more motivation. By listening or reading these testaments, you can take advice from people who have been there and conquered their battle. Also testimonies of failure, like my Poppy's, are also effective. Utilize them to instill fear and a drive to avoid the ultimate consequence, death.

Body Image:

We are all in a fervent search for the "magic pill", but why? Why is an increasing amount of emphasis and time put on appearance? Why do we feel it is acceptable to label one thing "perfection", while degrading things that fail to squeeze into the ideal, cookie cutter size 2? We live in a superficial society consumed with the importance of appearance. Everywhere you turn there are advertisements using models that do not reflect an average healthy customer but abnormally thin girls.

More than 80% of 4th grade girls have been on a fad diet.

The body type portrayed in advertising as the ideal is possessed naturally by less than 5% of females.

The average weight of a model is 23% lower than that of an average woman; 20 years ago, the differential was only 8%.

Each year the US spends over 33 billion on weight reduction programs, diet foods, and beverages.

95% of diets fail.

Ads on TV and in magazines tend to use the most idealized images of women-research has shown that exposure to these ads negatively impacts body image.

Victoria Secret Fashion Show:

The annual Victoria Secret fashion show that graces each holiday season ignites twitter newsfeeds. Tweets like…

- "The most entertaining and depressing night ever"

- "Goodbye any self-esteem I have and hello insecurities"

are too common; consisting of the majority of that nights posts. Hollywood stars are pressured to stay thin and comments like Kate Moss's, "Nothing tastes as good as skinny feels" brainwashes girls into believing that being skinny is the ultimate goal. All aspects of our media perpetuate the issue and only once in a blue moon do we have the opportunity to see a refreshing and down to earth celebrity such as Jennifer Lawrence. Like Jennifer Lawrence, Olay's beauty campaign has been another example of light in our pop culture. This company has advocated the message that "Everyone is beautiful, despite their age" and "Love the skin you're in". This attitude should be more prominent in our world of fame and glamour instead of shows, blogs, and more outlets of media devoted solely on ridiculing and critiquing individual's looks.

Eating Disorders: A size double 0 girl stands in front of the mirror and scrutinizes her body with a look of disgust. What others see as skin she sees as fat. No matter how thin see gets, she is still convinced she is the dreaded f word— FAT. Another girl loves junk food, but can't bear to keep down what she has veraciously consumed. She has become addicted to the cycle of binging and purging. These two scenarios depict the lives of many girls and women living with the burden of anorexia and bulimia. Eating disorders are any of several psychological disorders characterized by serious disturbances of eating behavior. A distorted or hated body image and low self-esteem are two of the most common roots to the development of eating disorders. The eating disorders of anorexia and bulimia are two very serious and prevalent issues in modern America. Just like obesity, people should be educated about the harmful effects of eating disorders. Overcoming any eating disorder requires support, a plan, a new mentality, being honest with and monitoring yourself, and discipline. Eating disorders are devastating to health, productivity, and relationships.

Anorexia can lead to…

- Abnormally slow heart rate, which means the heart muscle is changing
- Blood pressure too low
- Increased risk of heart failure
- Reduction of bone density
- Muscle loss and weakness
- Severe dehydration which then can lead to kidney failure, fainting, fatigue, and overall weakness
- Dry hair and skin
- Hair loss

Bulimia can lead to…

- Electrolyte imbalance
- Heart issues
- Gastric rupture
- Inflammation and rupture of esophagus
- Tooth decay and staining
- Constipation and irregular bowels

Binge Eating can lead to....

- Increased blood pressure and cholesterol level
- Heart disease
- Type two diabetes
- Gallbladder disease

My Ideas to Make a Difference

For the Future: This topic is near to my heart and very important to me although I cannot accomplish all the goals I want to at this point in my life. Over the course of time, I would potentially like to earn a degree in health and psychology or become a certified trainer. I also think an ambitious, but attainable goal, would be to set up a website that allows for anyone, anywhere, anytime can sign up for and talk to someone about their struggles, questions, and concerns. In addition to the website having a network of people that are going through the same struggles, I also feel it would be necessary to include expert advice and opinions on nutrition, exercise, and a complete plan for success.

Taking Action Now:

- Start a petition for anyone and everyone to sign stating they will love themselves. Hopefully, I will gather enough signatures to grab the attention of some modeling agencies to use healthy and average body type girls along with their existing models. Ideally, this will empower people to make a difference.

- Encourage girls to find worth and self-esteem in places besides their body shape and size. Looks are not everything. I want to help girls to focus on being healthy and being determined and focused in school and not on the scale or weight. People should be reminded they are in control of their life—don't wait for destiny to choose your path, but make your own. Girls need to be reminded that skinny does not mean healthy and healthy looks different on every body. Having our society's perception of a "perfect figure" is not attainable for everybody and that's okay. There are many body types and they are all beautiful and women and men alike should be taught to love what they are blessed with and to never attempt to abuse it or try to alter it for the worse.
- The thing I would love to do the most is start a no fee run to promote the importance of health and positive body image. I would want this run to be set up so everyone can participate in. That would mean dictating courses for beginners and experienced runners, for small children, elderly people and everywhere in between. The ultimate goal would to be to contact celebrities and fitness gurus as well as local business to support and sponsor this run. Maybe even someday it would go nationwide.

"God created man in his own image, in the image of God He created him; male and female He created them." - Genesis 1:27

Kelsey Freshour - Bio

Kelsey Freshour, a native to Marietta, Georgia, is a 16 year old student at Lassiter high school. There she holds the position of sophomore class president, is a member of the Renaissance club, and is a staff writer for Lassiter's newspaper, The Laurette. Her education is very important to her and she hopes to someday attend Vanderbilt. Kelsey is interested in criminology, political science, health, and psychology. She strives to be successful in every aspect of life and to find a career she will be happy to wake up every morning for. Outside of school she is involved with her church, Johnson Ferry Baptist. Every Sunday she acts as an assistant in a 1st grade Sunday school classroom and she a member of the high school choir. She has gone to Romania, Texas, New York, and the Dominican Republic for mission trips and hopes to go on more. In addition, she is currently an employee of Zaxbys.   Besides her job and her faith, her family and friends are very important to her. She lives with her mom, dad, two younger sister, grandmother, and dog. They all fuel her fire to succeed and reach for the stars. The topic of health and body image is close to her heart and she desires for everyone to live the best life they can and to love the body God has bestowed them with. Lastly, she would like to thank Gary and Adam for this amazing opportunity and her literature teacher for pushing them to seize it.

Aiding Our Elders
Nisha Lee

CHAPTER 24 - Aiding Our Elders

The Importance of Everyday Tasks

Oscar Wilde once said, "Youth is wasted on the young". I feel that this is true because we, as young people, are often inclined to take for granted many aspects of our lives that we assume to be everyday tasks. But I feel that the older generations put in perspective how much we should value our simple skills; such as driving, having a job, or even walking. Many senior citizens want so badly to participate in our community, but at times they are not given the opportunity. As a society, our culture is changing. There was a time where the elderly were given the deepest and utmost respect, because they were considered to be wise and mentors to the younger generations. Even though I have not been alive for very long compared to some people, I can still see this tradition is changing. In the constant rush of our busy daily lives, we find it hard to slow down and be polite to the senior citizen at the grocery store who takes a while to pay or the elderly person who drives a little slow. Of course there are people who go out of their way to help a senior cross the street, but in general I feel the that respect the elderly are receiving is slowly declining. This is not the only issue. Many seniors are put in retirement homes because they don't have children to take care of them, or their children are too busy. There are many superb retirement programs with happy residents, but I have visited a few, and from what I have seen depression runs rampant in these facilities. Many have this depression from loneliness, but others may be troubled by the fact that they are no longer independent, or no longer able to do simple tasks that were once second nature to them. It has got to be hard when one doesn't want to retire but stops getting hired because of age discrimination. Of course we must make sure we are keeping safety in mind; we should not let people who struggle with driving become school bus drivers. But many capable elderly are denied the opportunity to work. There are laws that try to stop this discrimination, but that does not mean that it has been eliminated. I'm not trying to paint the picture that all senior citizens are ill-treated and unhappy, because many of them are quite content. The issue that I am trying to face is that there is a large number of elderly people who struggle in today's fast paced society, and it is these people that I would like to help.

Reaching Out to the Elderly

Many elderly people withdraw from the community because they feel that they are not welcome. I feel that we should reach out and reassure them that this is not the case. There are many places where volunteer work is badly needed, from soup kitchens to animal shelters. Many people living in retirement communities are not aware that help is needed in charity organizations because they may not leave their homes very often. If the organizations that would like volunteers advertise in retirement homes more often, they would be likely to get more help from the people living there. Residents of retirement communities often have spare time and would absolutely love something productive to do. There could even be charitable organizations formed that are run specifically by senior citizens. There would be different levels of authority within the organization, like officer positions such as a president, vice president, and treasurer. Funds could be raised to donate time and resources to those in need, and perhaps if such organizations are successful, the members could have a modest salary. This would be ideal; they would be getting a small income while working to help others. I feel that if a salary is included in the positions within these organizations, it will simulate a working environment without the same amount of stress and demand as a real job. This income would not be enough to live on, but most retired people live on social security and money they have already saved. This would just be a little bonus to maybe raise their spirits. Money could be raised for these organizations through fundraisers and donations, keeping in mind that the majority of the profits go to the cause at hand, such as a natural disaster or children's hospital. If a senior citizen is religious, they should be encouraged by their church or religious group to be involved if they have not been already. In my personal opinion, I've realized that as the older people get, the more religion tends to be a comfort in times of trouble. Of course, this is completely a personal choice, but I feel that many times spiritual involvement is soothing when knowing that we may not have as much time left in this life as it used to seem.

Reasons for Depression

Many of the elderly suffer from depression. I am familiar with the constant heavy feeling, which feels as if one is slowly drowning, completely isolated from any light. I would not wish this upon anyone, especially not senior citizens, who are battling enough hardships as it is. In order to treat this depression, we must know the cause. People fall into depression for many reasons, but some of the common ones in the older generations are moving away from home, chronic pain or illness, children moving away, spouses and friends passing away, or the loss of independence or freedom that comes when the body can no longer function as it once did. There are many ways to help these people with their depression. For those who are lonely, visits from friends and family are obviously the best solution. But for those who have no remaining friends or family, new friends can be made. Children and young people especially can help when raising older people's spirits. Local schools can form clubs that go around and visit retirement homes. The visiting children will need a quick lesson on how to interact, and be cautioned that sometimes unexpected things may happen while visiting, but I feel that in the end only good things will come of it. It is not only the elderly that will feel better with visits, those who visit them will receive the great satisfaction of brightening someone's day. There will be people who live in retirement homes that do not want to be visited, and their wishes must be respected. I feel that in the later stages of life, health is definitely important, but happiness is something that everyone deserves as they make their transition into the next stage. There are those who take medications that make themselves miserable. But how is living in pain for a year better than having happiness for a few months less? Many times it is not the patient's decision which path they will follow, it is their children's or doctor's. I understand that this is not a black and white situation; there is a grey area where maybe the patient doesn't know what they want. Some people may not be mentally fit to make their own decisions, but if they are, I feel their opinions must be heard and at the very least compromises must be made. If someone is suffering from depression due to chronic pain, there is not much that can be done. We can try and distract them from their ailments by visits and doing activities (safe activities) that they enjoy. There are those who suffer from depression but do not live in retirement facilities. If they live with their families, the family can notice and seek out help for their senior family member. If the senior citizen lives on their own, it is hard for anyone to really know if they suffer from depression. We must be respectful of their privacy; if they seem to not be in a good state of mind we can maybe bring up the delicate topic of treatment, but in the end it is the individual's decision. The truth is that there are many seniors who live on their own suffering from depression, but no one is aware.

Being Friendly and Pleasant

What I try to do is just be polite and courteous at all times; who knows, maybe that little gesture could have a positive impact on someone's day. Of course, this is easier said than done, and I can freely admit that I am not a naturally cheerful and upbeat person. But I put in an effort, mostly around children and the elderly, because for me personally I only want to see them happy. I know that this should apply to all groups of people, and I have made it a personal goal to try and do so. But the elderly do tend to suffer depression more often than other adults, and I do feel that they deserve all the respect and courtesy that people can give them. Many times the older generations are depicted in movies and such as being grumpy and bitter. But this is only because some of them are treated as if they were children, rather than the adults they are. Now there are exceptions to every rule, and I'm sure there are some senior citizens who were unpleasant from the start, because let's face it, in this world there are some people who are just downright disagreeable. But I feel the majority of the elderly that are resentful become this way as a result of their depression, because they are unhappy with their lives. This is an extremely daunting problem to tackle, because it is not a physical condition that can be easily repaired. The mind is complicated and fragile, and must be treated as such.

Helping the Elderly With Technology

One way to help the elderly be more involved in today's culture is teaching them how to use technology as we do. I understand that some of them would prefer not to, and personally I don't blame them because the extent of my technological knowledge is pretty much the internet, my cell phone and Microsoft Word. But as much as we hate to admit it, we cannot get enough of our electronics and apps. It must be strange to feel like an outsider simply because one can't figure out how to set up a Facebook account. Many senior citizens don't need any help at all with figuring out today's technology, some of my friend's grandmothers are much more active than I am on Twitter. But for those who do struggle, the knowledge merely gives them an option to participate if they like. I taught my own grandmother how to text a few years ago, and now we have the cutest conversations from time to time. I'm fully aware that there are more pressing matters to attend to around the world like famine and war, but if there is time or resources I feel like classes for the elderly on using technology would be something nice for them. Not essential, but nice.

My Own Plan of Action

I have wanted to become a lawyer for quite a long time. Although they sometimes portrayed in a negative light, I have always admired the profession. There is a certain branch that I am particularly interested in pursuing because it combines many of my career interests with personal ones as well. It is called Elder Law, which includes helping the elderly with writing their wills, estate planning, healthcare, retirement planning, discrimination from employers, and protecting them from abuse, neglect and fraud. Aside from my professional interests, I hope to continue visiting retirement homes and volunteering for anything involving the elderly as often as possible. I would also like to be involved with non-profit organizations that help aid the elderly. Most people cannot dedicate their entire lives to their favorite cause, but if everyone gave a little of their time we could accomplish a great deal.

A Smooth Transition

We must remember that these people are senior citizens today, but years ago they were the working force and youth of our nation. We must also remember that we are tomorrow's seniors as well. We must treat these people with the respect and dignity that they so rightly deserve. It makes me angry when people treat them as children, because they are far from it. They are our elders, and even if they are not as fit as they once were they have more life experience than us, and we can still learn from them. If I live long enough to grow old, I hope that I will consider myself lucky, and not resent my last stage of life for my own loss of abilities or isolation. I believe everyone deserves to be content late in life. I would like to make a difference by trying to help the senior citizens of today make their lives a bit happier. This can be a frustrating topic because no matter how much we do, there will always be people that we cannot help. But we can't let this stop us from trying, because helping a little is better than not helping at all. To age gracefully can be a beautiful thing, and an opportunity to do so is what everyone deserves.

Nisha Lee – Bio

Nisha Lee was born in Clearwater Florida and grew up in Melbourne Beach, Florida until the age of ten when she moved to Marietta, Georgia. Although she loves her life in Georgia, Florida is still a large part of her life. She often goes back to visit her extended family and old friends, spend time at the beach, and walk the trails on her family tree plantation near Tallahassee, where she attends Florida State football games.

Nisha has always enjoyed outdoor activities, such as hiking and snorkeling. She has played soccer, danced and swam for many years and currently runs track as a sprinter. She is a sophomore in high school and enjoys learning about history and literature. Outside of academics, she attends Model United Nations conferences, and is a member of a Beta Club which takes on service projects for various charities. She enjoys traveling very much and so far her favorite destination so far has been Singapore. Her desire to aid the elderly started with her close relationship with her grandparents and became stronger after visiting retirement homes. As of now Nisha would like to continue visiting retirement homes and volunteer more with helping the elderly. In the future, she would like to pursue a career in law. The branch she is most interested in is Elder Law, which seeks to protect the rights of the older generations. It is a personal goal and passion for hers to make an impact and improve the lives of the elderly, no matter how small.

I Will Make a Difference

Annalise Dressel

CHAPTER 25 – I Will Make a Difference

Making a Difference

What does making a difference mean to me? Well, some people may ask "On what kind of scale are you planning on making a difference? Are you trying to make a difference in your home, your school, your town, your state?" However, I believe none of those are the right answer for me. You see, I want to make a difference in the world. My thoughts on my future are quite simple- I want to do something that puts others first before me. By doing this, I know I'll be making a difference in people's lives. I believe making a difference not only affects others but also affects yourself; with doing something for others, you're improving the way others see you and the way you see yourself. People that are planning to make a difference are the individuals who instead of saying "I'll try" they say "I'll do" and instead of saying "I think" say "I know". These people are doers and dreamers who want to make the world a better place. I know I have the capability to be one of those people and I believe with a little effort and a calling I can make a difference.

My Many Callings

I've received many different callings in the past 15 years of my life. When I was in kindergarten I wanted to become a ballet teacher with my best friend Jackie. It was the first year I had been doing dance and like everyone at that age, you have no clue that your view on your future was going to change…multiple times. During 4th and 5th grade I wanted to be an artist; I had been taking an art class and I really enjoyed it. The next few years were a blur; through my middle school years I didn't really think about my future. I was too busy trying to deal with all the problems that were currently at hand. In my freshmen year at Lassiter I wanted to be a marine biologist. Throughout the year I had enjoyed the biology course I was taking and wanted to take that knowledge further. Every time I said I wanted to be one of these things, my parents would always encourage me to take on some extracurricular activities that pertained to the certain job. I thought their constant nagging was annoying, but I now I realize they just want to make sure I'm going to end up doing something that I really want to do. So, I've tried multiple hobbies and every time decided it wasn't for me. For the longest amount of time I was really starting to worry if I was ever going to find something that I would actually end up to be.

Finding my Calling

Last year during the month of April, something happened that made its mark in history forever. At 2.49 pm, two bombs exploded 12 seconds apart from one another near the marathon's finish line on Boylston Street during the Boston marathon in Boston, Massachusetts. I remember going onto Instagram having my feed displaying the same pictures of the bombings that had just recently occurred in Boston. Under the hashtag millions of photos were displayed and within minutes, I soon knew exactly what had happened. Among those participating in the marathon, 3 were killed and more than two hundred were injured. Because of this and the knowledge of not knowing where the bombers were, I was permanently wounded. Why would someone do this to innocent people? Why would you put your own life on the line? Why would you risk your future? After that day, multiple investigative arms were out looking for the bombers. The FBI was one of these investigative arms and they were the first to have the images and names of the two bombers. They were also the department that discovered the appearance of the bombs and how they were set off. Once the identities and the locations of these terrorists were identified, all public transportation shut down in the area and tons of people were in their houses on lock down. After a car race between the bombers and the police department, one of the bombers was captured and later died while in custody. Shortly after, the other bomber was found and it was broadcasted on the television. My family and I were sitting down watching the television and I recall seeing police hats and FBI jackets. Tons of people were crying and cheering in relief and some even shared their experiences over the past few days. It was then, looking at the television at all the locals and the people being thanked who helped them that I realized what I was actually supposed to do with my life. I wasn't meant to draw, or dance, or study marine life, I was meant to help others. I was positive I was meant to protect others and to put others needs before my own. After that day, almost everything fell into place.

FBI

    I realized that I wanted to serve others by going to the FBI to work with forensics. The FBI stands for the Federal Bureau of Investigation. In all, the thousands of people that are a part of it work to protect the US from threats and to investigate particular crimes. The agents and people apart of the FBI must have skills in law enforcement, intelligence, foreign language proficiency, and other skills that would prove their selves useful in this particular field of work. To become a FBI agent, you must be in the age range of 23-late 30's when you enter. This and specific background checks determine the entry's ability to work hard and long. The FBI isn't really like a police force, it works more on a national scale and that's why I found that it was the place for me- it works on a bigger scale. Most people associate the FBI with the shows on television depicting a field detective and the big crimes they solve. However, there is a lot more that goes into the FBI then the people physically out on the streets chasing the criminal.

Forensics Science

Crime lab analysts and Crime scene analysts also play major roles in the FBI and other investigative departments. Because of my interest in Genetics and Forensics I could see myself working to protect others and making a difference in our nation through doing the things I love to do. During my biology class during the ninth grade, we did a crime scene unit. Basically, there was a story about a murder and there were different stations around the room. The stations were things like DNA fingerprinting, blood types, and hair samples. We spent a whole week going through each of the stations. I remember finding this unit very fun. I sort of took control in my group and started working to figure out who the killer was. This and many of the forensics articles and books found online, I really think I would enjoy doing something like that in my future. I believe I've found my forte and I've already starting to plan for the future and to work towards my goal.

Learning to Defend Myself

Although I've decided I may not want to be in the field, I've begun to take self-defense classes because I believe that with any position I do take in the FBI, I will need to be able to do certain things to excel at my job. I expressed some interest in these classes towards the beginning of the year and my parents held me to it. They made sure I didn't forget about wanting to do it and they took me to some places to check out the programs. The day we scheduled my first class, my dad took me to a fairly new restaurant and we sat down in a booth near the back of the restaurant. My dad told me that he's proud of me for trying something like a defense class; No one in my family has ever tried something like it before. When I first began, I got frustrated and upset beyond belief because I was in a class with bigger, stronger, and more experienced kids than me. However, after going for a while I realized that out in the world, if I want to be involved in investigating and dealing with crimes, I'm going to need to know how to deal with stronger and more advanced people than me. I'm going to have to deal with criminals that will do a lot worse to me than just punching me in the face. The thoughts of this and my dreams for the future help me preserve and keep a positive attitude in the class. I'm planning on making a difference and if I start off with accepting that things are going to be rough for me enable to get there, I'll be better off in the future.

Final Words

On top of all of the things I would like to do in my future, I hope I have the strength to survive high school.

Once I get out of high school, I have my whole future ahead of me, and I truly can't wait. Going back to my first thoughts, I do believe anyone can make a difference if they have the right motives and if they want it badly enough. There are no limitations to what a certain person can or cannot do. If you want it, work for it. I know that everyone was put on the earth for a reason, and I was fortunate enough to find out what mine was early enough in my life. Doing work with the FBI is sort of a dream job for me and although joining the FBI requires work and secrets to be kept, I'm willing to take on the challenge. Through taking defense classes, reading into information on the FBI and forensics science, and working hard in school, I've started to plan and prepare for what lies ahead. My final words are from the words of Robert Kiyosaki: "Your future is created by what you do today, not tomorrow."

Annalise Dressel – Bio

Annalise lives in Marietta, Georgia with her parents and two sisters. She is currently a sophomore at Lassiter High school and does multiple extracurricular activities such as DECA, kick boxing, study buddies, and mission trips with her church. She enjoys hanging out with friends, watching *The Walking Dead*, and traveling with her family.

The Invisible People
Emmalyn Dressel

CHAPTER 26 – The Invisible People

"You're the only one who can make the difference. Whatever your dream is, go for it."

Earvin Magic Johnson

What 'making a difference' means to me

Every person is put on earth for a specific reason. Each human being has an individual plan to help the world and the people living in it. Whether the person makes their plan a reality is left up to the individual. To me, 'making a difference' means acting instead of saying, performing instead of bragging, and producing instead of theorizing. To 'make a difference' requires motivation, dedication, love, and confidence. These qualities are needed to persevere during both the good and tough times. Without motivation, dedication, love, and confidence, the dream won't succeed. As a young child, I believed that 'making a difference' meant setting up a big foundation, raising multi millions, and sending the money to all the people that needed help. As I have grown older, I've come to realize that I can act, perform, and produce regardless of my personal status.

Definition and Stereotypes of the homeless

The typical stereotype placed on homeless people makes many individuals believe that the homeless are nothing but lazy alcoholics and drug addicts who are taking no measures to improve their way of living. Before I had served the homeless, I thought this too. In actuality, the homeless are people just like you and me. They have families, dreams, and preset plans to make a difference in the world. Every single homeless person has a story to tell, and every story is different. Some of these stories fit the stereotypical spectrum, but several people have stories that fall in a completely different category. Regardless of their background, every homeless person has a preset mission, and we should help them get back up on their feet and moving in the right direction. It is only after I served the homeless that I realized that the label placed on these people was false, and their condition was being overlooked by a mass majority of the population.

First-hand experience

Before my first mission to the homeless, I failed to realize how many people were living without a home. Even though homelessness in third world countries is more prominent, the homeless still wander the streets in the United States. I didn't realize that every single time I drove into Atlanta, I was passing the "homes" of hundreds of homeless people. Needless to say, I was extremely surprised when I first saw the people who appeared to be invisible to the rest of society.

My first time assisting the homeless was a couple winters ago, underneath the overpasses of Atlanta. I had bundled myself up in my winter coat and set out with my church to participate in an organization that specifically specialized in local homeless assistance. The guides led large groups underneath several underpasses to not only provide food and clothing, but also love and prayer. The sight of torn blankets, makeshift tents, loose shoes, and garbage bags met my eyes the instant I climbed underneath the first bridge. In addition to what I saw, I was greeted by the smell of urine and garbage. Even though I experienced the harsh conditions that the homeless had to deal with, I still saw a great deal of good. Everywhere I turned, I saw the eyes of the homeless light up with joy when a stranger offered to pray with them. Smiles erupted from the homeless when they were given a sack lunch and a new blanket. It amazed me how much of an impact a simple service project had brought to the people around me. Not only had we given them something warm to wear and eat, we had given them a burst of happiness and a great deal of joy.

Some people that were a part of that mission trip went home and completely forgot about what they had seen. Even though they had seen how little the people under the bridges had, they carried on with their life of constant complaining and unnecessary drama. On the other hand, I chose *not* to forget. I chose to accept the problem and I had decided that I was going to make a difference, one homeless person at a time.

Throughout the past years, I have made this particular mission trip an annual tradition. This past year, I participated in the same routine. I woke up early, got dressed in my winter finest, and drove to my church to prepare for the mission later that day. Once I had arrived in the sanctity of the church, I was put to work writing Christmas cards and putting together packed lunches. After loading the cars with the gifts and food for the homeless, our caravan headed towards a shelter in Atlanta, our starting point for the bridge route. As soon as we arrived at the women and children shelter, we were greeted by several kids who directed us towards the main sanctuary. The sanctuary was decorated with the normal Christmas decorations along with inspirational paintings which were hung from the walls. The cheerful atmosphere in the sanctuary showed me yet again how happy people can be even with the bare minimum. It was here that the bridge leaders explained the schedule and rules for the bridge route. During the speakers' presentations, bible quotes were said and personal stories were told to set everyone in the right mindset for serving. By the time the presentations ended, all of the people who were going on the bridge route were more than ready to put themselves out there and serve the individuals in need. The first couple overpasses were the same, we left gifts and prayed over the beds and then carried on to the next destination. One of the places we went to allowed enough space for the homeless to set up tents. I spread my love by giving comforting hugs and briefly praying for them. One woman in particular, who goes by the name Tasha, told me something that has had a lasting impression. My friends and I gave her a hug and then she looked down at us and began by thanking us for the food and love. Her appreciation was clear on her face, and her words made it quite clear that even though we hadn't given her fortune or fame, she was still grateful for what we could give her. Before we left, she looked us each in the eyes and told us that we were smart, kind, young girls that had so much potential in life to do something significant. She told us to stay in school, strive to do our best, and persevere even when times get tough, because she didn't want us to stumble down the path she took. Her words stuck with me throughout the rest of the trip and even today, I still remember who she was and what she said. Her words have motivated me to lead a better life, and she also gave me more motivation to make a difference. There was one more person on the mission that motivated me to continue to strive for a difference, a young boy around the age of 8. I met him in an abandoned apartment complex, living with his father. Both of them came outside into the cold to talk to us and receive our presents. The little boy's emotionless face immediately sprung into a cheek to cheek smile once we handed him a Christmas present and gave him a hug. His heartwarming smile left an impression on me just like Tasha and her words of wisdom.

Future plans

As the years go on, I want to continue to put aside time for missionary work. Regardless of my future jobs and plans, helping the homeless will continue to be an aspect of major importance in my life. I want to let the world know about the invisible people underneath the bridges of Atlanta and I want to do this my verbally spreading the word and using social media to show the importance of the matter. I hope that people will start to realize that even though the problem may be hidden, it is still thriving. Hopefully the more and more the population learns about the homeless, the less they will be able to turn around and hide from the problem.

More opportunities will continue to knock on my door as I grow older. I will be able to go more places, help more people, and experience new ways of life. I want to branch out from my hometown and help other people in foreign countries such as Africa and India. My end goal is to get to as many places as time allows.

Final thoughts

It is because of the joy I see and the people that I've met that motivate me to continue my journey of making a difference within the homelessness community. Without these experiences, my plan would just be another empty spoken phrase. Because of my choice to persevere, I am making one of my plans a reality. Even though I'm starting off small, my results will grow larger as time goes on, and I'll continue to help the homeless and those in great need of compassion and comfort. I am changing the phrase from 'I want to make a difference' to 'I will make a difference'.

Emmalyn Dressel – Bio

Emmalyn Dressel currently lives in Marietta, Georgia, with her parents, younger sister, and twin sister. She is presently enrolled in Lassiter High School as a sophomore. Emmalyn participates in several school activities such as orchestra, debate team, study buddies, and track and field. In her free time, she enjoys helping out at her church, participating in her church's life teen, and hanging out with friends and family. Her plans for her future include going to college, getting a double major in some area of biological science, and minoring in German. She also wants to continue helping those in need by going overseas to third-world countries and helping the environment through her occupation.

Start a Chain Reaction

Danielle Okonta

CHAPTER 27 - Start a Chain Reaction

"The purpose of life is to contribute in some way to making things better" - Robert F Kennedy

I would like to make a difference in society and in the world as a whole and using other community resources with the establishment of children-staffed help programs. This will help children have access to the resources of their environment and how to use it to benefit them. Although the idea sounds a little ironic, it is actually a great way for children to see what is actually going on outside their homes and will allow them to appreciate their lives and the sacrifices that parents and loved ones make each day. In all, children would be making efforts to help those who are less fortunate than them achieve success in their lives. In order to make this possible, I've got to start now. This past Christmas break, my family and I spent four days gathering items to donate to Nigeria. My dad, who is currently working in Nigeria, will distribute these items after they are shipped. In all, we filled about nineteen Home Depot boxes with close to three thousand items of clothing, shoes and bags that my siblings and I wore years ago. It was strenuous labor because on the first day we started at twelve in the afternoon and finished at close to two o'clock in the morning! I was absolutely exhausted, but I knew that what we were doing was for a good cause and I was glad to make an effort.

Children-Staffed Programs - Why?

This is what jump started my idea to make children-staffed programs for the help. Obviously, it doesn't necessarily have to be something laborious, but something that will be essential to families who are deprived of basic items such as clothing, food and shelter. At the same time if many children of all ages (or when they are old enough to do such) can come together to do things like this it will be even better.

"Community Service?"

I believe that even the youngest children can make a difference, so in high school teenagers certainly can too. In some high schools there are school clubs for teenagers to get involved in making efforts to get involved in the community and help out. At Lassiter it is BETA Club, Interact and FCA. Unfortunately, I wasn't able to join BETA club this year, but I have a friend that is involved and usually they sell goodies and items that will pay for food, clothing and shelter locally send to places around the world where there is a need. I make sure to buy any item, knowing that my little token will make a difference in someone's life. However, not everyone is involved in it and I am glad that all students in high school are required to have a certain number of community service hours. This will really give us an insight into how the other half lives. I think all teenagers should spend their summer time going outside to help people in their community and in other places of the world genuinely, instead of kicking back at the beach for two months. Making a difference does not need to involve monetary gifts, it can be as a mentor, counselor or even someone to talk to when in need.

Summer Solace for the Suffering (Teen-staffed help programs)

In order to change the typical lazy summers of some teenagers, we should all participate in state-regulated relief programs. Many of us take the "Driver's Ed" course during the summer. For us teens and students in high school, a great way for us to help others is by the creation of a "help foundation" similar to the "Driver's Ed" course. This help foundation should not only be about community service but we can be taught how to help others, and how it can and will make us better people. In order to do so, I think we need some exposure to some of the suffering both locally and globally (if financial payments won't be a problem and our safety is not in danger). At least then, most of us will feel the need to really take the time to make the lives of others better, once we see it for ourselves. To make sure this happens everywhere, I will send letters to the Georgia Federal Government and do the same to other federal agencies in the country. Overall, not only will we complete our community hours for graduation, we will also see that it is important to help others. Since this idea has not yet launched, I will continue to make my own efforts and encourage others to do so while I'm in high school.

Goals for College: Initiate Children-Staffed Programs

Once I'm in college, I will start launching these "children-staffed help organizations" by taking time to come to elementary schools to talk about how they, as young as they are, can help others. Before I do though, I will ask to become an exchange student for a period of time to a Third

World country, where I can view the suffering myself. I'm currently taking Spanish now and plan to speak it fluently by the end of my high school years, and I currently also have a math tutor who is Chinese and she will also teach me how to speak Mandarin. While I'm in college, I also plan to take other foreign languages as well.

Developing "Junior UNICEF"

The best way and most effective way of recruiting children is by sharing my ideas with public schools. In the periodic visits I make to the public schools, I will first start off by showing a film that I filmed myself from traveling abroad as an exchange student. Students can see what responsibilities other children their age have to take up to survive. On the next few visits, I will develop fundraisers aimed at making money for food and other items to be sold and shipped to other countries. In a way these will be like "Jump for Heart" fundraisers, in that prizes will be earned for their efforts. Most visits will be where the children are being active in helping out others, such as going out into the community and donating toy items that they no longer play with, making homemade dishes to be served out to the homeless and making care packages like first aid kits and sleeping kits to be donated to other countries and distribute to the people. To make sure all their efforts are being beneficial to others, I will go out locally and film people's reactions to the gifts given and I will go out to a country where we shipped items to see how thankful people who are suffering will be when they receive their necessities. To make this much faster and easier, I will meet up with my colleagues so we can set this up and make all this possible.

A Call to Action

In the future, I want to be a doctor. As I master my practice, I want to travel to the world and give the ill-stricken people medicine and the treatment they need to survive and heal. At the same time however, I want to be a spokesperson and speak out to others about this idea in other states in hopes that they will create organizations like these. We need to start this now because children may not be aware that others their age are suffering, and possibly don't even care. Worse, entertaining technological devices that are improving can keep teenagers from doing anything active and thus not being aware of what is going on locally and outside the United States. If we hammer on this now, children and teens of all ages will be more active in their communities and more lives will be saved.

When the time comes for me to launch my programs, I will send out this letter to public schools and homes:

Start a Chain Reaction with Kids

Everyday a typical American child wakes up to the smell of bacon and eggs, and maybe some buttermilk pancakes, steaming at the wooden dining table in mother's kitchen. A young child in the Third World wakes up to find that the week's supply of food has finished, and it is yet another day to go scour for more. The American child pours a glass of freshly squeezed orange juice. The child in the Third World fills a small clay vase with water in a nearby lake. The American child makes his way to the table. The Third World child carefully balances the water filled vase on his head while dragging the few meal items he could find back to the village. Most children don't know that kids their age have to take up responsibilities like that just to survive. Children receive many things, but when have you seen them give? This is why I propose that children should get involved in more community activities and services to help those who are suffering. It will teach children to provide for others, increases their self-esteem, and those who receive the care will be greatly benefited.

Children help organizations can teach children to provide for other people. Children don't like to share and complain about what they don't have. If children help organizations can make a child see his or her blessing, they will be more willing to help others. Children help organizations can teach a child to give to one another. A child can give away toys they no longer play with, clothing and food for families who cannot afford it. They can be taught to help feed others that are younger than them, to bathe them and even entertain them. Children can help clean up impoverished areas. These are typical things that children seven and eight years old do for their younger siblings while mom and dad look for food and shelter in Third World countries. Children can even practice these responsibilities with their younger siblings. This at least gives mom a break. In doing this, children will learn to do things for others at a young age, things that they can provide for themselves and others.

With helping others, children will grow to have better self-esteem. It is a good feeling to receive a gift but even better to give one, and when you give one as big as this, you'll be as happy as the person receiving the help. Children can get the same feeling. Some might be afraid to give their old clothes, toys, and belongings away but at the end of the day, they will be able to understand that they didn't lose very much, and those who needed their belongings gained much. Programs like these can be a great way to improve the self-esteem of many adolescents that might have been bullied in school or gotten in trouble with the law. The once great self-esteem brought down by their peers will rise back up for the time and effort they put into saving lives. It is very important that children can help save other lives in the process but in their time and work they put into doing that they also have to gain something from it: a great big heart.

If this "chain reaction" can grow, many more lives can be saved in the process. Even to donate a small sack of children clothes or shoes can provide for many children in a village or a couple of people in a local homeless shelter. With such programs we can reduce rates of malnutrition, famine and early mortality rates. With so many donations great things can happen; books and pencils will allow children in other countries to read and write; clothes can provide warmth and coverage for severe weather. All this and so much more. Even if you can't do so physically, give some donations, because they will go somewhere, and make sure to see how you may have affected, or even saved a life.

I call upon children, of all ages, to go outside and make a change for the better. Go donate one of your little toys, a baby blanket, or some canned soup. You will always have access to items like these in the future, but others may not. Teenagers engrossed in your cool gadgets and Apple products, stop texting and find a reasonable way to use those phones to make a donation, or find a way to help someone, or go out there and do it personally. Over many years, relief programs have developed, as big as UNICEF, and lives are being saved right now, and technology is still growing and improving for the future, but the staff and volunteers that are involved are a majority of adults. If conditions are not dangerous, and with parent permission and supervision, children can go out into their local communities to help others or travel with family and friends to areas in the world who need support.

If you're that typical American child that gets up in the morning to a delicious breakfast, stop and think about who doesn't, go outside, and *make a difference*.

From reading this rather expressive and informative essay, one might understand that age is no longer a barrier to help others. As time goes by, the environment changes, technology transforms, and people grow. The wars in global conflict, famine, malnutrition, and poverty seem to be getting worse. Why? As Americans, we value freedom, equality, strength, wealth and independence. We also try to make efforts in other countries so they can value the same. Most people use to think only U.S, soldiers, leaders, and ambassadors were capable of doing such, but in order to make these changes available, ALL American citizens need to get involved, *including children.* An ancient legend explains the Central Asian steppe raiders (Mongols) were united when the wife of the khan was trying to settle a dispute between her two sons and heirs to the throne by using sticks to explain the importance of a unit. She challenged her sons to break one stick, which they did easily, but when she asked them to break four together, they were unable too. This may or may not be true, but it is symbolizes the importance and strength of a unit working as one; in the end these central nomads formed a siege and unstoppable group called the Mongols, who created the largest living empire ever. Similarly, if children and teenagers start playing roles in helping people in their communities and beyond, we can help fight world hunger in the world.

According to John F. Kennedy" Let no one be discouraged by the belief that there is nothing one person can do against the enormous array of the world's ills, misery, ignorance, and violence. Few will have the greatness to bend history, but each of us can work to change a small portion of events. And in the total of all those acts will be written the history of a generation.".

Danielle Okonta - Bio

My name is Danielle Okonta. I am a Lassiter High School sophomore as well as an honors and scholar athlete. At school my favorite subject is AP World History because I am fascinated with the world, which is why I wish to travel in the future. I am also a varsity athlete on the track and field team. My favorite event on the track is the 300 meter hurdles. In my family of five, I am the oldest child of my two siblings. My mom owns a daycare that is very successful and still growing and my dad does business in Nigeria. My younger sister, who is nine years old, is also a writer, one with an even bigger imagination than myself and she is involved in many sports. My brother is fourteen years old, and a phenomenal athlete in basketball and soccer.

In my free time I usually hang out with friends and host sleepovers. But on any rainy day, I either sit with a good book, read, draw or write. If I'm reading a good book I would usually put myself in the book as the main character and change the story a bit to make it my own, but I found that if I wrote my own, I could create the character I wanted. I have a very big imagination, and I like to put together my imagination and inspiration from book and movies. I mostly enjoy writing short story narratives, whether they are for fun or for school assignments, as well as persuasive essays. I would say my persuasive essays are better than my short stories because they are usually based off important topics, such as this one. In my essays I don't just talk about why I want the change to happen but how it can be created.

When I grow up, I don't wish to be an author; I want to be a pediatrician. I am very good at analyzing many things and it will feel good to get a sick child up and running again. However, that does not mean that I will not write. I will continue to write informative essays because in writing one can address a problem, be creative and share ideas on how to fix it, and some of these ideas can change things for the better.

Be Kind
Paige Gorski

CHAPTER 28 – Be Kind

Plato said, "Be kind, for everyone you meet is fighting a hard battle." This is the motto I strive to live by, and I believe through this perspective we each have the opportunity to impact the people in our lives and the people we encounter every day. I believe every person has the ability and the responsibility to make a difference and encourage and support those around us.

Take Notice

As a young adult I know how easy it is to get wrapped up in our own little world; we get into a usual routine and it becomes customary to block out everything else and focus on what we know. But with this mindset we will miss out on infinite opportunities to influence or completely change the lives of those around us- The people who slide through life unnoticed and seemingly unremarkable, like the homeless man we ignore as we walk by, or the girl who sits alone at lunch, or maybe even someone who 'has it all' but truly feels empty inside. We never know if one of the people we encounter every day is going through a tough time. Just because someone is smiling doesn't mean they're happy. I am an example of the statement. I want to share my story with you, not because I want attention or sympathy, but because I want to make a difference. I want to share how others have made an impact on my life and how I plan on doing that in return. So, I hope my story encourages you to reach out to others and make a difference in someone's life.

My Battle With Self-Hate

I'm not good enough for anyone or anything. People don't care about me. I must be forgettable. No one cares. There's nothing special or good about me. I'm just like any other girl. Everyone I thought cared doesn't. Am I really so bad?

This is a journal entry I wrote in January of 2011. These are some of the thoughts I struggled with for almost three years. I walked around pretending I was okay, pretending everything was perfect and fabulous, but in reality I was a slave to my self-doubt and insecurity. Instead of reaching out to my friends and family, I dug deeper and deeper into a world of self-hate, self-harm, and depression. I pushed away those who cared about me, believing I was undeserving or that they didn't deserve to put up with someone as complicated and depressed as me. I began to cut myself. It started as a once in a while thing, but gradually became something I could not escape. I thought it was the only way to cope with my frustrations and ever-changing emotions. I looked for solutions to my pain in all the wrong places. Instead of turning to God and my friends and family, I tried to fill the emptiness I felt inside with boys and constant partying. As you may have guessed, these vices dug me even deeper into my depression, compelling me to try other things in order to find happiness. I felt alone, empty, sad and useless. As these feelings continued my depression worsened. I began to cut constantly, and I felt like life wasn't even worth living. I had hit rock bottom. I battled with these feelings for a while, struggling to find purpose for my life or really even a reason to live at all.

There Is Hope

    I eventually received help to fight my urges to self-harm and worked through the feelings that had caused me so much unbearable pain. It was a long, hard battle, but I'm in a much better place now and I definitely could not have gotten here on my own. There are so many people who made a difference in my life and are the reason I am even alive today. Most of these people were not even aware of what I was going through, but their love and kindness helped more than they will ever know. My friends who stuck by me through my bad moods and constant distant attitude; my parents, who loved me unconditionally even though I pushed them away from me as far as I could; my sisters, to whom I feigned happiness instead of trusting and continued to support me even though I refused to accept it. Even my church community, teachers, and complete strangers loved me though my struggles even when I faked happiness and pushed them away. They did not know what I was going through, and that is one reason why their love and kindness was so outstanding. I was fighting a battle that I tucked away far inside of me, and without the love, kindness, and hope I found in others I do not know where I would be today. The smallest things, like an unexpected smile from a stranger, or a text or call from a friend, could make one of my typical bad days just a little bit more bearable. This is why I love Plato's quote so much. Through all of the hard times, and believe me, everyone has their struggles; there will always be those people who lift up others. I desire to be that person to others. This is how I can make a difference. I aspire to be a sign of hope and a friend to those around me. Although my past has been shaky and filled with pain, I am a new person now. I want to make a difference by helping others to believe in themselves and believe that there are better days ahead. When I am angry or upset and want to take it out on those around me, I try to remember the effect this could have on them. Our pride and emotion is not worth causing someone else pain. You never know how your words can affect people. Why should we treat others badly just because we are able to? They may be going through a tough time, and showing them love and kindness could make their day, week, month, or even year. You never know how much a small act of kindness can mean to someone. I know I went through these experiences for a reason: to help others who are struggling and to show them that life goes on. It gets better; this is not a permanent condition. All of these experiences have taught me to be more forgiving, to be kind to others, especially those who I feel are undeserving, and to try and improve the lives of those around me in any way I can. I know how it feels to experience hopelessness and a lack of control. I don't wish these feelings on anyone and instead urge you to help those people who are suffering to feel renewed.

Together

Everyone we meet is fighting a battle. Sure, their battle may just be a grumpy boss or a spilled cup of coffee, but think of how easily we, as a best friend or as a complete stranger, can do something simple that could be exactly what they needed in order to move forward. It may take conscious effort and it may place you in uncomfortable situations, but I believe the impact you can have far outweighs anything negative that could bloom from kindness. I encourage you to be kind and love those around you unconditionally. Show someone who feels hopeless that there is hope. You can make a difference, and together, we can make a difference.

Paige Gorski – Bio

Paige Gorski is a senior at Lassiter High School. She will graduate in 2014 and then wishes to attend college and study to become a nurse.

Paige has always had a love for journaling and writing of any kind. She also enjoys poetry.

When asked why she enjoys writing Paige stated that she thinks words can hold power, and she likes the idea of sharing that power with others.

In her free time, Paige works, takes guitar lessons, coaches volleyball, and volunteers at a homeless pet shelter.

Helping to Inspire Future Generations
Sarah Lezaj

CHAPTER 29 – Helping to Inspire Future Generations

My Motivation

Inspiring people to be the best person they can be is harder than it sounds. Furthermore, becoming motivated to put your own needs aside for others is even more difficult to do in the world we live in today. However, if kids start learning what is important in life at a young age, it is more likely that they will prioritize and be the best they can be as they grow. If inspired in the right ways, children can learn to be the best person they can be, and pass it on to their children, which, in the best situations, will lead to positive affects generation after generation. It is for this reason that I take time working with kids to make a difference in their lives, and would like to continue working with them after I graduate.

The Key to Connecting

When I was nine years old, I began working with kids in my mom's preschool class. Every opportunity I got, I would go in and help her, and sometimes she would pay me a couple of dollars if I did well. However, the cash motivation was not necessary for me to help her out. To me, working with the two- year- olds was so much fun, it was hardly a job. The requirements were simple and fun. I got to play with them in the classroom with puzzles, building blocks, and Play-do, but most importantly I got to teach them. As a kid I loved to read, and so I was always excited to read to all the kids as they sat on the foam mat in front of me. With all the fun I was having, I did not realize that I had an impact on these kids simply by reading a story book. Studies show that reading to kids stimulates their imagination, and helps them develop language and listening skills, which are key elements in communication. Also, I would help them learn the letters of the alphabet, and make connections to words and pictures they already knew. With these connections, it is easier for kids to understand so they learn better. So, already at the age of nine, I was making a small difference in children's lives and I did not even know it.

As I grew older, I only became more attached to kids. I wanted to get more involved in helping them, and when I was 10, I found a way. I wrote a letter to my school principal asking if it would be okay if I held a drive to collect art supplies. She gave me the okay, and every morning for two weeks I collected art supplies from donations of the kids in my elementary school, giving them smiley face stickers in return for their donations. My drive got published in the school newsletter, which only increased the art supplies flowing in. After two weeks, I had several boxes of crayons, paints, markers, coloring books, and everything in between. The weekend after the drive, my family and I drove to the Children's Hospital of Atlanta and gave all the boxes to them for the kids to enjoy. As I was wheeling all of the boxes into the hospital, I passed a child in a wheelchair with a nurse pushing her. She asked the nurse what all of the crayons were for, and when the nurse told her that they were for her, the girls face lit up. Though I did not get to personally deliver the supplies to the children, just seeing that one girl made the whole thing worth it. After I dropped everything off, I received a medal from the hospital, and I felt like I really helped make a difference in those kids' lives, with something that most of us take for granted. Now that I am old enough, I plan to volunteer at the hospital this upcoming summer and hopefully many summers after that as well.

My Experience Working with Kids

This previous summer, I was old enough to work at Roswell Park, where I often help my mom out with her preschool class. Since I was 15, I could work part time as a Kindercamp counselor. This specific camp was for kids between the ages of three and five. At camp, we would play games, do arts and crafts, play on the playground and in the pool, and have a party every Friday. Being with these kids for a week at a time was so much fun, and it was effortless to make them enjoy it with all the fun I had. Being a camp counselor really makes a difference in young kids' lives, because they look up to you. I got to teach them things, show them different ways to do things, and most likely disciplined them differently than their parents. Being away from their parents allows them to grow in the smallest ways, make new friends, and learn new things. Being a part of that is so important to me, because children need to learn things young and have positive influences throughout their lives. Through this wonderful job, I got the opportunity to work with so many different kids, make them laugh, and help them when they fall down and need a band aid. It allowed me many other opportunities to babysit, and helped me mature and take responsibility for other people that need help. Through this job, I not only made a difference in kids' lives, but they made a difference in mine. Luckily, I was asked to come back again next summer full time, so I will be able to continue making a difference with them.

Because of my love for kids, I babysit frequently and volunteer in my church's nursery. I love babysitting and babysit for multiple families. I love working with the younger kids, and it makes my day when they run to the door whenever I ring the doorbell calling out "Miss Sarah!". It confirms to me that I am a positive influence in their lives, which really matters especially when they are learning to make their own decisions. Playing with them and having fun with them is also important. These days, technology often keeps kids inside, and knowing that I could get them outside and active makes a small difference in their lives. When I help out in my church's nursery, I make a difference not only in the child's life by interacting with them and teaching them their faith, but also I affect the families who want to celebrate mass in peace. Teaching a child religion, no matter what faith it is, is beneficial and definitely makes a difference in their lives. Exposure to different faiths can change the morals and life choices that one makes. It also gives a child something to believe in and have faith. It teaches them commitment and exposes them to different cultures of the world. By volunteering in the nursery, I not only make a difference in children's' lives by interaction and positive influence, but also by teaching them faith. For these reasons, I would love to continue babysitting all throughout high school, along with volunteering.

Goals for the Future

For a few years now, I have dreamed of becoming a pediatrician. To me, this is the best way for me to help kids in need after I graduate. I would get to work with kids every day, help them get better and keep them healthy. The job includes regular checkups as well as prescribing medicine when the kids do not feel good, and potentially saving their lives if it is serious. Also, people tend to trust their doctors, and letting a child know that they have someone they can trust is always beneficial. This would make such a difference in their lives, and it would be so fulfilling to me. Knowing that I could help a child feel better from just a little cold, or save their lives from is so important to me. To achieve this goal requires eight years of school after high school graduation and a two year internship. However, even though the process of becoming a pediatrician is hard and long, it is worth it. Saving a child's life and letting them know that they always have someone that they can trust is the biggest difference I feel I can make to not only them, but to their family and friends as well.

Though becoming a pediatrician is my ultimate goal in making a difference in children's lives after I graduate, I have others that are in the nearer future. As I said previously, I would love to volunteer at a children's hospital. This is a step towards my biggest dream of becoming a pediatrician. After I graduate, I will still be young, so I feel like I would be able to bond with kids better. The chance to interact with kids and make them feel emotionally better as well seems like it would help them so much as well as being personally fulfilling. When working with sick kids in a hospital, they most likely want a friend more than anything. Being in a hospital as a young child is scary, and being alone without seeing friends regularly is probably unfamiliar and stressful. The chance to connect with them and make them feel like they are not alone while helping them get better at the same time is a great opportunity to make positive impact on their emotional being. Additionally, working at the hospital would give me more experience in medical treatment as well. This way I can help them become physically better and get more experience so I could be the best pediatrician possible, which in turn offers children the best care I can give them. Overall, volunteering in a children's hospital will not only affect my short term goals of making a difference in children's lives, but also my long term goal.

Another closer goal of mine is to make a difference not only in America, but all over the world. After I graduate from Lassiter, I would love to go on a mission trip out of country to work with kids who are not as fortunate as we are. Some places in the world do not have half the things or comfort that we have in America, and I would love to help those children and give them hope. Sometimes, giving emotional help to kids affects them in the best ways, and I believe that working with kids in less privileged places would inspire them to help others as well. Working with less privileged kids would give both me and them joy, and I feel that it would be a very humbling experience. Making a positive difference in their lives simply by playing, talking, or joking around with them, washing their feet, or cleaning up their community and home would probably mean the world to them. These actions are so small to us, but to kids who grow up with nothing, they offer hope for better things to come.

Why Kids?

All children deserve a chance in life. They are all innocent and so eager to learn that they need positive influences to help guide them so they can become the best people possible. Ultimately by making a difference in kids' lives while they are young, you make a difference in the whole world because eventually they will grow older and hopefully pass on the things that they were taught and shown as they grew. When children are taught right and make good decisions, they are more likely to have a successful life. So, by working with kids, I affect not only their lives at the moment, but also their lives in the long run. Even making the smallest contribution such as reading to them is enough to inspire something inside of them. It is for this reason that my goal is to continue making a difference in children's' lives now, and even more so after I graduate and am able to take it a step further.

Sarah Lezaj – Bio

Sarah Lezaj is a sophomore at Lassiter High School, set to graduate in 2016. She is very involved in both competitive and high school soccer, along with FCA and multiple AP classes. Sarah has always been very interested in writing, and even has an online book that she enjoys writing in her free time. When she isn't playing soccer or studying, Sarah loves to babysit or help out at Roswell Area Park. She is very interested in medicine, specifically pediatrics, and hopes to follow that career path throughout high school and into college.

The Power of a Simple Choice

Caroline Knight

CHAPTER 30 – The Power of a Simple Choice

The Things We Can Change

There are many diagnoses for the problems in our world today. We ask ourselves what we are doing wrong as a whole, and we try to find answers in all the wrong places. We blame scapegoats such as television, government, and celebrity icons. Yes, there are many problems that can be found in each of these categories, but are these things really the root of our problems? What if we look past all the things we cannot control and start looking into the things we can control? We have become so engulfed in others' problems that we have overlooked our own. If each and every one of us took the time to evaluate the most private parts of our minds, to test every value and intention, would we be happy with the results? What problems would we find and how would we fix them? There is a single, common antidote that lies in every single one of us. Not in the way we eat our food, do our hair, or arrange our t-shirt drawer, but in the way we go about thinking. There is one thing we all have in common—the free will in the way we use our minds. I cannot control anyone's mind but my own, but I can say this: if we all had better attitudes, not only would the world be a better place, but there would also be a different way of life everywhere. If we opened our hearts in love rather than in judgment, if our motives were genuine instead of self-serving, if we offered a helping hand rather than a blind eye to the needy, if we did things for the welfare of others rather than the money in our pocket—the world would never be the same. Through values such as honesty, generosity, courage, optimism, and acceptance, we can together make the biggest difference the world has ever known.

The Fire Rages

We live in a world where it is morally acceptable to many to be dishonest. Dishonesty is fueled by selfishness—a destructive fire ignited with one single self-glorifying purpose. This fire rages as more and more people decide it is okay to sacrifice their honor to the shame of being untruthful. This fire rages when we would rather lavish in the pleasures of a cheated victory than face the miseries of the failure that we deserve. This fire rages when we make excuses for the wrongs we commit, no matter the extent. There is pride in an honest lifestyle, and it should be everyone's luxury to know that pride. It was said so long ago by the Greek philosopher Chilon of Sparta, "Prefer a loss to a dishonest gain; the one brings pain at the moment, the other for all time." In other words, desire to earn your rewards, not steal them. It is much more than a victory that is gained from working hard to earn something. If everything we have is truly ours, accomplished through our own sweat and blood, we absolutely deserve everything we have in life. With honesty, we can uncover the true harmony and pride in the life we earn.

Value of Generosity

There is one single thing that can be credited for maintaining the survival of the world in its most dejected places. This one thing gives hope to the helpless and support to the desperate, and it comes from the most gracious, caring people. It is not commonly found, but has tremendous impact in even the smallest cases. This one thing is the value of generosity. To act generously, one must care enough about an issue to where they are willing to put forth their own belongings and ability to help. It is a way to give back to the world. Generosity does not depend on the size of one's wallet, but the size of one's heart. In some cases, it is found that the people with the least give the most while the people with the most give the least. These compassionate people value the lives of others so much that they are willing to sacrifice their comforts for the aid of the less fortunate. These people are absolutely selfless. There also other ways one can be generous without reaching into the pocket. Taking time to volunteer is undoubtedly substantial. Whether it is for a local charity or a simple act of kindness for a neighbor, it is something that everyone is capable of doing. We need to apply ourselves to the good of things other than ourselves, to commit our talents to help the disadvantaged. This should be a priority for everyone. It is said that giving is a gift in itself, and I am a strong believer of that statement. For one to see the benefit of the gift in the life of the acceptor is truly better than any material gift one can receive. The world is absolutely dependent on kindhearted, philanthropic people, for those are the people with the courage to spend time on others rather than themselves that make changes for the better.

The Strength We All Need

Conformity is the chain that keeps us from excelling in our own unique ways. As individuals, we feel the need to remain safely inside our comfort zones—to blend in with our peers. If we blend in, our own specialties will not be known, and the world will never know what we personally have to offer. If we blend in, we stand by and watch as justice is not served to the neglected. If we blend in, we do not live as the people we believe we are in our hearts. In these cases, it takes courage to stand up to conformity. Clearly, no person on this earth is made the same or thinks the same as another. We need the courage to be okay with who we are even if it is different than what is traditional or is considered normal by others. We need the courage to be independent when rejected, proud when degraded, and confident when questioned. With this courage, we can prosper in the ways that are exclusive to our different types of talents. If one has enough nerve to step away from the crowd, half the battle is won. The other half, however, is staying away from the crowd, and that takes the bravery to a whole new level. Peer pressure is one of the hardest things to resist. It is much easier to make a terrible decision if our friends are also contributing, for it is said that misery loves company. Standing up to our friends can be extremely tough. We have to have the courage to be a righteous example for our peers, and the confidence to be sufficient for our own selves. Nothing original and innovative is accomplished as a follower, only as a leader. Have the courage to be the example. Stand up for what you believe in or who you are, not what other people want you to be. If we do not, how will we be proud of the people we are? Have the courage to support the fragile when no one else is. Be there to stand up for someone, even if you are the only one. Immense strength lies with the courage we seek, and it is absolutely necessary we all find it.

A Chance to Improve

About three years ago, I met one very special family that had the absolute best attitude. They instantly stood out to me as people who look at life in a different way than most people do. As I got to know them better, I found that the mother was a twelve-year-and-counting cancer survivor. Every day is an uphill battle for her, and she fights with more courage than I can figure. To this day, she has bravely persevered and is getting through her fifteenth year. This family is an absolute inspiration. They take every negative and turn it into a positive. They go by one dictum, "If you're kind to the world, then the world will be kind to you." This is an interesting thing to think about. Whether or not you agree with the saying, "you get out what you give," I think it is safe to say it raises a good point. If we were all positive and friendly, would we not all receive positive and friendly in return? Positive attitudes are tremendously encouraging, and absolutely contagious. The power of a smile is way too often underestimated. You never know, one smile can change someone's day completely. Be optimistic! Harry S. Truman once said, "A pessimist is one who makes difficulties of his opportunities and an optimist is one who makes opportunities of his difficulties." Life is a two-way street, one way or the other. You can move forward with improvement, or you can go the opposite way in retrogression—your choice. Only with optimism are past mistakes easily forgotten, and a little fire of hope for the future is kindled. Positive people with great attitudes stay happy and see only the joy in life.

Coexisting

The restrictions in our world today can be blamed on one thing—intolerance. When we are closed and opinionated to the point where we cannot accept people, we are limiting ourselves. Not only are we doing ourselves wrong, but also we are obviously doing the individual wrong. We live in a society where people will not display their personal beliefs in fear of being criticized. This fact reflects negatively on each and every one of us. It is sickening that we make people feel lesser because of their differences. We judge because we think that our ways are superior, and what we believe is entirely true. We point fingers people who sin differently than us, and we label them degradingly. We throw blame for our societies problems at people that have different views and ethics. We need to wake up and realize that the problem lies in the fact that we are so selfish that we cannot accept someone because of his or her irregularities. Be open to differences even if you consider them wrong or immoral to your standards, and do not be quick to judge. Too many times people are identified as not worth associating with based on a single characteristic, choice, or fault. The reality of all of it is that we are all the same. Some choose to accept others, and those are the people with the advantage to expand their horizons in knowing and coexisting with various types of people. However others choose to limit themselves to a select few that fit their standards and never know the positives of being around different, unique people. If we accept others, others will accept us. If we change the way we look at the people in this world, we will coexist in harmony, and we will learn to appreciate what each person has to offer despite their differences.

Making a Difference

In order to change this world, we must start with our own selves and make the change in our hearts. If we improve ourselves in each of these ways, the world will on its own change into a better place. How will I, myself make a difference? I will be one of the few to change my ways in the areas I have discussed. Not only for myself—as I will be living a life with good character which is very important to me—but also for others. Because by doing this, I will undoubtedly make a difference, for it is so easy for all of us to do. Also, it is one of my ambitions to create a program focusing on bringing these values to children. Through this program, I will help children by teaching influential decision-making skills, teaching acceptance of themselves and others, leading misguided and underprivileged children to better situations through charity, and giving knowledge of ways to handle tough circumstances with confidence and courageousness. I will bring morals to children by leading by example and showing them that it is beneficial to themselves and everyone around them. We do not need magic to change the world, only the strength to realize where the problems in our world derive. If we take care of ourselves in these ways, we will automatically take care of others and our surroundings. The content of our character is what determines where we go in life and if we will honestly achieve it. Be an example to others. Let the goodness of your heart be a light to your surroundings and an inspiration to your companions. The power to change the world lies solely in the decision. If we choose to change ourselves for the better, we will make a tremendous difference. If we all make this choice, we as a group will transform this world into the greatest it has ever been. It is a simple choice, but we have to be willing to carry it out. We will then find in the power of this simple choice a revolution that will bring us an extraordinary world.

Caroline Knight – Bio

Caroline Knight was born in Georgia in 1998. She lives with her parents and two sisters in Marietta. She is a sophomore at Lassiter High School, and is a very enthusiastic student. She enjoys spending time with her family, playing softball, traveling, reading, and studying. Competing at a very high level in fastpitch softball, she travels with her team to play in tournaments in the spring and summer, and she plays on the Lassiter softball team in the fall. Staying active and fit is one of her most important priorities, and she enjoys running. She participates in the Lassiter Chorus and plays the piano. She attends Johnson Ferry Baptist Church and is very involved in her youth group and both international and domestic missions. Holding a very keen interest in biology and other sciences, she aspires to attend a medical college in the future to pursue her dream of becoming a doctor.

Giving to the Less Fortunate
Varsha Padmanabhan

CHAPTER 31 – Giving to the Less Fortunate

A man comes home from work. He kisses his wife and hugs his children, and then he pulls his wife into the kitchen. He slowly tells her that he got laid off that day and that he is now unemployed. One month later his neighbor sees a foreclosure sign on the man's front yard. Another month later, the neighbor is walking in the street and sees a man in dirty, unkempt clothing holding a sign saying he is unemployed and asking for donations. The neighbor looks at him for a second until he realizes that the man on the street is the old neighbor he used to know. This is the sad story that many Americans are facing today. Millions of people are losing their jobs and their homes due to the economy. The worst part of it all, however, is that their friends and family often stand by and watch, but are unable to help. Poverty rates in America today are steadily growing, and this is an area where I want to make a difference in my community. I would like to motivate my community to help the less fortunate by collecting donations, encouraging volunteer service, and creating employment opportunities.

First, I would like to collect donations for food, clothing, and water, and distribute them to the homeless. These donations would not entirely have to come from generous citizens, however. I have gone to many restaurants in the past, and I have noticed that at the end of the day, all the leftover food gets thrown out. This food is usually perfectly fresh, and can be packaged and shipped to a donation center. To make a difference in my community, I would like to arrange with local restaurants to donate and package leftover food from the end of the day. However, transporting prepared food creates the issue of refrigeration. Due to this, I would like to donate food that does not always require refrigeration, such as many types of bread and other dry foods. Although it may be difficult to donate all leftover food, I believe that even the small donations will make a difference. Then, I would hold collections for non-perishable foods, like canned and packaged food. By collecting and donating this food from all around the community, I believe that I will be able to help those in need.

Next, I would like to hold clothing drives. I know that growing up, I have outgrown quite a lot of clothing. Usually, I like to donate this clothing to a thrift store or charity organization. However, often times my old clothes are handed down to a family friend's daughter, who frankly has enough clothes to begin with. This passing down of clothes happens a lot in society today. Although it is good to give old clothing to a young boy or girl that you know, often times those kids do not need the extra clothing and may not actually wear it. Instead, one should donate their clothing to a young boy or girl who cannot actually afford the clothing he or she needs. I would like to collect some of this old clothing from members of my community and donate it to a children's charity. By doing so, I would not only be helping the child who receives the clothes, but also the parent who no longer has to buy it.

Also, I would like to start a service project to give clean water to people. A surprisingly large number of people do not have access to clean water every day. I could hold collections where people donate bottled water, and I could then get volunteers to help distribute the water to people. Coming from Atlanta, I have seen many homeless people on the streets of the city. If, perhaps on weekends, I could have volunteers each go through various streets of Atlanta and give out free water, I believe I could really help many people. I find it absurd that water is a necessity of life, and yet it costs someone in need four dollars just for a bottle. I know that some people can afford this, but I would like to give water for free to the people that cannot. Recently, I volunteered at an event where parents of less fortunate families could go and get free toys and bikes for their children for Christmas. All the toys were in prime condition, and they were all donated by the community. Many had applied for this, and on the day of it, hundreds of people were lined up outside for hours. Seeing the smile on the parents' faces as they found the perfect gifts inspired me to want to give more to my community. Also, the parents all left with cars full of gifts, and seeing this made me realize how much a small donation from a household can benefit someone else's life. After realizing the impact of a donation, I believe that by getting more people to give, I can make a difference.

In addition, receiving donations will do almost nothing if they are not distributed to the people who need them. However, it is very difficult for one person give out donated items without any help. So, I would like to encourage people in my community to volunteer. To do this, I could spread flyers around notifying people of volunteer opportunities. I could also even create a blog or web page to spread the word. I know many people who want to volunteer and help out, but they do not know how or where to do so. Thus by creating this blog and spreading flyers, I could spread the word of places to volunteer. It is interesting to see how many people who donate items do not know what happens to their things after they donate them. Usually, these items are sent to packaging and distribution centers which many do not know about. However, these centers often do need volunteers to help. So, if one does not have much to donate, they can still help by volunteering at these centers. Since many people do not know about them, I would like to create a website where one can locate the nearest center to them where they can volunteer. By doing so, I believe I can spread the word about volunteer opportunities and encourage people to get involved. Along with at donation centers, individuals can volunteer at many community service places around town. There are many local soup kitchens and homeless shelters that always appreciate extra help. I would like to add these locations to the website so people can know of any volunteer opportunities around them. However, spreading the word about volunteer opportunities may not be enough to encourage people to volunteer. So, I would like to encourage people to volunteer by making it seem more enjoyable to the average citizen. To do so, I could give out prizes or have theme days at certain events. I know that the purpose of volunteering is not to win a gift certificate but rather to help out others, but by giving out prizes, people may become more motivated and excited about volunteering. If I can get more people to volunteer, I can make a significant impact in the lives of many. I know that to truly make a difference, it will take time, but if I start small, eventually the effects will be considerable.

Lastly, I would like to create employment opportunities for those in need. Of course, it would be difficult to give careers to people off the street. However, there are many odd jobs that people need done. I would like to help create an organization that hires unemployed people to do small odd jobs for citizens around the town. I know it would be hard for families to trust a total stranger with babysitting their children, but the people hired could mow lawns, repair small things, paint walls, etc. Proper background checks and identification would be run so the employees could be trusted. I know that by giving small jobs to people I am not fully rebuilding their lives, but by giving small wages, I could help a family who is trying to get back on its feet. For example, while a man is out looking for a job, his wife or teenage son could be planting flowers or trimming bushes in someone else's lawn. I have also seen many volunteer projects where people go out and build houses for the less fortunate. I would like to "flip" this system, and have the unemployed people go to work on building these houses. I would use my organization to ensure that workers would be fully trained and paid proper wages, and I could collect donations and hold fundraisers to help pay these people. Also, I would ensure that all projects abide by state and federal law. I could also start a website where unemployed citizens post profiles of their skills, and when someone would need a job done, they could look on the site for the right worker. Of course, to give employment opportunities to people I would have to start small. However, by opening up a few job opportunities with people I know or who live in my community, I could start to make a change.

Making a difference is something I find very important. The unemployment and poverty rates in America are rising, and many people are still not working to make a change. A few ways I could start to make a change include gathering donations, inspiring volunteer work, and creating employment opportunities. To do any of these things requires a lot of work, and I know that it would be incredibly difficult to make a significant change through these ways. I also know that many of my ideas are very ambitious, and I cannot fund a successful and influential organization in a few days. However, I believe that over time and through small contributions, I can truly make a difference. I would like to work so that the man from the beginning, who represents any unemployed citizen in America, has hope for a better future. This is because I believe that by helping others, we also help ourselves, for we realize that we have achieved something. We have not just won in our smart phone game or received another follower on social media, but we have actually done something worthy of our efforts. We will have actually achieved something significant that will actually make a change. I understand that many have not succeeded in making a lasting change, but I want to work against the odds. I will not look only to the past to define what I can do, but rather to the future where the possibilities are endless and the bar has not been set. It will be a great feat for one person to make a long-lasting impact in the community, but if a great venture does not start with one idea, how will it start at all? I think that I have the power to discover that one idea, for all the great standing wonders of the world all started with an idea. I know that I can succeed because I believe that it only takes one drop to make a wave, and one wave to move the ocean.

Varsha Padmanabhan – Bio

Varsha was born in St. Paul MN but her family moved to Atlanta, GA when she was a month old. She is a sophomore at Lassiter High School. She loves dancing and spending time with her friends and family. She also enjoys performing with the Lassiter Women's chorus.

Improving Your Quality of Life
Erica Jackson

CHAPTER 32 – Improving Your Quality of Life

Although there is good in the world, it is easy to be overwhelmed by the human hatred and violence taking place in our society. One never has to look too far to find violence and it can often be found in our own communities. Throughout my life I have heard stories of children and youth who have been hurt by an adult, a bully, or sometimes even themselves. Knowing this, I feel compelled to defend the vulnerable from these horrors, and if I could change just one child or youth's life for the better, I would be satisfied. But I know I am capable of improving many people's lives, and by doing this, I would be happy.

"Childhood should be carefree, playing in the sun; not living a nightmare in the darkness of the soul." - Dave Pelzer, author of <u>A Child Called "It"</u>

ABUSIVE RELATIONSHIPS WITH ADULTS

On the news we have all heard stories of children living with abusive parents. There is one particular story about a little girl that has stayed with me. This girl's mother would verbally abuse and degrade her by saying things like, "I shall never love you as much as I love your sister." and "We had to pay Santa this year because you have been so rotten." Cruel words to say to anyone, especially a child who had not even started elementary school. Unfortunately she did not just suffer from her mother's sharp tongue. Whenever her parents would be in an especially foul mood, she would be brutally beaten repeatedly and whenever an outsider would inquire about her cuts and bruises, she would cower back in fear and begin to whimper. Locks were even added to multiple interior doors so that she could be confined within various rooms. The horrors did not stop there though. Whenever the parents believed that their little girl should be punished, they would neglect to feed her. This little girl died at the age of five of starvation.

In My Future

Stories like this are often broadcasted on the news or get an article in a newspaper, but the majority of us choose to ignore these nightmares and try to forget that they are some children's realities. The idea that an adult would physically abuse their children appalled me, but encouraged me to find out how I could help children and youth like that little girl who was horribly neglected. An association that my mother is a part of helps set up an annual run for a local nonprofit called the Anna Crawford Children's Center. Having helped out with the run before, I already knew a little about the children's center, but wanted to find out more. So I called the center and was fortunate enough to get an interview with a clinical child specialist. The Anna Crawford Children's Center receives cases from the Department of Family and Children Services and the county's district attorney's office. The victims are brought into their secure location for an interview to retrieve information that may be used in a lawsuit. The Anna Crawford Children's Center provides therapy for the victim as long as it is needed. This special place also offers two types of programs for adults. The first helps parents who have been charged with abuse, so that they can learn to control themselves and maybe one day regain custody of their child. If a child is unable to return to their parents, the center assists with the adoption process so that the child may live with a new, safe family. The second program teaches parents how to keep their children safe from dangerous situations where they could potentially be physically abused. One day, the center is hoping to be able to go into schools to help teach children how to avoid abuse, as well as what to do in case of abuse. One of my goals is to one day work with a nonprofit like the Anna Crawford Children's Center as a psychologist or counselor to help youth and children be safe from abuse.

What I Can Do Now

Donations to organizations like the Anna Crawford Children's Center are always helpful, but as a full time student, financial donations are not always possible. However, after visiting the center, I learned of more ways to volunteer my time and energy through their fundraising activities. Now I know that finding the free time to volunteer can be difficult with the heavy school workload, and extracurriculars, but the Anna Crawford Children's Center, like most other non- profits, has multiple fund raising events where I can easily find one that fits into my schedule. If you too have an interest in finding a local non-profit , all you have to do is go to VolunteerMatch.org where you can find nearly 20,000 non-profit organizations where you too can volunteer your time and talents.

Finding Help

Now what can you do if you are in a situation where you are being abused? Try to find an adult you trust like a teacher, counselor, or someone in your place of worship and tell them about your situation. Then this individual can contact authorities before the situation gets worse.

ABUSIVE RELATIONSHIPS WITH PEERS

Most people can say they have been involved in a bullying situation, either as a victim, a bystander, or as the bully. I personally know what it feels like to be the victim. My first year in high-school started off pretty well. As a social person, I was able to make new friends fairly easily and I enjoyed the overall school experience. Then a girl I previously considered a friend started being rude and outright hateful towards me. This is when my school experience took a turn for the worse. I would carefully avoid this girl, but it was difficult since we had classes together. As I became more and more stressed with this particular relationship, I started to have trouble in my classes. I became so angry for allowing this relationship to have such a negative impact on me that my anger morphed into depression. At this point, I began to move away from some of my other friends so that I could avoid the bully, and what hurt me almost as much as the bully did was that none of my closest friends noticed my changed behavior or showed that they cared. However, my mom noticed the changes in my behavior and these included;

- Feeling sick
- Not wanting to go to school
- Confused emotions of anger
- Unexplained tears

I felt so alone and helpless. Having classes with the bully, it was impossible to avoid her forever so I went with advice that I had heard as a young child; Treat others the way you want to be treated.   So that's what I did, and I didn't try to be good friends with her, just nice whenever our paths happened to cross. This worked for me, but for a lot of people this doesn't work. Most importantly, I recommended you find someone to talk to about the situation in order to prevent from feeling alone in your struggles.   For me, that person was my mom.

In My Future

Unfortunately, bulling does not appear to be a problem that will disappear. To help kids who find themselves in a situation with a bully or even as a bully, I might one day want to be a school counselor. I did some research online and got some information on how counselors address bullying situations on kidshealth.org. When made aware of a bullying situation, as a counselor I would speak with the victim on strategies to deal with the bully. I could also speak with bystanders and the bully to see multiple perspectives of the situation. I would alert teachers and parents of the situation and share information with the appropriate individuals or authorities if fearful for a student's safety.

What I Can Do Now

As a youth, there are some things that I can do to help individuals that are being bullied. In school, we have been taught what to do as a bystander.

Don'ts:

- Do not join in on the bullying
- Do not encourage the harassment

Do's

- Try to distract the bully to turn their attention away from the victim
- Support the victim privately
- Support the victim publicly
- Confront the bully's poor behavior

Finding Help

If you are being bullied, remember not to emulate the bulling behavior. You can try what I did and be kind to the bully or simply ignore the person. If this does not work, you need to let someone know so that you can have a support system. It is critical that you do not feel alone during this time for things can get bad quickly.

SELF ABUSE

The two previous types of abusive relationships could possibly lead to self-harm, but there are other reasons that people feel like they have to hurt themselves as well. When you don't feel good about yourself, it's easy to take the anger that you have, and use it to hurt yourself. If done enough, your brain becomes trained to release chemicals called endorphins which make you feel better. This is how addictions start. People begin to associate self-harm with feelings of calm and relief that come from the endorphins. This happens all the time in our society, probably even to someone you know. There was a story that I read in a newspaper about a boy who loved his big sister. The sister was depressed and decided that the best way to escape the pain was to take her life. This had a huge impact on the little boy who had so admired his sister. Her decision made him depressed as well, which he associated with weakness. So he decided to become angry because that was better than feeling weak. Needing to release the anger but not wanting to hurt anyone else, he began to cut himself. After doing this for a while, he lost all emotion and his motives for cutting changed. Instead of trying to relieve anger, he simply wanted to feel something. This however was only a temporary solution, for he would begin to feel guilty for cutting which would add to his depression and return the impulse to cut, forming a vicious cycle. This little boy grew into a troubled teenager and followed his sister's footsteps. He killed himself at the age of fifteen.

In My Future

When I grow older, I would like to try to help others that feel the need to self-harm. As a neuropsychologist, I could learn how certain chemicals like endorphins are triggered, what they do, and how to control the timing of their releasing.

What I Can Do Now

Now, all I can do to help out people like that little boy is to be a good friend. A listening ear can really mean a lot to someone who is depressed. Listening helps them know that they are not alone and are cared for. As a good friend though, you take partial responsibility for that person's safety. If you are afraid for their safety or even life, you need to let an adult who also cares for them know.

Finding Help

Suicide can sometimes seem like the easiest solution or even only solution to someone suffering from depression, but it never is. No matter how bad a situation seems to be, it can and will get better, sometimes it just takes some time. You have to remember that each day provides a new opportunity to make life better and that the decision to take your life not only affects you, but everyone you love as well. One way to kick out depression is with a change in diet or exercise. Talking with friends or relatives can also be helpful when trying to find solutions to problems. Often severe depression requires professional help from a psychiatrist, psychologist, or counselor. These professionals have a lot of training and experience in helping people with life problems.

My Calling

I feel that my goal in life is to have a positive impact on as many people as I can, and although I may not be able to improve everyone's life, if I could do something as small as make someone smile, it will mean that I am one step closer to making a difference, but I know that I am capable of more than simply making one person smile. I want to help children and youth in dangerous relationships whether they are with an adult, a peer, or themselves. Knowing about the experiences of others along with my own encourages me to take a stand and pursue a career in counseling or psychology, but I can do things now to help prepare me for those careers. Besides volunteering at non-profits, I can simply be a compassionate person, and that is my challenge to you. Stand up for the vulnerable, be a supportive friend, and as Mahatma Ghandi said, "Be the change that you want to see in the world."

Erica Jackson – Bio

Erica Jackson was born in Marietta, Georgia and is currently a Lassiter High School honors student. At this time, she is a part of the Renaissance leadership team in her school which provides opportunities for students to develop strong leadership skills. She also volunteers her time with an annual fundraiser for the Anna Crawford Children's Center for abused children. Her other volunteer activities include assisting with the Special Populations Tennis Program which helps children and young adults with disabilities develop skills and a love for tennis. She enjoys playing the viola and has had the privilege to be first chair in one of her high school's orchestras. She also plays viola in a small ensemble group which performs in the community. Erica assists in leading children's worship and has been training to become a counselor at a Christian camp over the summer. Some of her hobbies include traveling, photography, reading, watching old movies, and listening to various types of music.

The Power of Reading
Luke Bentley

CHAPTER 33 - The Power of Reading

In American society today, the power of reading is underappreciated. Hopefully, this chapter will aid in seeing its importance and what can be done to change its negative connotation. I will make a difference in how reading is viewed, show why it is beneficial, and provide solutions that will improve the state it is in today.

A Look at the Reading Condition within Education

The first and more minor reason many dislike reading is because of language arts teachers and their decision makers. That's right, I'm calling out some of my favorite teachers, because in many cases, school makes students detour from out of school reading, and take another route. Now this is the defense- not everybody likes the same books, so a general book, as a compromise to everybody must be chosen. So, most often, the teacher is not passionate about the book they are teaching, and this lack of enthusiasm is put upon the students. How can students be expected to like something when even the teacher enforcing this assignment is unhappy about it? Another problem with these, "General," books is that sometimes they are repeated. For example, I liked the book, *Al Capone Does My Shirts*, the first time it was an in-class read. Hell, I liked it the second time. But by golly, the third time it rolled around, there was no way I would read it, for I basically knew it cover to cover. So I did what every delinquent reader would do in my situation. I opened the required book on my desk, had my friend, Travis, flip the pages every few minutes, and I'd read my own book below the desk. Books that are chosen every year, year after year, are not only unappetizing, they turn students away. My peers say similar things, all adding up to, "I used to like to read for pleasure, but required reading ruined it for me." There is a reason that the sentence, "Students, we have a book report coming up," is the bane of classrooms from 1st grade to senior year. The books just aren't cutting it.

Issues Sprouting from Our Culture

The other and major problem people have with reading is that it goes completely against the impulsive and answer-needy society we have today. When you pick up a book and read the first chapter, it's already about how it ends. Nobody values the journey anymore- it's all about the destination. This problem has its roots in the endless struggle between instant and delayed gratification. A book is the latter. Usually, a book takes weeks to finish, and the problem is solved near to the end. Therefore, it takes a while to get the treat of a conclusion, but once you get there, the work is justified. If we liken this gratification to candy, it would be a king-size Snickers bar. There is a certain pride that comes with finishing a weighty book. Conversely, things like TV shows, especially sit-coms, are instant gratification, and take no work at all. The catch is, the satisfaction gained is much lower, for there is no hubris that comes from sitting on a couch and watching last night's recorded show. In the candy metaphor, this satisfaction would be an after dinner breath mint- sweet, but barely mentionable. Comparing the payoff of delayed versus instant gratification; it's hard to see why anyone would choose instant. That's where our culture has to be addressed. This philosophy we have, in which we're always looking to make a quick buck, or find the shortest route is as

American as baseball. Fortunately, to show which gratification is more beneficial, Stanford University and Walter Mischel did a study on the two types of gratification, and it went like this. It was called the, "Marshmallow Experiment," and pre-school kids were given a choice between one marshmallow immediately, or two marshmallows in fifteen minutes. The kids were then studied ten and twenty years later. The teens that had chosen to wait fifteen minutes in pre-school had higher SAT scores, better planning skills, were better able to cope with stress, and were rated more mature by their parents. Teens who had taken the immediate mallow were more aggressive and had higher levels of hyperactivity. As adults, those who waited had lower levels of divorce, and were less likely to be overweight or have drug problems. Obviously, there are advantages to being patient. I believe that through reading, a greater appreciation for delayed gratification is obtained, and the spoils as well.

Benefits of Reading

Now that we've seen reasons for the decline in reading, it's important to see the benefits of reading, why it is such a big deal-

Immediately, a wider vocabulary is developed. One's vocabulary has a great influence on one's life. Many judgments, positive and negative, are made on our articulation and word choice. It is also important to be able to convey emotions, an area in which many people, especially teens, have trouble. So, it makes sense that every possible aid be pursued. An easily accessible opportunity in this area is simply to read. I can remember reading many words before I ever heard them. Sure, this meant that in second grade, or so, I said words like "colonel" and "melancholy" completely wrong (and let's be honest, colonel should sound like the body organ and not a piece of corn), but this also meant I knew words like "colonel," and "melancholy" as a seven year old! This, however, is only one advantage of reading.

Another plus of reading is the learning of life lessons. For instance, take *Aesop's Fables*, the collection of short stories, where each selection has a specific moral. This is the source of, "The Tortoise and the Hare." If everybody read this medley of morals as a young child, we would have an base level understanding of truths, such as, "Slow and steady wins the race." Many teachings can be found in a whole range of books. From standing up for the weak in *To Kill a Mockingbird*, to female empowerment in *The Hunger Games*, to believing in one's self in *Oh, The Places You'll Go*. Regardless of what book is read, there is bound to be an ethical schooling buried in it somewhere.

An additional aspect is the intellectual gain. The more you read, the more information goes into your noggin and up goes your knowledge. The more knowledge you have, the easier everyday life becomes. For example, it is much easier to converse with someone wearing a triathlon shirt when it's known that it refers to the 3-part athletic event requiring you to swim, to bike, and to run. As well as knowledge, reading has a positive effect on intelligence. The SAT, an intelligence-based test is run by The College Board, who suggests extensive reading outside of class to improve test scores. Bottom line, if you read more, you've got a better chance of getting into a prestigious college and having a high intellectual quotient.

Finally, reading is entertaining. It can take you away to lands only meant for dreaming, or to lives worth observing. Losing yourself in a book is a great experience, one that surpasses that of a movie or a TV show. With books, it's an interactive entertainment, where the reader gets to decide their feelings on a character or a situation, and create them in your mind. Imagination has free reign. It's one of the oldest forms of fun, and there's a reason it has been around for so long. While reading, all worldly cares are taken away, and it is a reprieve from mundane responsibilities. It's a stress-free environment that can still make your blood pump and your emotions respond. These are only a handful of reasons why reading is important, and there are many others.

Luke Bentley and Reading, the Best of Friends

Before the end, I'd like to share my story, and why I'm so in favor of reading-

From a young age, I enjoyed books read to me by my mother, and from then on, books were always available to me. I used to get in trouble during grade school for setting my alarm clock to 4 am, just so I could read before school. Everywhere I went, I read. The size of my vocabulary was quite large for my young age. This gave me many opportunities, such as having older friends, and being able to talk my way out of trouble. When you can talk intellectually and humorously, people will listen, so I got to be heard. I kept reading. When I started holding conferences with my teacher during kindergarten nap time about books we had read, I would spend the whole naptime in these conferences. I hated nap time, so this was a good deal. I kept reading. Eventually, when grammar, spelling, and writing assessments appeared in school, I never had to worry. Because I read so much, these assignments made sense. This is still true today. I kept reading. Throughout middle school, reading was my refuge from boredom and bullies. I kept reading. Now, as I'm starting to take SAT and ACT tests, the amount of reading is a big advantage. So trust me, it's worth the time and the late nights of page-turning fun. I can't imagine where I'd be without it. I'm glad to say that reading is my passion, and it could be yours too.

Solutions to the Sad State of Reading in Schools

Solutions to the aversion to reading in schools are easy-peasy lemon-squeezy. First, teachers must have the freedom to choose books they are passionate and enthusiastic about teaching, which will increase their student's excitement. Secondly, reading time must be treated like a valuable gift, instead of a death sentence, as it is viewed in middle and high school. I remember in elementary school, many students' favorite time of the day was D.E.A.R. time. This stood for Drop Everything and Read. Another opportunity for the proliferation of reading includes all teachers encouraging reading when work in their classwork is completed. The fact that school is actually turning people away from reading is frightening to me, and hopefully, through these solutions, school and books can enter into a long term, amicable relationship.

Wrap-up to the Cultural Calamity

If books are introduced to young kids when they are still obedient, as opposed to stubborn teens, they will finish the books to make teachers and parents happy. After this, they should and will find that sense of earned satisfaction and pride that comes along with the sweet jumbo chocolate bar that is a story's conclusion. So what happens, if you're a teen or adult, and this chance has already passed? Honestly, this is the tougher, football-coach solution. Suck it up, and get through it. Yes, I know, reading, especially required reading, can be boring, but there are ways to alleviate that hardship while pushing to the end. First, find a book that suits you. Don't choose a book because it's on the bestseller list, choose one that interests you. Find a book based on what you like and is at your level. Also, find somebody to read with. Not physically, just the same book. My dad, who hasn't read since college, recently started reading the same books that I read for class, because it's fun for us to discuss the story, and it helps us get through the less dynamic sections. Third, get into your book. Let yourself be completely absorbed in foreign lands it takes you to, become friends with the protagonist, and hate the villain. Another tip, keep your book with you as much as possible. Many opportunities arise during the day to slip in a few pages, such as downtime in class, or as a substitute to counting sheep, or simply waiting for anything. These things can help in getting through the first book, and once done with that the satisfaction comes. And then, there are no limits or boundaries on what can be read. Go crazy! Try a four-incher, or a ten-fonter. It's worth it. That's all that can be said. Enjoying a good read is like the movie *Inception*. You just don't get it until you watch, or in this case read, twice. That's the answer to starting a reading passion.

Ultimate Notes

Finally, to sum up my thoughts, reading is an important, life-affirming, enriching experience. Break the chains of society and taste that delayed gratification. It will make a positive difference in your life. It can improve your behavior, improve academic achievement, and improve your state of happiness. Sometimes it will be difficult, but there's nothing like the feeling of polishing off another novel. I think it's best to leave you with this thought- Imagine reading as the first step in a Rube Goldberg machine: It is a switch for many things to occur, and once triggered, those benefits will make themselves known. All you have to do is enjoy the journey. And, oh yeah, read.

Luke Bentley – Bio

Luke Hansen Bentley hails from Roswell, Georgia, and is a sophomore at Lassiter High School. He is very involved in his school, as well as his community. Luke is a proud member of the Lassiter Trojan Marching Band and Symphonic Band, spending many of his afternoons and weekends rehearsing. An avid percussionist, he is also part of the Lassiter High School Percussion Ensemble and drum line. This year, he auditioned and made the Georgia All-State band. He is also a part of Lassiter's Math Team, Model U.N. Club, Academic Bowl Team, Track and Field Team, and FCA. Luke is currently a nominee for the 2014 Governor's Honors Program in the area of communicative arts, one of his many interests. Achievements in school include highest GPA in his freshmen class, multiple highest average awards, and an Academic letter. Eager to learn, Luke is taking an extra class this year, Comparative Religions in his first semester. Recently, Luke has become a staff writer for *The Laureate*, Lassiter's very own newspaper. Outside of school, Luke is an active Boy Scout, and enjoys helping with service projects, camping, and, of course, doing a good turn daily. Luke can be found almost anywhere on the weekend- running a 5k or sprint triathlon with his dad or brother, spending time with good friends, boating, and often, curled up with a good book. It's hard to exaggerate Luke's fascination with all things literature. Since childhood, he has been staying up late, getting up early, procrastinating, and simply wiling away the hours with his nose buried deep in a thick book. Consequences of this are predominately positive, but he also has found himself using a book for a pillow and reading in an abandoned classroom after an unheeded bell. Luke is also very interested in sports, both watching and participating in them. He is one of the Michigan State Spartan's biggest fans, and loves to watch their football and basketball teams. He has competed in a long list of sports, such as football, fencing, lacrosse, soccer, and he now throws shot-put, discus, and the hammer. A main influence on Luke comes from his family. Starting with his nuclear family, he has supportive and caring and goal-driven parents that have pushed Luke to obtain his goals since day one. He has an older sister and brother who have helped teach him the laws of the land and always have his back. Spreading further out into his family, he has received life lessons from each and every one of them- his grandparents down to his youngest second cousin. He also receives much support and inspiration from his close-knit friend group. Luke really believes that a strong family and circle of friends leads to a strong person, and therefore is very appreciative of his own. Luke's main motto is that knowledge can be gained from anyone anywhere, and that it's important to take an opportunity to learn whenever possible. In a nutshell, Luke Hansen Bentley is a passionate lover of knowledge and learning.

Enviro-Girl
MacKenna Butler

CHAPTER 34 – Enviro-Girl

My deep passion for animals sparked when I was just three-years-old. My family and I were staying at an overnight African-themed zoo in Michigan. After fumbling out of my rainbow snail sleeping bag at dawn, everyone else and I walked over to a bridge and watched about eight or ten hyenas laugh their way out onto the open plain. Then the real fun began. Feeding giraffes! I still love to watch the video of myself doing this because it is such a great memory and hilarious to see three-year-old me with bright blonde hair jumping up and down, giggling, and being way more excited than most people get! Giraffes today remain my second favorite animal (between leopard seals and West Indian manatees) and their print can even be found on a pair of my sunglasses!

However, I have never intended to work with giraffes. My passion for countless years has been marine zoology and environmental conservation. Too many species have become extinct and are endangered. This is due to mainly direct and indirect human contact with the environment. Homo sapiens sapiens (the current human species) have been polluting the earth since the invention of fire over an eon ago. One of my dreams is to reduce the size of the amount of toxins that are added on to earth's carbon footprint per year to ensure that future generations will be able to prosper in a way like we do today.

The Struggle to "Go Green"

I do not want a world of gadgets and gizmos to ever control us unless everything is wind, water, and solar powered and creates no pollution. This way we would be using clean and natural energy with no toxin production and release, allowing little to no pollution, helping our environment in ways people today can only imagine. If technology is moving anywhere, it should be in this direction.

In Walt Disney's EPCOT (Environmental Prototype City of Tomorrow), Siemens is a large sponsor of rides, such as Spaceship Earth, and Illuminations, the nightly show at nine pm. They are a power company who are experimenting with ways to spread clean energy worldwide. The thing is, Illuminations is a colossal fireworks display and fireworks are one of the worst pollutants out there! When you sponsor a green and clean planet as well as a large contributor to the earth's carbon footprint, how much do you really care about the environment? This is a situation in which many companies and ordinary people fall in to. As usual, my advice is, "Go green!"

Sirenia Order

Marine zoologists do not usually do everything in their field. So, I have chosen to focus on the Sirenia order, which consists of the trichechidae family (the West Indian, West African, and South American manatee) and the dugongidae family (the dugong and the extinct Steller's sea cow). However, I will discuss mainly the West Indian manatee.

There are approximately 2,640 West Indian manatees left. That is less than the polar bear, Sumatran orangutan, cheetah, snow leopard, and the white rhinoceros, just to name a few. Their population is declining by nine to 20 percent each year; 16 percent in 2013. Unfortunately, the population sizes for the other living Sirenia are unknown. However, scientists do know that at least the South American manatee population is decreasing. All can be found of the IUCN (International Union for Conservation of Nature) red list under "vulnerable."

    Every member of the Sirenia order, with the exception of the Steller's sea cow, is on the endangered species list. The West Indian manatee (located from the coast of Brazil to North Carolina) population, at least, is significantly impacted thanks to human interactions with the environment. Humans litter, go speed boating through and around manatee zones, poach manatees, and more. If you got to places where people can see manatees, you can spot speedboat injuries in abundance. Most are just scars, but a SeaWorld Orlando there is an adult female manatee with no right flipper. In Walt Disney's EPCOT there is a manatee found in The Living Seas building that is missing more than half of their tail. The threat of humans poaching manatees is very real. It is part of the ancient Amazonian culture to hunt and kill the South American manatee. Apparently their meat is "delicious." Manatees are legally protected mammals as well, which causes the value of their meat to be through the roof! Some other human-related causes of death are entanglement in fishing lines and nets, being crushed by flood gates and canal locks, and fishing hooks. Natural causes of death include cold stress, red tide, gastrointestinal disease, pneumonia, and so on. Cold stress is when the water becomes even a few degrees colder than usual. The colder water causes "a cascade of physiological events and diseases."[1] Manatees are not yet able to adapt to temperatures below approximately 70 degrees Fahrenheit. The symptoms are a slowed metabolism, which triggers weight loss, decreased appetite, and digestion problems, and a weakened immune system. In early 2010, at least 193 manatees died from cold stress. Red tide is when there is a bloom of a certain species of toxic, usually micro, organisms. This causes illness among manatees, eventually leading to death like in the 2013 case where at least 170 manatees were found dead due to red tide. Manatees are expected to live approximately 60 years. However, today in the wild manatees are lucky to live past 30.

After being discovered in 1741, the Steller's sea cow became extinct by 1768. They were about eight to nine meters in length, more than two meters broad, located in the Bering Sea, and was a subspecies of the dugongidae family in the Sirenia order. They were discovered by Georg Wilhelm Steller who was aboard the St. Peter when is became separated from the St. Paul during a storm in the Bering Sea and inhabited what is today known as Bering Island. Steller and the remaining crew survived for a year while rebuilding the St. Peter on the meat of Steller's sea cow. New spread about the scrumptious meat of these animals, whose population then was estimated at about 1,500, and annual hunts went out. This eventually led to their extinction in 1768.

Many people, including myself, deeply care about the Sirenia order! To get involved and help, contact the local government of whichever region you wish where manatees or dugongs dwell and express you concern. For West

Indian manatees try Florida's governor and/or a U.S. senator or representative, preferably from Florida. You can also spread the word, not litter, educate yourself even further, not fish in manatee zones, not poach manatees, participate in beach clean-ups, not 10 miles per hour in watercraft around manatee zones, and so much more! Maybe even become an adult or youth volunteer at your local aquarium or zoo! There is more than you think out there to do, so go out and do it!

My high school science courses include a mixed topics year in ninth grade, Advanced Placement (AP) biology in tenth grade, (hopefully) AP chemistry and zoology in eleventh grade, and (hopefully) AP Physics and AP Environmental Science my senior year! I hope to go to one of the best schools for marine biology/marine zoology when I leave for college. These schools include Stanford University, University of British Columbia, Simon Fraser University (British Columbia), Newcastle University (England), University of Hull (England), and University of Tasmania (Australia). All of these are in locations I love (even though the only place of these which I have been to is Hobart, Tasmania) and offer bachelor programs which target environmental sciences and/or genetics and evolution on top of marine biology/marine zoology. All of them are located near a coast and offer many field research opportunities as well! I am still looking though, as any sophomore in high school is!

At my new school in Marietta, Georgia I participate in Academic Bowl, where I can practice working my mind quickly as well as teach and learn new thing related to science and a wide range of other topics, Model United

Nations, where in the 2014 Kennesaw State University conference I am representing the People's Democratic Republic of Algeria in the United Nations Educational Scientific and Cultural Organization's committee, and the Lassiter High School chapter of the Science National Honor Society (SNHS). I go to science days at a local elementary school with others from my chapter of the SNHS to teach children about all different kinds of science out there and have fun while doing it. I also participate in park clean up days and tutor my friends for free. When I turn 16 in April I can start volunteering at the animal shelter (without an adult with me) and become an adult volunteer at the Georgia Aquarium, the largest aquarium (by gallons of water) in the world! Both of these I shall eagerly take up! I have been mentioned on Twitter by people such as WWF! I also run a Tumblr blog called Enviro Girl where I inform people about environmental situations, careers in environmental fields, such as environmental engineering and marine biology, how to go green, and tips on being a vegetarian as well as sharing beautiful pictures and reblogging from people like WWF and Ellen DeGeneres! It is such an amazing feeling whenever I log on to see that more people have checked out my page and have commented, reblogged, and favorited something of mine! I recently went through my last round of interviews (this one was state-wide) for the Governor's Honors Program (only available to high school sophomores and juniors in Georgia) where I plan on spending four weeks of summer 2014 at Valdosta State University majoring in biology. There I can collaborate with other students and professors who love biology like I do and even conduct and independent research project! I have also been a vegetarian for about six years and am a budding humanitarian! This is just the beginning of my impact on the world!

Through seventh, ninth, and tenth grade (I skipped eighth) I lived just outside of Sydney, Australia in a suburb named Mosman. Mosman holds arguably the best zoo in Australia (which has a branch in Dubbo, New South Wales, Australia) called Taronga Zoo. Not only is it large, outdoors, well organized, and is home to an abundant amount of species, but it has a spectacular view of Sydney Harbor, a Great Southern Oceans area, and a renowned adult and youth volunteer program! I myself was a Youth at the Zoo member for the two years in which I was eligible! In the program I was able to take classes on endangered species, ancient Aboriginal life, animals husbandry, careers, where we met people who worked around the zoo (I went three times before meeting a marine biology staff member!), and so much more! I could even take care of certain exhibits for a few hours, monitor animal behavior, work with the children's day program, and help promote campaigns throughout the zoo! Don't even get me started on the time I got to enter the lion enclosure! I also represented Mosman High School with a few other students at Taronga Zoo's EnviroForum 2013! These are just two major things which I did while living in Australia that changed my life!

When I grow up I will be satisfied not working with manatees or dugongs as long as I am still a marine biologist, spreading the word and making a difference! I could work at SeaWorld, Marine Institute Ireland, Florida Fish and Wildlife Research Institute, becoming a professor in environmental conservation, marine biology, or zoology, or something else, like joining an organization such as the

IUCN or the Save the Manatee Club. My ultimate dreams are to open up a manatee and other marine mammals research and rescue center, most likely to be located in Florida, and to reduce the amount of toxins added to the earth's carbon footprint per year, hopefully ultimately making a better name for my generation! It also would not hurt to take the remaining Sirenia order off of the endangered species list as well!

****

Countless environmental matters, such as Earth Overshoot Day (when earth will run out of natural resources), are not publicized on television, in newspapers, in magazines, or on the radio. I found out about it via WWF's Twitter page. Did you know that humans are currently using a year's production of natural resources in eight months? I bet that that is new to you. Educating is part of making a difference in the world. People have to know what is going on around them before they know to take action. Try hosting an environment day at any local public building, beach, or park. Maybe set up a fundraiser at an ice skating rink, bowling alley, or ice cream parlor. Imagine how much cleaner the ocean and beaches would be if every time you or someone else goes to the beach, you or they will pick up at least two pieces of litter. There is a whole world of opportunities just sitting out there waiting to be spotted and taken up by you. Use them! So, whether you like snakes or penguins, zooplankton or elm trees, do something about it, because you can bet your bottom dollar that I will be!

[1] www.sciencedaily.com/releases/2003/08/030805071937.htm

MacKenna Butler – Bio

MacKenna Butler is currently a sophomore attending Lassiter High School in Marietta, Georgia. She was born in Granger, Indiana in April 1998 and moved to St. Peter's Village (near Pottstown), Pennsylvania and attended French Creek Elementary School and Owen J Roberts Middle School. She left OJR in seventh grade and moved to Sydney, Australia, living in Neutral Bay and Mosman and attended Mosman High School for the remainder of seventh, ninth, and a term of tenth grade (she skipped eighth). MacKenna moved to Georgia in July 2013. While living in Australia MacKenna participated in Youth at the Zoo and her schools Enviro Club. She runs the Enviro Girl Tumblr blog, volunteers at park clean-ups, and is a member of the Lassiter chapter of the Science National Honor Society. MacKenna has multiple accomplishments in music and athletics as well, including being chosen to sing with her Australian high school on a music tour around Italy and Austria and is a two-time national champion cheerleader. She has big plans for her future that involve changing the world!

Random Acts of Kindness
Stephanie Lilly

CHAPTER 35 – Random Acts of Kindness

"Unless someone like you cares a whole awful lot, nothing is going to get better. Its not."

Dr. Seuss

Can's help but smile

Everyone has bad days. Sometimes the slightest thing can set you off for no logical reason. Now imagine you are having one of those days. Your alarm didn't go off so you were late to school. Then you got yelled at in front of the entire class for your tardiness. After that, you found out you failed a math test. Now picture yourself walking through the halls with all your books and someone inconsiderate bumps into you, and of course everything flies out of your hands and all over the hallway. This day just keeps getting worse and worse. Then, out of nowhere, a perfect stranger starts picking up your things for you. Even after everything that has happened, you can't help but smile. That person did not have to help you, but they did. And they did it out of the kindness of their heart without seeking any sort of personal gain. This small act of kindness turns your whole day around and suddenly your horrific morning doesn't even matter.

Random acts of kindness, in my opinion, make all the difference. It's the little things that matter. If everyone takes it upon himself or herself to be nice to others, whether its something big or small, we could easily change the world. It could be a small gesture such as holding the door open for someone. If you are feeling more ambitious, you can pay for a stranger's meal or go sit with someone at lunch that is alone. Another option is volunteering to help in a soup kitchen or donating your hair to locks for love. Big or small, any contribution makes an impact.

People in society today are very self-centered. They are so busy looking out for themselves that caring for others is no longer a priority. The world will be a better place when we all start looking out for others. I can make a difference by being kind and doing all that I can to remove some of this selfishness from my own life. And hopefully I'll eliminate selfishness in others. The best way to accomplish this goal is through random acts of kindness. The mentality of self-preservation above everything else is ruining the world.

Changing the World Has to Start Somewhere

I got my idea for this chapter when I was watching the movie version of <u>The Lorax</u> by Dr. Suess. Spoiler alert! I don't want to ruin this but the premise of the story is that there is a town called Thneedville. The entire town is made of plastic and rubber, nothing is natural. In fact, they even sold fresh air. The main character in the story, Ted, has a crush on a girl who wants to see trees, Audrey. So he sets out to find one. All he wants to do is make the girl of his dreams happy with something as simple as finding a tree, which is a small act of kindness for her. Along the way his act of kindness became more difficult as people tried to stop him. But he persevered and ended up planting a tree and changing the whole town. His determination to find a tree to make Audrey started out as a little gesture, but ended up being something much more monumental and important. Changing the world has to start somewhere and usually, it starts as something small.

You never know when someone is feeling down and a simple compliment could brighten his or her whole day. When you are nice, people are more likely to be nice to you. That, in turn, makes them more likely to be nice to other people. A sort of chain reaction occurs. In fact, Princess Diana once said "Carry out a random act of kindness, with no expectation of reward, safe the knowledge that one day someone might do the same for you". Lets say you go out of your way to be nice to two people. Then, those two people are each nice to two other people and so on. This network of good deeds takes very little effort from each individual person yet so many people are touched by it.

There is a club that I'm a part of at my high school that is called P.A.N.T.S., which stands for People Acting Nicely Throughout Schools. The goal of this organization is to make the school a happier place with random acts of kindness. We accomplish this in many different ways such as leaving positive notes around the school for anyone to find or baking cookie or cupcakes for the janitors and bus drivers as a thank you. These things may seem silly but they were easy to do and made a huge impact.

I have experienced all of this first hand. One day I was having one of those bad days. I studied really hard for a huge test all night in order to bring up my grade only to find that I studied the wrong chapter. On top of that, I got in a fight with my mom on the way to school that morning and I knew that when I got home from school she would ground me. I was sitting in chorus class dreading the day ahead of me when I glanced down at the floor and saw a little purple piece of paper. I picked it up with the intention of throwing it away but I noticed there was a note scribbled on the back that simply said "Smile Jesus love you :)". I had no idea who wrote it, and I still don't know but it made me cheered me up. Why did I let all my petty pointless problems get to me? In hindsight, none of that mattered. I put that little sticky note in my folder so that I would see it everyday and be reminded to smile, because I am loved. Whenever I was upset or stressed or angry I could look at that note and instantly feel better. On the last day of class when we were cleaning out our folders I saw my little note and decided it was someone else's turn to enjoy the uplifting feeling it brings. So that day I put the note somewhere in the school. I can't remember exactly where but I can only hope someone found it and appreciated it as much as I did. This happened two years ago and I still remember it. It must have taken someone less than a second to write down those four simple words on a sticky note but I'll remember that little note forever.

Making a difference doesn't mean you have to cure cancer or solve world hunger. Doing something small for someone else can only take a second but it may have a lasting impact on a person's life. If boys ever wonder why girls appreciate it so much when they open doors for us or give up their seat for us, its because it shows that they care. Everyone wants to matter to somebody, even if it's a stranger. Some people even end their lives because they feel as though they don't matter and a random act of kindness could save them. It is impossible to know what others are going through. People often hide their emotions so you can never tell who needs your kindness. But you never know when you can save a life. We've all heard stories of people who are contemplating ending their lives and then, somebody does something nice for them or even just smiles at them, and they decide not to do it. So why not extend a smile to a stranger? Its crazy to think about how something as simple as that could make the difference between life and death. Nothing but good things will come from that simple gesture. Some people may shy away from things like this because they are embarrassed or afraid that someone will judge them. If someone thinks you are "weird" for being nice, you should feel bad for them.

"Smile..."

I think it's really tragic that being mean, to appear cool in front of your peers, is the norm in society today. People are so unnecessarily cruel to one another. Teenage girls especially are terrible to each other for no good reason besides their own insecurity. Sometimes the most significant acts of kindness are the ones that nobody sees. For example, if your friends are gossiping and talking bad about someone behind their back you have the choice to not participate. Or better yet, you can put an end to it and change the subject. The person who was unfortunate enough to be the subject of the gossip may never know that you stood up for them. But that's the whole point. Do the right thing because you know it's the right thing, not because you want recognition. When we remove this hate from our lives, we will all become better, happier human beings.

Being kind isn't limited to being nice to others, it can also mean being kind to you. What I mean by that is that in order to reach your full potential, you need to not be critical of yourself and treat yourself the way you would want others to treat you. Some people may say that this is the most important thing you can do. Believe in yourself. Do not look in the mirror and notice all of your flaws. Instead notice all of your good qualities, not only in appearance but also in your heart. Would you want to be friends with someone who judges you as harshly as you judge yourself? I know I wouldn't. So cut yourself a break every once in a while, you'll be much happier for it. When I was an awkward middle schooler I would have those days where I'd feel really insecure. In order to get over that terrible feeling I would make a list of all my good qualities and all of the things in my life I had going for me. It made me feel a whole lot better about myself and I could look back at that list if I every felt like that again.

When you're old and gray, sitting in your rocking chair on the front porch looking back at your life, you will not remember everything. You will only sit back and think about the important stuff in your life; the things that shaped who you are. You will remember the people who were good to you. The little moments that made all the difference. You will recall the positive people who picked you up when you were down and helped you through hard times. The people who went out of their way to help you, even when they did not have to. Those people are the ones that matter. Every one of us should make it our goal to be one of those people. Try to be the kind of person that impacts people's lives for the better without expecting anything in return.

A Little Goes A Long Way

Most importantly, be kind to everyone. Every single person on this planet will experience hardship in his or her life. Some less than others, but hardship all the same. You could despise someone mean with every fiber of your being, and you should still be nice. Why? Because it's the right thing to do. Who knows what happened to the other person that made them so sad inside. Don't give that person more bad little things in their life, give them some good little things to help tip the scale in a positive direction. By reacting nicely, instead of mirroring the meanness, your kindness may change them.

Every day we have on this earth is a gift. Yet people still spend their days breaking others down instead of building them up. Make the most of every day by being the best that you can be. Your example may inspire others to do the same. I challenge each person who is reading this right now to make a point to be nice to someone today. For example, in our family we have a new tradition where everyone shares one random act of kindness that they performed that day. Eventually, this habit of one nice deed a day will become second nature. When it does, make it two nice deeds a day. Eventually you will start seeing a change in those around you and within yourself. Give it a try; I think you'll find it's worth it.

Stephanie Lilly - Bio

Stephanie Lilly was born in Marietta Georgia where she currently resides. She has two siblings: an older sister, Alexandra and a younger brother, Morgan. She is sixteen years old and a junior at Lassiter High School. She hopes to attend the University of Georgia after she graduates high school in 2015. She is focused on making a difference in her activities and has chosen to take leadership positions that allow her to pursue her passions and act as a positive agent of change.

Stephanie's maternal grandparents immigrated to America, from Greece, in the nineteen sixties. She is a Greek Orthodox Christian and very involved with her Greek heritage. She was elected the Vice President of her church youth group (Greek Orthodox Youth Association or GOYA) and has been learning traditional Greek dancing since she was four years old. In addition, she participates in the Southeast GOYA basketball tournament over the winter holiday every year. Stephanie enjoys doing community service, which includes volunteering at community soup kitchens and also serving food at various luncheons to raise money for her church. She has made an impact on her church community by volunteering as a counselor for the Vacation Bible School for a week over the summer and Greek dancing during the annual Marietta Greek Festival.

Stephanie is also very involved in the Lassiter High Chorus. She is a chorus officer and during her sophomore year she was a part of four different groups within Lassiter Chorus. One of the groups is the select ensemble called Choraliers. Her favorite experience with Chorus was during spring break of 2013 when she travelled with the Lassiter Tour Choir to Italy. There they performed in Saint Peter's Basilica in Vatican City as well as two other venues in Tuscany. This was a life changing experience because of her deep connection with her own religion. In addition to the Italy trip, during January of 2014 Stephanie and the Lassiter Tour Choir went to New York City and performed at multiple venues.

An Ever Changing World
Madeleine Sewall

CHAPTER 36 – An Ever Changing World

I will make a difference in how society treats minority groups and how we should learn to accept them and not discriminate them for who they are. This is a difficult topic to talk about as a high school student, because it is extremely challenging to sway peoples' opinions that are already set in stone. As a whole, our society has projected a unique image upon all minority groups. Because some people feel insecure about them, they tend to shame them, degrade them, and discourage them of anything that they do in their life. Do some people deserve to be treated like this? Is it really fair that someone, a human being, is shamed or stripped of something just because they do not look the same as everyone else, act the same, believe in the same things, or talk the same? I certainly do not think it is right, and that it is why I will make it my mission to educate people to become open minded and accepting to others.

In the modern world today, people do not think twice before judging someone based on the way they look or act. It is easy to notice differences amongst certain members of society, and it should be a priority not to judge them based on their differences. I feel like a large number of people view minorities groups as a flaw to our society, a parasite, that is tainting the minds of people and destroying the previous character of the world that they were familiar with. This is far from the truth, because they do anything but that. Instead of focusing on what separates them from the general population, their positive features such as their personalities, accomplishments, and interests are what needs to be looked at. My point is, is for people to try and understand a person before blindly saying things that have a negative impact on someone.

One of the most important things that people need to understand, is that the people are changing along with the world. A little too fast for some people, if I dare say. Let me explain what I mean by that "the world is changing". The people are changing along with their views, thoughts, and ideas. Humanity is slowly evolving, and there are some people who refuse to change with the rest of society. When the word 'change' comes to the minds of many people, they usually see it as something negative and interfering with their life. Honestly, I think the reason why people do not like change, is that it makes them feel uncomfortable and not familiar to what they are accustomed to. Change should be a sign of progress in our society and looked at with positivity, because every person is being forced to face and live in diverse environments that expose them to different elements of the world. Even though there is a percentage of people that feel uncomfortable or opposed to the changes with the people in the world, it is our job, as a community, to teach these people that change can be a good thing.

Making a difference in the way a certain group of people is seen is difficult, but it is worth a try. I do not want to make a difference for just the sake of doing it. I want to wake up one day and not see people struggling with the restrictions people place on them for simply living. There are people in the world that place restrictions on specific groups just because it offends them and makes them feel uncomfortable. These people need to open their eyes and realize that the world does not revolve around them, and that they should just accept change. I am trying to make a difference so that arrogant people do not restrict and destroy the lives of good people. The road to a society that completely accepts changes and differences is a challenging one, but if society take this step by step if does not seem that bad or far off.

While addressing the topic on how I plan to help people understand minority groups and accept them, I had a difficult time coming up with ideas that could change the way somebody thinks about them. Throughout my life, I gradually plan to open peoples' minds to help them understand the people of the world. Whether me making a difference involves performing little every day tasks or huge projects that promote people to be open-minded is something that I plan to do in the future. One of my main rules in life is that everything I do should affect someone in a positive way. Hopefully if I am able to broaden a person's perspective, they will be able to spread what they have learned. With a chain effect like this, the world will not seem that big to conquer with my goals.

One of my goals is to make a difference in doing small tasks that can show people how we should treat each other equally. Tasks like defending someone who is being discriminated in a non-aggressive way or just simply treating someone like everyone else. Some people become rude and mean when they encounter a person who acts or looks different, and they do this without knowing anything about them. I want to set a good example for everyone who lay eyes on me, because whenever I see someone acting neutral and nonjudgmental to any stranger I feel at ease. Being a good role model will help show others that anybody can treat everyone the same without there being any problems.

Another big way I can make a difference is getting my opinion and voice out into the world. I can do this in a number of ways, and one way is to give speeches that educate and teach people about subjects that need to be brought to the attention of the public. Whether I strive to makes speeches through a TED talk, which has a massive audience, or through little speeches between me and another person, I have realized that every little difference I make in the world counts and effects people in a positive or negative way. As a population, we should know that it is not acceptable to treat a person in a negative way because of a difference that distinguishes them from a majority of people. Hopefully, if I help people understand and digest this concept, then maybe our society might be able to move forward.

Whenever something or someone attempts to move forward and progress, there are usually obstacles that interfere with it. One good example of this would be attempting to get marriage equality and gay right in the states. Some states allow it, and others do not. I think eventually people will realize that there is no point in preventing marriage equality and being hostile to these people just because they feel like they are tainting society is pointless. Hopefully this will happen sooner or later, and people will be able to do as they please. With the hope of progression on this topic, there are actually people who want to crush this hope. Kansas, especially, is a state that wants to and hopes to succeed in discriminating against these people. Recently, they attempted to pass a law that basically legalizes all discrimination against these people that are fighting for their rights. This law not only will not allow marriage equally, but it will openly allow people to deny gays and lesbians to work a certain job, perform certain tasks, and much more. This is a tremendous issue not only in places of America but in other countries as well. Look at Russia, where people are getting physically harmed for being themselves. This disgusts me to no end, and the world desperately needs to change before things get out of hand.

As of right now, some people are using all their time and energy to hate and discriminate against certain people. I think these people invest too much of themselves into this sort of thing, and should be using their energy for more positive things. With all the other bad things in this world like war, hunger, poverty, and much more, it is a wonder why people are spending so much of their time filling the world with more hate than it already has. If people spent as much energy on helping and improving the world around us, the world would be a better place for all who live in it. I am baffled and will always be baffled by how much someone can hate another person for being who they are. If a person is bothered by it that much, then they should just ignore them. There is no reason why they should go attacking and hating something or someone because they feel uncomfortable with them. One thing that I wish to teach people is that if they do not like something, then they should just leave it alone. This rule applies to everyone.

They should focus on the people that make them feel loved and the things that they love. If they spend their entire lives worrying about something they do not like, then what is the point of living a fulfilling life? If everyone focuses on things they love instead of the things they see unfit for the world then people would be a lot happier in their life.

Showing people and helping them understand that everyone is equal, regardless of everything that says other wise, should be a common goal in every place of the world. I want to makes this difference not only for the sake of the people around the world today, but for future generations that will soon grace our earth. Nobody should live in fear for being who they are. It is not they who have the problem, but the rest of societies mentality towards them that has the problem. There is no question that it will take a great deal of time to change the mentality of the people on earth, but one day we are sure to get there. With hard work and dedication, I believe that I and anyone who is willing to put forth the effort can make a difference in the world one small step at a time.

Madeleine Sewall - Bio

Madeleine Sewall is a sophomore at Lassiter High School who is striving to make the most of her high school years through her participation in activities in the school and around the community. Her greatest interests include playing various sports, such as soccer and tennis, and playing the piano in her leisure time. Madeleine is an active member in her school and is involved with the sports program as well as several clubs. She also enjoys volunteering on her off weekends when she is not working.

Final Thoughts
Adam Weart

CHAPTER 37 – Final Thoughts

Removing Stumbling Blocks

When Gary Martin Hays called me on the morning of October 10th to discuss the speech he had prepared to give the students of Lassiter High School for their academic letter ceremony, it didn't surprise me for a second that Gary wanted to offer the students an opportunity to become authors. Since I began working with Gary over 5 years ago, he has never stopped looking for ways to give back to the community and this was just one more instance of Gary's good nature shining through.

Gary offered the students an opportunity to become *published* authors. This is no small task. As a business professional, I have seen people of all ages struggle mightily with the prospect of writing a book or even a chapter in a book. One of the major fears associated with writing a book is that once you publish something, it's out there for the world to see forever. I was very curious to see what kind of feedback we would receive from the students. One of the first questions I asked Gary was "Should we put a limit on the number of students we allow to take part?" We decided that this would be available to everyone, even if they all accepted. From the very beginning, Gary and I were always passionate about removing any obstacles that would have impeded the students' desire to take on this opportunity.

Age is No Excuse

Within the first few days, we were inundated with questions and requests to learn more about the opportunity. It became clear to me very quickly that these kids were not going to let their age get in the way of their confidence in themselves. Many of the students were sophomores in high school and we even had the pleasure of accepting an 8th grader into the project. It reminded me of something you might read on a motivational poster: If you start telling yourself at a young age that you can't do something, regardless of the reason, chances are you never will.

The Process

When we had our first meeting to discuss the project with all of the students that signed up, we had over 50 who had filled out the sign-up form. Gary and I stood in front of a packed room full of bright-eyed potential authors with lots of questions:

"How many words?"

"How long do we have?"

"Does everybody get picked?"

"Is it weird having your personal writing out there for the whole world to see?"

We answered everyone's questions and outlined the process.

As you know by now, the theme of the book falls in line with Gary's speech that he gave on October 10th that focused on making a difference. We talked to the students about what it meant to them to make a difference. We emphasized the importance of creating an outline and then letting their proverbial pens flow. Even if it isn't pretty right away, it's important to get your rough ideas out so you can organize them.

Over the course of the next few months, Gary and I met with students who had questions, set up a website where we posted reference material, created a Facebook group and reviewed rough drafts. Every student received editing feedback about their chapter and we also encouraged them to discuss their content with trusted teachers and their parents. We didn't want them to take this opportunity lightly. The entire process took approximately 3.5 months and I am extremely proud of the work that was put into this book.

Goals For "We Published That"

When Gary and I started our publishing company, We Published That, one of our main goals was to use the endeavor as a way to raise awareness for causes we were passionate about. Gary started a non-profit called Keep Georgia Safe (KGS) back in 2008 and many of the proceeds (in some cases 100%, such as the case with this book) that are raised from our book sales go towards child safety initiatives that are the core mission of KGS. We even wrote the book "The Authority on Child Safety" to help parents start the conversation with their kids about personal safety.

We also wanted to give potential authors the opportunity to establish themselves as the authority in their respective fields by publishing books that allow them to unveil their knowledge. We trademarked the phrase "The Authority On" and use it to help our authors stand out from their competitors.

Gary and I have both co-authored books through independent publishers in the past and on several occasions we found ourselves asking "What's stopping us from doing this ourselves?" This was something that we talked about with the students when writing this book. We stressed the importance of "simply trying." So many ideas are never seen through because good intentioned people aren't willing to take the first step.

Personal Goals

One of my personal goals in taking part in the "I Will Make a Difference" book was to teach aspiring young authors that they can do anything they set their minds to. It sounds cliché, but it's true. I also wanted to help establish, for a handful of aggressive young minds, a cornerstone to build their resumes on. It's not every day that a college is going to field an application from a 17 or 18 year-old, best-selling author. At the time of me writing this sentence that is not the case but I am almost certain that when this book is published, that dream will come true for 35 impressive authors.

Thanks

I would like to thank Gary Martin Hays for his genuine support in fostering these youths to become future leaders. Thank you to Ann Rives for being the liaison between the students and our team's publishing efforts. Thank you to all the parents of these bright students. You have raised them to be intelligent, polite and respectful and there is alot to be said for creating that foundation in this world. A final thank you to all the students who poured their hearts into these chapters. You have shown the world a microcosm of what the future holds when inspiring young minds come together to MAKE A DIFFERENCE.

Adam Weart - Bio

Starting with a BS in Industrial Design and a Certificate in Marketing from Georgia Tech, Adam Weart has spent the past decade providing unmatched design and services to his clients as well as leadership and loyalty to his employers.

Adam spent 4 years running Design and Engineering for HomeWaves while leading the initiative for branding, marketing and sales. During his leadership, HomeWaves achieved their industry's most prestigious recognition by receiving 3 National CEDIA Awards.

He also co-authored the best-selling books, "CHAMPIONS - Knockout Strategies For Health, Wealth and Success," "The Authority on Tout: How to Use Social Media's Newest Video Sharing App to Engage Your Community and Grow Your Business," "The Authority On Child Safety: How to Talk to Your Kids About Their Personal Safety Without Scaring Them" and has been featured on Yahoo News, CBS News' Moneywatch.com, The Miami Herald and The San Francisco Chronicle.

Adam continues to extend his leadership and marketing creativity by leveraging all aspects of Social Media Marketing and Web Usability Design as a key leader at the Law Offices of Gary Martin Hays & Associates, P.C. as well as being co-founder of We Published That, L.L.C.

www.ingramcontent.com/pod-product-compliance
Lightning Source LLC
LaVergne TN
LVHW051541070426
835507LV00021B/2348